INSTITUTE OF PSYCHIATRY

Maudsley Monographs

ABNORMALITIES IN PARENTS OF SCHIZOPHRENICS

INSTITUTE OF PSYCHIATRY

MAUDSLEY MONOGRAPHS

Number Twenty-two

ABNORMALITIES IN PARENTS OF SCHIZOPHRENICS

A review of the literature and an investigation of communication defects and deviances

By

STEVEN R. HIRSCH

B.A., M.D., M.PHIL.(PSYCH.), M.A.C.P., M.R.C. PSYCH.

Professor of Psychiatry, Charing Cross Medical School, University of London. Formerly Attached Worker, Medical Research Council Social Psychiatry Unit, and Lecturer, Institute of Psychiatry, London

and

JULIAN P. LEFF

B.SC., M.D., M.R.C.P., M.R.C. PSYCH.

Assistant Director, Medical Research Council Social Psychiatry Unit, Institute of Psychiatry. Senior Lecturer, Institute of Psychiatry, and Honorary Consultant, The Maudsley Hospital, London

LONDON
OXFORD UNIVERSITY PRESS
NEW YORK   TORONTO
1975

Oxford University Press, Ely House, London W. 1

GLASGOW NEW YORK TORONTO MELBOURNE WELLINGTON
CAPE TOWN IBADAN NAIROBI DAR ES SALAAM LUSAKA ADDIS ABABA
DELHI BOMBAY CALCUTTA MADRAS KARACHI LAHORE DACCA
KUALA LUMPUR SINGAPORE HONG KONG TOKYO

ISBN 0 19 712144 6

© *Institute of Psychiatry* 1975

*Printed in Great Britain by
The Camelot Press Ltd, Southampton*

CONTENTS

ACKNOWLEDGEMENTS   vii

PART I

REVIEW OF THE LITERATURE

INTRODUCTION	3
I. CLINICAL STUDIES RELYING ON CASE STUDY AND INTERVIEW	5
II. QUESTIONNAIRE STUDIES	34
III. SMALL GROUP INTERACTION STUDIES	43
IV. PSYCHOLOGICAL TESTS OF ABNORMAL THOUGHT PROCESSES	63
V. ABNORMALITIES OF COMMUNICATION AND LANGUAGE	72
VI. SUMMARY AND CONCLUSIONS	93

PART II

AN INVESTIGATION OF COMMUNICATION DEFECTS AND DEVIANCES

VII. ABNORMALITIES OF SPEECH IN THE PARENTS OF SCHIZOPHRENICS: A REPLICATION STUDY	113
Section I. Introduction	113
Section II. Selection of Subjects	115
Section III. Methods	119
Section IV. Results	125
Section V. How can we account for the difference between groups on the Deviance Score?	141
Section VI. Comparison of National Institute of Mental Health and United Kingdom results—some hypotheses which could explain the differences	156
Conclusion	169

Appendices
1. Additional Conventions for Use of the Singer and Wynne Manual	171
2. Education Scale	174
3. Social Class Occupation Scale	175
4. Categories of Communication Defects and Deviances	176
5. Raw and Transformed Data for the 80 Subjects	178

References	182

MAUDSLEY MONOGRAPHS

HENRY MAUDSLEY, from whom this series of monographs takes its name, was the founder of The Maudsley Hospital and the most prominent English psychiatrist of his generation. The Maudsley Hospital is now united with Bethlem Royal Hospital, and its medical school, renamed the Institute of Psychiatry, has become part of the British Postgraduate Medical Federation. It is entrusted by the University of London with the duty to advance psychiatry by teaching and research.

The monograph series reports work carried out in the Institute and in the associated Hospital. Some of the monographs are directly concerned with clinical problems; others, less obviously relevant, are in scientific fields that are cultivated for the furtherance of psychiatry.

Joint Editors

PROFESSOR SIR DENIS HILL
F.R.C.P., D.P.M.

PROFESSOR G. S. BRINDLEY
M.D., M.R.C.P., F.R.S.

with the assistance of

MISS S. E. HAGUE, B.SC. (Econ.), M.A.

ACKNOWLEDGEMENTS

OUR thanks are due to a number of people who assisted us in the conduct of our study and in the preparation of this monograph. We are very grateful to the following, who read individual chapters and offered their comments: D. Cantwell (CHAPTER I), D. Hawkes (CHAPTERS II and III), N. McConaghy (CHAPTER III), J. Orford (CHAPTERS I, II and III), M. Singer and L. Wynne (CHAPTER V). Professor J. K. Wing read through the entire manuscript and gave us continuing support and advice during the project. We are extremely appreciative of Miss Kathleen Jones' painstaking work in transcribing the subjects' responses, and of the accurate typing of Miss Carol Perkins and Miss Christine Durston. Miss Jane Sproule kindly scored the intelligence tests for us. Mr. W. J. Robertson and Miss Edwina Porter of the West-minster Medical School Library were of great help in checking the references.

We would particularly like to record our gratitude to Dr. Margaret Singer and Professor Lymann Wynne, without whose co-operation the study could not have been mounted nor carried through.

We gratefully acknowledge the permission of the Editor of *Psychological Medicine* to reproduce TABLE 4 and FIGURE 2 from our article in Volume 1 of that journal; and the permission of the Editor of *Excerpta Medica* to publish TABLE 1 from Professor Wynne's article on page 403 of *Problems of Psychosis*, edited by P. Doucet and C. Laurin, 1971, and the list of Communication Defects and Deviances from Dr. M. Singer's article on 'The origins of schizophrenia' in *Excerpta Medica International Congress Series* No. 151, 1967. We also acknowledge the permission of the Editor of *Archives of General Psychiatry* to publish TABLE 6 from Singer and Wynne's paper 'Thought disorder and family relations of schizophrenics. IV Results and implications' on page 206 of volume 12, 1965 (copyright 1965, American Medical Association).

We are very grateful to Professor Wynne and Dr. Singer for their generous permission to publish the above-mentioned and also the table on page 80 and TABLE 27 on page 127 of this monograph which have not previously been published.

London   S. R. H.

1974   J. P. L.

Part I

REVIEW OF THE LITERATURE

INTRODUCTION

RESEARCH into the role of parents in the aetiology of schizophrenia began in 1934 and has had its greatest expansion since 1960. Although several previous reviews have covered various aspects of the field, research has been proceeding within a number of different disciplines using a variety of approaches, and a comprehensive review has not been attempted. We see a need for a review which considers in particular the methodological aspects of the studies and on this basis assesses the solidity of the evidence to date. Our interest in this area of research was aroused by some striking findings of a series of studies which seemed to be the most promising of their kind, and which we felt demanded replication. It is appropriate to combine these two projects, a survey of the studies in this field and a specific piece of research, under one cover in so far as the former emphasizes the relevance and importance of the latter.

In previous studies a multiplicity of methods have been used, but they can be assigned to reasonably well-defined categories, each with its own inherent strengths and limitations. Under each category of method, we look at the relevant studies from the points of view of both their form and content, and try to conclude what facts, if any, have been reasonably established.

In CHAPTER I we begin with the historical background and the earliest studies in the field, and then review papers which have employed a clinical and descriptive approach. In general we have chosen to review only work which has attempted to approach the problem systematically with some form of scientific methodology. This means we have not included simple anecdotal clinical descriptions and in general have not discussed theoretical papers as such. However, in a middle section of CHAPTER I we set out the main psychoanalytically derived concepts because these have made an important contribution to the field and have given direction to most of research which followed. The theories of Bateson, Lidz, Alanen, Wynne and Singer, and Laing are therefore given special attention. The final section of CHAPTER I comprises the main methodological considerations which affect the interpretation of work in the field. We ask how far existing methods can take us and consider recent work which has overcome some of the previous problems and limitations. This establishes the pattern into which we can then fit the results of experimental studies considered in the ensuing four chapters. Each focuses upon the results of a particular methodological approach: questionnaire studies, small group interaction studies using social psychological techniques, formal psychological tests for abnormal thought processes in parents, and recent work on abnormal communication. The work reviewed in these chapters is aimed at establishing whether or not there is a link between parental abnormalities and schizophrenia. The nature of the link is considered in CHAPTER I. In view of the diversity and complexity of the material, we give our conclusions at the end of each chapter. In CHAPTER VI we bring together the results from all the different methodologies and relate them to the principal concepts in this field. We then present various models which set out ways in which the established factors may interact, and we discuss their bearing on the issue of the parents' role in the aetiology of schizophrenia.

In PART II we present a detailed account of our attempt to replicate the work of Wynne and Singer, who have made the most promising contribution to this field of inquiry.

CHAPTER I

CLINICAL STUDIES RELYING ON CASE STUDY AND INTERVIEW

EARLIEST BEGINNINGS

THE emphasis given by Freud and his colleagues to early life experiences in shaping individual development led to an interest in parental behaviour as a factor in the pathogenesis of psychiatric illness and personality disorder. However, it was not until 1934 that a systematic attempt was made to study the environmental effects of parents in the pathogenesis of schizophrenia. Kasanin, Knight, and Sage (1934) in their paper 'The parent–child relationship in schizophrenia' anticipated many key issues which were not dealt with again until the past decade. They adopted criteria of 'over-protection' which Levy (1931) laid down while discussing in a didactic fashion the consequences of over-protection for the developing child. His criteria included prevention of the development of independent behaviour by the child; excessive maternal contact, such as sleeping with a child until age 14; prolonged infant care, such as breast feeding to age 4; and an excess of or lack of maternal control, such as over-indulgence of the child's whims. Using these criteria, Kasanin *et al.* examined the case notes of 45 unselected schizophrenics and found evidence for maternal over-protection or rejection in 60 per cent of them. They noted that 'with unusual frequency over-protection was occasioned by some illness or anomaly in the child', such as 'poor development, malnutrition, birth injuries, etc.' or 'obvious intellectual weakness'. They concluded that 'the biological inferiority of the schizophrenic child is easily detected by the parents and serves as one of the principal causes of over-protection . . . the pre-schizophrenic child invites and solicits the extra care and attention on the part of his parents'. There is a clear recognition here of the circularity of cause and effects, a concept that was lost sight of by subsequent workers for some time.

In the same year Witmer (1934) and her student social workers conducted interviews with the relatives of 20 manic-depressive patients and 28 schizophrenics. They tried to get a picture from their informants of the emotional relationships which characterized the patient's early family life. The groups did not differ in the proportion of parents who showed over-protection, maternal dominance, or extreme friction. At least one of these measures was found to be present in the parents of 83 per cent of the manic-depressives and 67 per cent of the schizophrenics. When mild degrees of over-protection and dominance were eliminated, the proportions became 55 per cent and 51 per cent respectively. An interesting ancillary finding was that about two-thirds of the children in *both* groups were found to have been 'unusually sensitive or close-mouthed'. Although this study was not sufficiently systematic to give weight to the incidences reported, and interviewer bias was in no way excluded, the importance of using a control group emerges clearly. The need for one is particularly important because many subsequent authors have regarded the above-mentioned parental characteristics to be of specific aetiological significance in schizophrenia.

Two other early papers deserve mention, principally because they are often quoted and seem therefore to have been influential in the development of thought in this field. In 1940 Hajdu-Gaines reported data from the psychoanalysis of four female schizophrenics. He found that they had in common the experience of a 'cold, rigorous, sadistically aggressive mother', combined with a 'soft, indifferent, passive father'. Drawing on the psychoanalytic literature, he related the patients' schizophrenic state to a lack of real parents in their childhood. In the climate of post-war American psychiatry, in which psychoanalysis was pre-eminent, the theory that schizophrenia could be due to early life experiences became readily acceptable, and the concept of the 'schizophrenogenic mother' was coined, almost as an aside, in a paper by Fromm-Reichman (1948) in which she referred to the mothers of schizophrenics when discussing the problems such patients present in psychoanalytic treatment. The catch-phrase and the concept it embodies rapidly became popular and dominated theoretical and research publications for many succeeding years.

CLINICAL AND DESCRIPTIVE STUDIES EMPLOYING INTERVIEWS AND ANALYSIS OF CASE RECORDS

The rapidly growing interest in early life experiences as determinants of mental disturbance stimulated research in this area. Lidz and Lidz (1949) heralded their later work in this field with a retrospective study more systematic than that of Kasanin and his co-workers, but still with many defects. They examined the case histories of 50 consecutive schizophrenic patients (23 men, 27 women) at the Phipps Clinic who became ill before the age of 21, and found that 40 per cent had lost a parent by separation or death before the age of 19. They included a study of 50 schizophrenics from the same clinic whose illness began after the age of 21. Of these patients 36 per cent had been bereaved of a parent by age 19 compared with 20 per cent of 50 severely depressed patients. It is noteworthy that if a chi-square test is done on these figures the difference is not significant. Of 33 schizophrenics for whom adequate information was available, 61 per cent had histories of marked strife between their parents, 48 per cent had at least one severely unstable (psychotic, neurotic, or psychopathic) parent, and 41 per cent were found to have had bizarre or unusual rearing 'by normal standards'. Any conclusions drawn from these figures must be tentative since they are based on retrospective analyses of case histories without controlling for observer bias or comparing the incidences reported with a matched series of patients. The effect of bias is likely to be particularly marked because the criteria for parental disturbance are not defined.

Tietze's study (1949) of the mothers of 25 schizophrenics was seriously marred because he only included intelligent mothers who were willing to come for several interviews and hence biased his sample towards individuals who were interested in talking to a psychiatrist. Consequently it is not surprising that 13 of the 25 marriages were unhappy and all the mothers were insecure. No criteria were given for these judgements or for other assessments of the mothers' personalities. The same defects are present in the material contributed by Reichard and Tillman (1950), who added 13 cases of their own to the 66 derived from their review of the literature. They did not mention how they selected their cases nor did they have a comparison group, and they failed to state the criteria on which they based their personality assessments. Despite obvious shortcomings these studies have been quoted repeatedly as supporting the view that the mothers of schizophrenics are over-protective and domineering (e.g. Alanen, 1966; Lidz et al., 1965a).

The problem of a control group was tackled by Gerard and Siegel (1950), although they failed to match the control parents adequately with those of the patient group. They interviewed the parents or closest available relative of 71 schizophrenics admitted to Brooklyn State Hospital in 1948-9. The control group was drawn from the parents of young persons about to finish high school. In the area studied only 50 per cent of the students reached this level of education so the control parents would be expected to be at a higher level of social class and education than the schizophrenics' parents. In fact the control group was on average 6 years younger than the experimental group and of decidedly different ethnic and racial background as well. Furthermore the interviews were neither blind nor structured, thus allowing additional bias in the collection of the data. Two positive features of the study deserve attention. First, an effort was made to reassure the relatives of the patients of their lack of responsibility for the illness, which was an attempt to control the effect of the situational context of the interview (see Schopler and Loftin, 1969; Mishler and Waxler, 1968a). Secondly, the reliability of the rating of the information sheets was estimated for a sub-sample of 20 cases and was found to be satisfactorily high ($r = 0.89$). The authors of this study found that the marital relationship of the parents of 27 per cent of schizophrenics was openly discordant and hostile, as compared with 13 per cent for the controls. In 62 per cent the marital relationship of the parents was quiet, passive and judged to be 'good', but nevertheless was categorized as cold, as compared with 23 per cent for the controls. Thus 11 per cent of the schizophrenics' parents had warm, active marriages, whereas 63 per cent of the controls did so. In 91 per cent of the families of schizophrenics, but in none of the control families they found a heightened relationship between the mother and the patient, as shown by excessive contact such as sleeping in mother's bed, prolonged mothering, or excessive attachment. It is of interest that like Kasanin et al. (1934) these authors felt that in many cases this was in response to a child who was in need of special care or was thought to be sickly and weak.

The need for an unbiased sample and a comparable group of controls was recognized by Prout and White (1950), who studied 25 consecutive admissions for schizophrenia. The patients' mothers were compared with 22 mothers chosen at random from the community. Though the groups were again ethnically different, this does not detract from the finding that a good marital relationship was reported by at least 20 of the mothers in each sample (i.e. 80 per cent of the parents of each group). The mothers of schizophrenics were *less* critical of themselves, the patient, and life in general. One might query whether the difference between these results and those of previous authors could be accounted for by a less intensive interviewing technique, or by more stringent criteria for parental abnormality. Unfortunately insufficient information is given in the paper to enable us to resolve this question.

In a study of the case notes of 126 subjects equally divided between normality, neurosis, and schizophrenia, McKeown (1950) found parents of schizophrenics and neurotics to be more demanding and antagonistic than parents of normals. However, there was no significant difference between parents of schizophrenics and neurotics. Broken families, families of delinquents and families with less than two or more than four children were excluded from the study, which tended to eliminate the more aberrant families. As in other studies of a similar kind, it is an open question whether the attitudes of the parents are a result of their child's illness rather than a cause.

Nielsen (1954) conducted an interesting study of 55 schizophrenics at Gaustad Mental Hospital during the years 1948 to 1951. He matched his sample of patients with 110 healthy women, controlling for age, marital status, urban rearing, and occupation. Unfortunately he used different methods of obtaining the information from the two groups, so that the findings are not truly comparable. Information on the patients was gathered by interviews with the patient and his family and from hospital notes. The agreement between these different sources was good. Information on controls was obtained from a questionnaire which was not assessed for reliability or validity. The main finding was that the mothers of controls were *less* quiet and affectionate than the mothers of schizophrenics, but were equally domineering. No differences emerged between the fathers in each group. The incidence of mental illness was found to be twice as frequent in the parents of patients as in the controls, but alcoholism and divorce were equally uncommon in both groups. The finding of a low incidence of alcoholism is in direct conflict with the findings of Vaziri (1961). He studied 219 schizophrenics who had a relative hospitalized with oligophrenia, psychopathy, alcoholism, or attempted suicide, and found that of these conditions only alcoholism showed a higher incidence than in the general population. This result is only of limited value, however, as the sample was heavily biased by including only schizophrenics who had a relative with a mental illness.

Wahl (1954, 1956) did two extensive case history studies of hospitalized schizophrenics and found a high incidence of parental rejection or overprotection in both series. Little weight can, however, be attached to his figures as his criteria were not defined, no control group was used, and no precautions were taken to exclude rater bias. He also reported data on parental bereavement and separation, which are of more value as at least the criteria are well-defined. Parental bereavement or loss of a parent by separation before the age of 15 was found in 44 per cent of patients. This proportion compares closely with Lidz and Lidz's figure of 40 per cent. These findings will be evaluated in CHAPTER VI, where the evidence for the importance of parental separation is reviewed. Kohn and Clausen (1956) and Clausen and Kohn (1960) dealt with some of the problems of sampling and controls met with in earlier studies, and recruited additional sources of information. Their work represents a definite methodological advance principally because of their attention to the influence of social class. They interviewed 73 per cent (45 patients) of all schizophrenics admitted between 1940 and 1952 to the mental hospital exclusively serving Hagerstown, Maryland, a community with a relatively static population. Seventeen patients were too ill to be interviewed or were not available, in 12 of these a relative was seen. Controls were persons individually matched with patients for age, sex, and father's occupation (where possible) prior to the patient's illness. The groups did not differ in family size or area of residence, and in more than half of the cases the control subject attended the same school as the index case. Information was gathered by an interview in which the respondent was directed to focus on his early teens and was asked about his parents' attitudes towards child rearing. An attempt was made to check the reliability of this information in the case of patients by comparing it with information in the hospital notes gathered from parents and relatives at the time of the patient's admission. Only one major discrepancy was found.

In marked contrast to the findings of previous studies in which social background and sampling bias were not controlled for, Kohn and Clausen found the families of schizophrenics and normals to be similar with regard to frequency of marital breakup or parental bereavement before the child was 13. Moreover, the two groups did not differ in the amount of parental discord reported retrospectively by patients and controls.

An important new finding was that when parental authority was rated on specially constructed scales, social class differences emerged. Control subjects from lower social class background saw their mothers as the principal

BAPS

authority figure, whereas controls from higher social class backgrounds saw their fathers in this role. By contrast, schizophrenics of both lower and upper class backgrounds saw their mothers as the authority figure—restrictive of their freedom, dominating, and making most of the day-to-day decisions. Thus, only the higher class parents of schizophrenics differed from the control parents. Although these findings have not been repeated by other workers, they are the result of the first of several studies in the field which pay detailed attention to demographic and social variables, and they highlight the importance of relating family data to the social setting.

Some of the pitfalls awaiting those who neglect to take social factors into account are illustrated in a study by Gibson (1958) who compared a group of schizophrenics with a group of manic-depressives in the same hospital. Ratings of parental behaviour were made from interviews and it was found that the parents of the manic-depressives were more concerned with social approval and social prestige than the parents of the schizophrenics and were also more envious of others and more competitive. One would expect social class to have a strong influence on these characteristics, and in fact the author found that the parents of these schizophrenics scored between those of the manic-depressives drawn from the same hospital and manic-depressives drawn from another hospital, suggesting that the diagnosis was less important than other characteristics determining admission. Fisher et al. (1959) paid attention to demographic differences between the groups they studied, which comprised the parents of schizophrenics, neurotics, and normals. They found that the parents of normals had a significantly higher educational and social attainment than the other parents. However, they did not relate this difference to their main finding, which was that the parents of schizophrenics verbalized more hostility towards their spouses and were less accepting of sexual expression in their offspring.

McGhie (1961a) compared the mothers of chronic schizophrenics, neurotics and normals, all the families being middle class by occupation and education. In interviews with these mothers it was noted that the mothers of schizophrenics lacked social control compared to the other groups; for example, they commented on the interviewer's health or invited him to their home and their interests centred narrowly on the family, their marriages were more often unhappy with poor sexual relations, and they were lacking in social contacts. Their husbands were described as avoiding responsibility in the home and lacking ambition and drive.

Lu (1961, 1962) introduced a methodological innovation by selecting families with a sibling of the same sex and approximate age as the patient so as to study differences in rearing techniques and parental attitudes towards the affected and unaffected offspring. Intensive interviews were conducted with the parents by interviewers who were aware, not surprisingly, of which child was the patient. It was found that parents more often reported that the schizophrenic child was more submissive and dependent on the mother. As an infant, the index child had cried more, had been more excitable, and had not got on as well with his peers as did the normal child. The mothers had appeared to be more dominant and over-protective towards the index child, but had also harboured greater expectations for him. It was concluded that this subjected the index child to greater intrafamilial tension of a 'double bind' type. This study reinforces the observations of Kasanin *et al.* (1934) of differences between the pre-schizophrenic child and its sibling from an early age. However, it is subject to the criticism that the parents' accounts of the child's early years were retrospective and might have been influenced by his subsequent illness.

Pollin, Stabenau, and their colleagues (1966, 1968) took the research approach of Lu a step further by collecting a series of families with monozygotic twins discordant for schizophrenia or borderline schizophrenia. This design allowed them to compare individuals sharing the same genetic, ethnic, educational, and social class characteristics within the same time span, so that significant crises occurred in both twins at the same developmental stage. They studied 15 patients, 5 of whom were designated 'probable' or borderline schizophrenics and the remaining 10 'hardcore'. They were concerned with biological and behavioural differences between the twins from birth, as well as the parent–child relationship. There were some striking findings: the schizophrenic twin was the smaller in 11 out of 11 cases, was born second in 8 of 11 cases, and was usually the slower to develop, less resistant to illness, more anxious, and less successful socially. Five of the index cases but none of their twins was cyanotic at birth. A significant preponderance of soft neurological signs, such as difficulties with praxis, hyper- or hyporeflexia, had been noted in the early childhood of the schizophrenic twins. The results from the study of interpersonal relationships were far less impressive, and the only relevant finding which was not wholly speculative or interpretative was that the parents favoured the smaller, pre-schizophrenic twin, and remembered having more concern about his eating habits, success at school, etc. These findings are in accord with the hypothesis put forward by Kasanin *et al.* (1934).

In a later paper by the same group (Mosher *et al.*, 1971), global judgements of the degree of illness, submissiveness, and type of cognitive style were employed to rate the patients, their twins and their parents. The reliability of the ratings was low ($r = 0.3$–0.6) though significant, and the ratings were not done blindly. It was found that the schizophrenic twin was more similar to the parent who was considered the more disturbed of the two, but this adds little to our understanding of the aetiology of the condition.

Oltman and Friedman (1965) examined the incidence of parental death and separation in a large number of schizophrenics admitted to hospital between 1946 and 1962. They scrutinized the case notes and discarded 10 per cent as being unsuitable. The incidence of parental deprivation before the age of 19 was 34 per cent, identical to their finding in a previous study

(Oltman *et al.*, 1952). However, the incidence did not differ significantly from that found in a large group of hospital personnel.

Several other more recent studies have involved the provision of controls, closely matched on a number of demographic variables. Lucas (1964) carried out a carefully controlled study of 100 young adult schizophrenics admitted to hospital for the first time. He matched each patient with a classmate from his sixth year of school, of identical age, sex, and race. As a result of this procedure there were no differences between the experimental and control groups in social class or age difference from the closest sibling. A multiple regression analysis was carried out using the data collected and a number of variables were found to be associated with schizophrenia: the degree of remoteness of the relationships within the family of rearing, absence of the father during the first 6 years of life, and being reared by distantly related persons. There was a positive correlation with absence of the mother in the first 6 or first 20 years, but this was highly correlated ($r = 0.63$) with being reared in a bad psychological climate, and so did not emerge as an independent factor in the multiple regression analysis. The effect of observer bias was investigated by having a rater eliminate any matched pairs whose protocols contained cues to the diagnostic group of the family. As many as 39 of the 100 pairs were eliminated in this way, but the correlations did not change significantly. Thus the findings of this study appear to be based on a sound methodology, but there is a problem of interpretation. It is possible that the environment of a foster-home engenders schizophrenia, or alternatively that the need for parents to send children away from the family for rearing reflects the effects of inherited factors in the parents which, when present in the offspring, predispose them to schizophrenia. Nevertheless, this study does suggest that remoteness on the part of the adults rearing the children and absence of parents are related in some way to a propensity to develop schizophrenia.

Rogler and Hollingshead (1965) also took great care to provide a demographically similar control group in their study of 20 lower class Puerto Rican families containing a schizophrenic husband or wife. The control and experimental groups both had intact marriages and were also matched on age and the proportion of slum and public housing dwellers. The usual American diagnostic criteria were employed, including the term pseudoneurotic schizophrenia. A number of features of childhood rearing and relationships with parents did not differ between the two groups. However, more schizophrenic than well women had experienced a severe beating as a child from a parent in a rage. This was not true for the men. Other factors which differed between the groups were the frequency of physical illness in the spouses of the patients in the 5 years before and after the onset of schizophrenia, and the incidence of the death of a child. Six of the 20 patients had lost a child before the onset of their mental illness compared with one of the normals. In interpreting these findings one needs to take into account the nature of the sample.

The subjects came from a very deprived sector of the population in a country with a predominantly rural economy. They were selected on the basis of an intact marriage despite the presence of schizophrenia in one of the partners. Data from other studies (Hirsch et al., 1973) would suggest that married schizophrenics as a group have a better prognosis and hence may represent a milder form of the condition. Moreover, as shown by Kendell et al. (1971), a group of schizophrenics diagnosed by American psychiatrists may contain up to 50 per cent of patients who would be given a diagnosis other than schizophrenia by British psychiatrists. Consequently the failure to demonstrate many differences between the experimental and control groups in this study may have a limited general significance.

Another study which failed to find many aspects of personal history, social adjustment, or family structure which differentiated schizophrenics from non-schizophrenics was reported by Costello, Gunn, and Dominian (1968). They scored the case notes of 29 schizophrenic and 28 non-schizophrenic patients admitted under one consultant at a postgraduate psychiatric hospital during 2 years. Only males age 15–25 years were included. No differences between the two groups were found in their I.Q., employment history, or social class of their fathers. No trends appeared to differentiate the groups in terms of the patients' relationships with either parent, the consistency of both parents' attitudes towards the patient, the leadership of the father or mother in the family, or their degree of authoritarianism. There was a high rate of marital discord in both groups. The only difference which did emerge was the more frequent absence of the fathers of the schizophrenic patients when the patients were between the ages of 11 and 15, and the lesser concern of these fathers over their son's illness. The failure to find differences between the parents of these two groups on most of the measures studied suggests that these factors do not determine the form of psychiatric illness, although they may be important in the aetiology. However, one must have reservations about the assessment of the quality of interpersonal relationships from routine case-notes, even if the information has been collected meticulously.

Up to this point we have described a number of clinical studies employing a wide range of methodology and gathering information from various sources on the basis of very different kinds of hypotheses. The information has always been obtained retrospectively, after the patient has fallen ill. Despite these limitations, and others discussed above, the data have always been factual in nature, such as those concerning parental separation, or descriptive information on parental attitudes, etc., which could in theory be operationally defined. We now come to a series of studies of quite a different kind, which have had a great influence on psychiatric theorists in this field. This body of work depends on psychoanalytically oriented techniques for its procedures. These studies continue to depend on retrospective collection of data but are at a logically different level, because the data presented are principally interpretative, determined by the observer's theoretical concepts.

STUDIES DEPENDING ON CONCEPTS AND INSIGHTS DERIVED FROM PSYCHOANALYSIS

Although many workers have examined the role of parents in producing schizophrenia in their offspring, it has been the more psychoanalytically oriented literature which has gained the widest acknowledgement and been the most influential in shaping professional and lay opinion on this matter. Various psychodynamic theories have been put forward. Some have permeated psychiatric thinking more successfully than others, but almost all begin with an unquestioned acceptance of the central importance of environmental, parental factors; an assumption that the way parents handle, interact, and communicate with their children is of central importance in the development of schizophrenia. Of the various conceptual frameworks put forward, those of Lidz and his co-workers at Yale and Bateson and his co-workers at Palo-Alto have had the greatest influence. We will consider these first; then other authors who have made contributions of a similar kind, some of which are well known and others neglected.

Although we have expressly limited ourselves to discussing work of a scientific, experimental or descriptive nature, we must make an exception at this point of those purely theoretical and speculative writings which have had a widespread influence in this field. The most important of these are the early papers of the Bateson group, who formulated the 'double-bind' hypothesis. They set out the terms of their theory and illustrated them with examples from their clinical work. It was not until recently that work was done to try to verify their hypotheses experimentally. These studies will be discussed in a later section with other work employing the techniques of social psychology.

THE DOUBLE-BIND HYPOTHESIS

The double-bind hypothesis has had considerable impact and appeals to many psychiatrists, possibly because it can be stated simply with reasonable logic and clarity (Bateson et al., 1956; Haley, 1959a and b; Haley, 1960; Weakland, 1960; Watzlawick et al., 1968). It focuses on the interactions and conflicts which develop between individuals who share the intense relationships characteristic of the family. Weakland (1960) states several conditions which he believes must all be operating for true double-bind communication to occur. First, the relationship of the persons involved must be such that the recipient of the communication feels it essential to understand the nature of the message accurately so that he or she can respond appropriately. Second, the speaker must express two or more messages which are incompatible at different levels of communication; an example is the mother who verbally expresses love and concern while showing lack of interest and lack of concern through her facial expression and movement. Third, the context of the situation must be such that the individual is prevented from commenting on the inconsistencies he or she is presented with, or else is unable to discriminate the order of message to respond to. Finally, if the victim of such double-binds responds to the ambiguities, then he or she is met by condemnation which creates an even more confusing bind.

Haley (1959b) makes a distinction between contradictory messages which occur within the same level of discourse—for example, in one breath the mother says her child may go to the cinema but in the next breath forbids it—and in congruent messages which occur at different levels. Examples of the latter are contradictions which arise between what is stated verbally and what is implied by intonation or gesture. Moreover, contradictions can emanate from an individual or develop between individuals with respect to a third person who is receiving these communications. The essence of the concept seems to be that the individual is presented with an intolerable conflict from which he cannot extricate himself because of constraints inherent in the situation.

Central to this approach to the aetiology of schizophrenia is a re-definition of the nature of schizophrenia as a specific pattern of communication rather than an illness of the mind (Watzlawick, Beavin, and Jackson, 1968, p. 214). Haley (1959a) states that a characteristic feature of schizophrenic behaviour is the incongruity between verbal meaning and content, for example, when a schizophrenic accuses a friend of being a spy, or when 'the patient denies his presence in hospital by saying he is in a castle or prison'. 'The classic psychiatric symptom of schizophrenia can be defined interactionally as indicating a pathology centering around a disjunction between the person's message and the qualifications of those messages.' Similar disjunctions also occur in non-schizophrenics but 'they tend to be temporary'.

The family is viewed as a system with a limited range of behaviour which is maintained by the rules and prohibitions laid down by the various members. Schizophrenic behaviour is seen as an integral part of the system, or sometimes the result of a breakdown in the system. Schizophrenia is a 'strategy of behaviour' by which a patient can extricate himself from a series of incongruent communications or demands from which there is no other form of escape within the rules of the system.

None of the papers mentioned above employs an experimental or systematic approach designed to test the hypotheses advanced. Direct observations, tape recordings, and films of families in group discussion with therapists are used to provide illustrations of the kinds of communication and interaction which the authors postulate are crucial to their theories. Unfortunately, the clinical experience drawn upon comes from only a small number of patients, most of whom have come for private treatment. Though experimental techniques have been employed in recent years (see CHAPTER V) there is still no evidence that double-bind interactions are more common in the families of schizophrenics than in other families. One cannot therefore rule out the possibility that prolonged exposure to double-bind situations may be harmful to individuals predisposed to schizophrenia because of a non-specific stressful effect rather than any particular quality of distorted communication.

FAMILY INTERACTIONS: LIDZ AND THE YALE GROUP

The work of the Yale school, including Lidz, Cornelius, Fleck, Terry, and others, has been as influential as that of Bateson and his colleagues. The influence has been felt considerably less in Great Britain than in the United States, possibly because of the psychoanalytic framework of the studies, and the fact that they employed neither control groups for comparison nor 'blind' precautions. Nevertheless, these papers are important in demonstrating the possibilities and limitations inherent in an intensive extended study of families from a psychodynamic viewpoint. Their findings therefore merit careful consideration.

It is well to emphasize that the authors, in the introduction to their collected papers, disclaim scientific exactitude for their work and state that they view it as an exploratory study from which they hope that they and others can move on to testable hypotheses. Despite these qualifications, the contents of the book and subsequent papers present their findings and conclusions as forming the basis of a sound and established theory of environmental factors in the aetiology of schizophrenia (Lidz, 1967, 1968). As such, their work deserves to be examined critically from the point of view of methodology and findings.

In all, 17 families were studied, 14 upper-middle and upper class and three middle class. The former group were all able to pay private fees for the hospitalization of the sick member which lasted several years. There were 9 male and 8 female index cases of schizophrenia, all aged 15–30 and unmarried, with the mother and at least one sibling living. A team of psychiatrists, social workers and others interviewed the family members repeatedly over months or years and also obtained information from people outside the family such as maids, friends, etc. The investigators were all psychoanalytically oriented and employed no control group. One reason advanced by these workers for the lack of controls was the difficulty in finding a suitable comparison group who could afford and were prepared to persist with treatment over the extended period of the study. This emphasizes the considerable bias of the selection procedure.

It is easier to appreciate the findings of these studies if one knows the theoretical position from which the material was approached. Schizophrenia is viewed not as an illness in terms of the medical model, but as a normal and understandable reaction to an abnormal environment. The conflicts, ambiguities and inconsistencies of the external world are seen as becoming internalized, resulting in a distortion of the patient's perception of meaning and logic. The condition is regarded as a deficiency state in so far as the individual has lacked what Lidz believes are the essential experiences of parental nurture: an adequate family social structure, and clarity of communication between family members. The studies to be reviewed are thought to support this theoretical formulation by recording observations of various ways in which the personalities of family members and their interaction are abnormal. The basic reasoning behind this method seems to be that the association between abnormality of interaction in the family and the presence of a schizophrenic must be a causal one. The direction of causality is assumed to be from the former to the latter. These assumptions are buttressed by discussion as to how and why such a connection is reasonable and understandable.

Let us consider first of all the findings reported on the fathers of 14 schizophrenic patients (Lidz et al., 1957a). None of these was judged to fill the parental role effectively. They were assigned to five descriptive categories according to the kind of personality they exhibited and the role they played in the family. One category comprised fathers with exalted concepts of themselves, who were described as having 'paranoid grandiosity'. This loose usage of the term paranoid is misleading, and indeed in later papers these fathers are referred to as 'ambulatory schizophrenics' without further justification. The classification of 14 individuals into five more or less mutually exclusive groups leaves the number in any one group so small that in no case could it be said that the occurrence of that particular category of father among families of schizophrenics was any more than a matter of chance. We are left then with the conclusion that the fathers are abnormal according to the intuitive norms of the investigators or compared with some general standard of effective functioning which is not defined.

The position with respect to the mothers is no happier. The problem here is seen as a need to understand the effects individual mothers have had on the patients over the years (Lidz et al., 1965). The three functions they believe to be basic to mothering were propounded and every mother in the study was found to be wanting in all three and grossly deficient in at least one. These functions are described as: (1) maternal nurture in providing a foundation for the child's development; (2) contribution to the family as a social system which provides directives for the child's development; and (3) transmission of the adaptive techniques of the culture to the child, especially the shared system of meaning and communication. These functions are so broad and general that most people are likely to agree with their importance, but it is quite different to contend that even a gross inadequacy in these spheres is essential to the development of schizophrenia, and no evidence is offered to support this crucial contention. Certainly, some of the case descriptions of the mothers present a picture of very abnormal personalities who are likely to have a disturbing influence on a child. But the biased selection procedure favoured parents with severe problems who were willing to commit themselves to the expense and effort of intensive therapy and investigation for several years.

The authors present a similar analysis of these subjects at the level of family interaction. Two types of marriage were seen to characterize 14 of the families studied (Lidz et al., 1957b). The term 'marital schism' was applied to eight parental pairs and 'marital skew' to six. 'Schism' refers to marriages characterized by conflict between the partners, whose personality difficulties lead them to pursue their own needs while ignoring the other's. 'Skew' refers to marriages in which one partner yields to the abnormalities and eccentricities of the other, which then dominate the family so that no conflict is apparent. Of the eight female patients, six were thought to have parents whose marriage was schismatic. In these, the mother's self-esteem declined because the father disparaged her worth as a wife and mother (Fleck et al., 1963). Consequently the mother was anxious about raising her daughter and tended to be aloof, though not rejecting. This forced the daughter to turn to her father for affection and placed her in a dilemma, feeling that she was more important to her father than was her mother yet despising herself to the extent that she felt similar to her mother.

Skewed relationships predominated among the parents of male patients. In such cases the father was passive to the dominant mother and provided a poor masculine model. The mother turned to her son for the emotional satisfaction she lacked from her husband.

These formulations of the Yale group carry a strong flavour of Freud's oedipal situation and of Bateson's double-bind. In another paper (Lidz et al., 1963) these workers attempt to understand why the patient and not one of his siblings was the particular family member to develop schizophrenia. They found that the schizophrenic patient had played a pivotal role in some family conflict, such as acting as a scapegoat, or caught in conflicting parental loyalties. In this paper, great emphasis was laid on the relationships between the child's sex and the sex of the parent who had particular needs engendered by the conflict between the marital partners. It follows from this that siblings of the same sex as the patient should be more disturbed than siblings of the opposite sex. There were not enough siblings of the appropriate sex in the group studied to provide evidence on this point.

The question of why these family abnormalities should lead to schizophrenia and not to any other psychiatric disorder is also dealt with by these workers. This is, of course, a critical question for their theories and it is in the nature of the method that an answer is readily forthcoming (Lidz et al., 1958; Lidz, 1968). The distinctive feature of schizophrenia in their view is the irrationality of thought and the abandonment of reality. Individual family histories are reviewed to demonstrate how the parents distort reality and provide their children with models of irrationality. Some systematic studies were undertaken by other workers to test some of these ideas and their work will be discussed below in the section on psychological methodology in the study of schizophrenic families [see CHAPTER IV].

LIMITATIONS INHERENT IN A DESCRIPTIVE–INTERPRETIVE METHOD

Having considered separately the principal clinical studies of the Yale group, one can ask what may be learned from studies of this design and what conclusions should be drawn. There is an obvious drawback if investigators who have a definite theoretical viewpoint try to make objective observations on patients with whom they are involved clinically in treatment. The observer's clinical knowledge of the patient leaves his observations of the family open to his theoretical bias. The papers by the workers at Yale made no reference to findings which might contradict the authors' hypotheses and failed to suggest alternative interpretations of the data.

Even if we accept the validity of the observations, it is doubtful whether the presence of intra-family conflict and abnormalities in the parents of schizophrenics is necessarily of significance in the aetiology of schizophrenia, as conflict exists to some degree in almost every family. The authors imply that the specific nature of the family constellation is significant yet the combinations and permutations of their typology are so numerous within the small number of cases in their material that no two observations between type of parents and type of child correlate at a statistically significant level. Moreover, characteristics very similar to those described in the Yale families have been found in the study of other conditions (Hersov, 1960). (These findings will be discussed below.) We cannot judge whether the degree of abnormality within these families is pathogenic for the authors have not offered comparative data on families with an offspring suffering from a different psychiatric condition.

Bearing all these criticisms in mind, one is still left with the impression that the families described are very disordered. The importance of this observation depends on the criteria for selection of these families. The bias inherent in their self-selection has already been mentioned, but it is also possible that those families willing to undergo investigation were in some way screened to rule out the less interesting (relatively well) families and to include the very disturbed ones. Even if one could establish that the frequency and quantity of abnormality were significantly greater in the parents of schizophrenics than the parents of normals, this would still not elucidate the nature of the link between family disturbance and schizophrenia. Any abnormalities in family members could be the result of a common genetic endowment, fully expressed in the schizophrenic patient and partially expressed in the other relatives, rather than indicative of the presence of a pathogenic environment. When we review all these considerations we can appreciate how far the observations of Lidz and his co-workers are from throwing any light on the aetiology of schizophrenia.

The studies so far reviewed in this section represent the best known and most intensive investigations using uncontrolled purely descriptive techniques, but many others have employed variations of the same approach. The studies of Delay et al. (1957, 1962), Brodey (1959), Bowen et al. (1959), Parsons (1960), and Wolman (1961) are subject to the same criticisms as the work of the Yale school.

PSEUDOMUTUALITY: WYNNE

Another influential concept has been that of 'pseudomutuality', described as an important characteristic of the families of schizophrenics by Wynne et al. (1958). In an intensive study of four families in an in-patient unit, Wynne and his colleagues noted that there was a high investment by family members in maintaining the idea or feeling of intra-family mutuality, the reciprocal fulfilment of expectations, even though true reciprocity and mutuality were in fact absent. The need to maintain the illusion of mutuality took precedence over perceiving and responding to each other's real but changing needs. Bowen et al. (1959), in contrast, from a prolonged study of four families, found that they were characterized by 'emotional divorce', but that 'the family pattern changes in varying individual and family circumstances in the course of daily living'. These conflicting observations illustrate the weakness of developing extensive theories on the basis of what can at best be called preliminary studies.

The work of Laing, Esterson, and Cooper has achieved considerable acclaim among many lay and some professional persons interested in the relationship between the family and schizophrenia. In view of current interest in their ideas, their major publications will be reviewed here, although none of them can be considered to be experimental work.

In his first book, Laing (1960) presents schizophrenia as being on a continuum with the schizoid personality, and by inference rejects the view of schizophrenia as an illness. He attacks the clinical approach to schizophrenia from an existential standpoint and argues that by seeing the patient as a collection of symptoms, the clinician is denying his existence as a person. He describes people of schizoid personality perceptively and in great detail, distinguishing between a false self that is presented to the world and a true self that remains unexposed and protected. He assumes that his understanding of the schizoid personality can be extrapolated to schizophrenia and states that 'it is, of course, not always possible to make sharp distinctions between sanity and insanity, between the sane schizoid individual and the psychotic'. Cases of acute onset of schizophrenia in a previously normal person would seem to provide an obstacle to his argument, but he disposes of them by assuming that 'outwardly "normal" appearance, dress, behaviour, motor and verbal (everything observable), was maintained by a false-self system while the "self" had come to be more and more engaged not in a world of its own but in the world as seen by the self'. He then applies his understanding to the speech and behaviour of schizophrenics, stating that 'delusions contain existential truth'. His crossing of the boundary between schizoid individuals and schizophrenics is made so smoothly that the reader is easily lulled into acceptance of an assumption of considerable magnitude. This assumption, which is crucial to Laing's argument, is that there is no qualitative difference between the speech and behaviour of schizoid people and that of schizophrenics, but only a difference in degree. 'A certain amount of the incomprehensibility of a schizophrenic's speech and action becomes intelligible if we remember that there is a basic split in his being carried over from the schizoid state'. One of the logical consequences of this assumption is that the schizophrenic has a certain measure of control over his symptoms; 'the schizophrenic is often playing at being psychotic, or pretending to be so'. The schizophrenic 'is playing at being mad to avoid at all costs the possibility of being held *responsible* for a single coherent idea, or intention'.

Although Laing and Esterson (1964) emphasize that schizophrenia is not an illness, they nevertheless concentrate on people that clinicians have diagnosed as suffering from schizophrenia. They do not view the individual schizophrenic as the unit of illness, but the family, or even society at large. Along with their rejection of the concept of schizophrenia as an illness, they explicitly renounce scientific methods of study. This is hardly surprising as it would be difficult to make the object of a scientific investigation a condition that they are not prepared to define. Laing and Esterson present the case histories of 11 families with the intention of demonstrating that the patient's experience and behaviour make sense when viewed in a family context. However, behind this neutrally stated aim of furthering understanding lies a much more specific implication: that is, that the behaviour of the family has resulted in the 'schizophrenic' behaviour of the patient. This is stated quite explicitly in places; 'Has what is usually called "her sense of reality" been torn in shreds by the others?' Two themes emerge strongly from almost all of the case histories presented. Firstly, that the parents are imposing their will on the patient and trying to saddle him or her with their idea of what he or she should be. The patient is seen as struggling to achieve autonomy and finally only achieving this in some measure by becoming 'ill'. The second theme is one of mystification by the family, involving an overt and covert denial of what is going on. This set of ideas has a lot in common with Bateson's 'double-bind' hypothesis [p. 14]. Laing and Esterson write, 'each parent is simultaneously imputing and denying ambivalent feelings towards her (the patient), denying they are imputing them, and imputing that the other is denying them'.

Rachman (1973) points out that the abnormal behaviour of the patients described by Laing and Esterson in this book remains largely incomprehensible even in the light of the family disturbances documented. He suggests that the link with schizophrenia may be a non-specific one and that similar abnormalities may occur in families with members suffering from other conditions, such as delinquency, obsessional neurosis, etc. He also believes that these disturbances of family interaction may be commonly found in families throughout the population, whereas schizophrenia is relatively rare.

Siegler, Osmond, and Mann (1969) have attempted to specify the models of schizophrenia that Laing employed in his book *The Politics of Experience* (1967). They identify two more or less complete models, and a fragment of a third. The first model they describe is a Conspiratorial model in which schizophrenia is conceptualized as a label pinned on certain people as a result of a social process. This process is one whereby some people reject the experience of others and call it schizophrenic. In these terms schizophrenia is not an illness but a form of socially unacceptable behaviour which results in the person being forced into 'a career of patient' by the family and the psychiatric professionals. The family and community fail to accept the schizophrenic's experiences as authentic and therefore banish him to a psychiatric institution until he learns to see things their way.

The second model is called a Psychoanalytic one, the essential features being that the source of the person's difficulties is seen to reside in his disturbed family relationships, and that treatment consists of a special kind of corrective relationship between two people, patient and therapist. Both these models can be seen to underlie the case discussions in Laing and Esterson (1964), mentioned above.

The third, incomplete, model that Siegler et al. describe is the Psychedelic one. In this scheme schizophrenia is viewed as a breakthrough rather than a breakdown, 'a natural way of healing our own appalling state of alienation called normality'. As such, the schizophrenic process is valued as a therapeutic experience through which the patient should be guided. Medical treatment of schizophrenia, aimed at removing symptoms, is therefore seen as anti-therapeutic. Both Siegler et al. and Rachman (1972) point out a major contradiction between Laing's Psychedelic model of schizophrenia as a valuable experience and the treatment he actually gives his patients, which appears to be close to conventional psychoanalytically oriented family therapy.

From the mixture of existential philosophy, clinical insights and mutually contradictory models one finds in Laing's writings, a number of testable hypotheses can be derived. For example 'our impression, comparing the families of schizophrenics with other families, is that they are relatively closed systems, and that the future patient is particularly enclosed within the family system' (Laing and Esterson, 1964). However, no scientific studies designed to test Laing's ideas have been published.

A more systematic attempt to make observations of parents in an uncontrolled setting is the study by Hotchkiss et al. (1955). They studied 22 mothers of male schizophrenics, selected because it was easy for them to travel to the hospital. The mothers were then observed unobtrusively during visits to their sons and in interviews with social workers and medical staff. Observations of the type and duration of the interactions were systematically recorded on charts. Note was taken of the direction of the mother's attention, whether towards the patients or elsewhere, the nature of her verbal or motor activity, such as arguing, feeding, grooming, the apparent affect she showed, and the apparent response of the patient to her. Descriptive summaries were then compared with material from the social workers' interviews and comments made by nurses, and good agreement was found. Only 3 of the 22 mothers were characterized as being over-solicitous, over-anxious and domineering, the qualities supposed to be typical of the schizophrenogenic mother. However, 12 mothers were considered to be over-involved. Unfortunately, there are no comparable observations on the mothers of patients suffering from psychiatric disorders other than schizophrenia so that it is impossible to say that this finding is specific to schizophrenia. Furthermore, it is reasonable to view the mothers' over-involvement as a consequence of their sons' illness rather than a predisposing factor.

ALANEN'S FAMILY STUDIES

The studies reviewed in this section have all employed some form of non-blind, clinically oriented interview as the principal means of eliciting information. Alanen and his colleagues in Helsinki have probably made more extensive use of this method than any other group investigating the families of schizophrenics. Alanen's orientation is close to that of Lidz, but Alanen has studied much larger numbers of patients and has invariably used control groups (Alanen, 1958, 1966, 1968). In his first study he interviewed the mothers of 100 schizophrenics, 20 neurotics and 20 normals. He assigned the mothers to five diagnostic groups, ranked according to severity. Disorders graver than neurosis included subjects with 'schizoid or borderline features whose egos are very weak giving rise to a tendency to unbearable anxiety and unrealistic thought and behaviour patterns'. Significantly more mothers of schizophrenics than mothers of controls showed disorder of this severity (p<0·001), and these disorders were significantly more frequent in the mothers of process schizophrenics than in mothers of patients with schizophreniform psychosis. Such mothers had a 'schizoid pattern of interpersonal relationships characterised by a limited affective life, poor self-control, and an inability to feel themselves into the inner life of other people'. They were found to be lacking in understanding and respect for the child as an independent person. They were over-protective in a possessive way if the patient was male ('possessively protective') but in a hostile way if the patient was female ('inimically protective').

In a further study (Alanen, 1966), he and his co-workers interviewed the families of 30 schizophrenics aged 15–40 years who had primary symptoms as defined by Bleuler. A control group comprised 30 families of typical neurotics, all in hospital. Each diagnostic group had 15 male and 15 female patients and each patient had one to three siblings. Chronic patients were not excluded. In this study 75 per cent of the parents of schizophrenics were either suffering from schizophrenia themselves or 'exhibited other psychotic or borderline psychotic traits, or disorder graver than psychoneurosis'. Only 20 per cent of the parents of neurotics were so classified and none had schizophrenia. The siblings of the schizophrenics were also significantly more disturbed than the siblings of the neurotics.

In terms of family dynamics, 10 schizophrenic families but no neurotic families were characterized as 'chaotic', that is, incoherent and irrational, often dominated by one parent's abnormal or psychotic thought processes. Eleven more schizophrenic families were found to be 'rigid', which indicates an 'inelasticity of role constellations' with unbending attitudes and fixed expectations. These families often contained a possessive and/or paranoid father. Only 4 neurotic families were thought to be rigid in the same way.

In considering the relationship between family configurations and the sex of the patient, Alanen thought that his findings supported the theories of Lidz *et al.* (1957b) with regard to the numbers of skewed and schismatic families. However, a statistical test of even the greatest of the differences fails to show that the findings are significant.

Possibly the most substantial of all Alanen's results is the greater disturbance found in the marriages of the parents of schizophrenics than in those of the parents of neurotics. But the question is still open as to whether the parental disturbance directly affects the offspring by environmental means, or whether the abnormality in the parents, the offspring and the family in general is the consequence of a common genetic factor. An additional criticism relates to the manner in which the information was collected. The workers were not blind to the diagnostic groups of the families interviewed and the descriptive nature of their observations involved a high level of abstraction and interpretation which raises serious doubts about their reliability.

RECENT METHODS AVOIDING RETROSPECTIVE BIAS. IS TRANSMISSION ENVIRONMENTAL OR GENETIC?

All the studies reviewed so far have had the disadvantage of relying on retrospective information, recorded after schizophrenia had become apparent in the patient. Under the circumstances it is difficult for the investigators and informants to avoid being biased by the knowledge of the patient's condition. In this section, studies are presented which have avoided some of the problems of retrospective bias.

The main strategy of the studies that follow was to use the records of Child Guidance Clinics to obtain material about the patients that was collected before schizophrenia became manifest. O'Neal and Robins (1958) conducted a 30-year follow-up of 526 children who had attended a Child Guidance Clinic. They obtained information from the clinic records of 28 former clients who subsequently developed schizophrenia and 57 control clients, matched for age and living area, who were found not to be psychiatrically ill at follow-up. The rate of broken homes was found to be very similar in the two groups: 68 per cent in the pre-schizophrenic children and 56 per cent in the controls. A number of significant differences were found relating to illness in the pre-schizophrenic children. They showed significantly more pathological lying, physical aggression, eating disorder, phobias, tics, and mannerisms. However, only one difference emerged in the parent–child relationship. The pre-schizophrenic children were more often dependent on their mothers than the controls, as shown by a fear of letting their mother out of sight.

Waring and Ricks (1965) used the records of 18,000 clients seen at the Judge Baker Child Guidance Clinic from 1917 to 1965 prior to a time that any of them became schizophrenic. From these, the records of 50 children who were hospitalized for schizophrenia an average of 6 years later were identified and matched with 50 control children who were not subsequently admitted to a mental hospital. The matching was in terms of age, sex, I.Q., social class, ethnic background, and presenting symptoms at the clinic. Forty per cent of the sample was from socio-economic Classes I to III and the remainder from Classes IV and V. 'Parent' was defined as the principal caretaker during the subject's childhood. Subjects were categorized as chronic schizophrenics, in hospital at the time of follow-up, released schizophrenics, currently out of hospital, and non-psychiatric controls. The diagnoses were based on hospital records, and supplementary information was gathered from various agencies and by interview with the subject wherever possible. Sixteen per cent of the mothers of released schizophrenics and 22 per cent of the mothers of the controls were found to be psychotic or to have schizoid or borderline character disorders. The mothers of the chronic schizophrenics differed significantly ($p < 0.01$) from both these groups in having a much higher proportion (55 per cent) with these characteristics.

Gardner (1967) used material from the same clinic but enlarged the sample to include 103 children who later developed schizophrenia and 57 non-psychiatric controls. The clinic workers paid special attention to family factors that were considered important in psychiatric disturbance. From this material, maternal pathology was graded for abnormality and was found to be significantly correlated with the later mental status of the female child, but not of the male child. The mothers of the chronic schizophrenics were described as shy, inadequate, withdrawn, vague, worried, fearful, incoherent, unreliable and suspicious. This is quite unlike the usual characterization of the schizophrenogenic mother. In fact, the cold, dominant, threatening mother was found most commonly among the control group.

Waring and Ricks (1965) employed the concepts of 'emotional divorce' (Bowen et al., 1959) and marital 'schism' and 'skew' (Lidz et al., 1957b; Fleck et al., 1963) in their analysis of information in the patients' former Child Guidance Clinic records. They found that the type of marriage most closely associated with subsequent mental illness in the child was characterized by emotional divorce, in which the parents lived under the same roof but in a state of mutual withdrawal. This situation was present in 35 per cent of their chronic schizophrenic group but in only 4 per cent of the controls ($p < 0.01$). Skewed and schismatic marriages [see p. 17] were no more common in the pre-schizophrenic group than the controls. However, none of the family environments of either the chronic or released schizophrenics was considered to be normal, whereas 16 per cent of the control group were thought to come from normal homes. In looking at the intra-family environment, the authors discerned symbiotic relationships in which the child was socially isolated and unduly helpless at home, making no attempt to escape. Excessive dependence of this kind was found to be significantly more common among the chronic schizophrenics than the controls.

This point was enlarged on by Ricks and Nameche (1966) who found that prolonged over-dependence of the child on the parent was common and characterized it by such acts as the parent bathing the child even in adolescence, isolating the child from its peers, and not allowing the child privacy. Nameche, Waring, and Ricks (1964) also reported that 65 per cent of twenty eventual chronic schizophrenics taken from the Judge Baker sample had never been separated for even one night from their parents by the time they were seen at the clinic. This compared with 23 per cent of the released schizophrenics, and was attributed by the authors to parental reluctance to let go of the child. An environment of prolonged neglect, on the other hand, was more often found in delinquents than in the schizophrenics.

Waring and Ricks' paper is of particular interest because the authors employed a number of measures of parental disturbance defined in the papers reviewed earlier in this chapter. However, they utilized information gathered before the child fell ill by persons unaware of the concepts behind these measures. This method eliminates an important source of bias operating at the data-gathering stage, and it is noteworthy that no evidence was found to support the hypotheses of the schizophrenogenic mother or of marital schism and skew. Unfortunately those authors were aware of the eventual outcome of the children whose records they were analysing, so that this particular bias may account for their finding of 'emotional divorce' in the families of chronic schizophrenics. Moreover, the measure is a global one and involves the usual snags of high level theories discussed above. If we allow for these deficiencies, the findings of this group of studies appear to add weight to the evidence that the parents of chronic schizophrenics more frequently show signs of mental disturbance than the parents of normal controls. Their marriages are more likely to be abnormal and they are more likely to have had an intense overprotective relationship with their pre-schizophrenic children. As pointed out above, the nature of this relationship may be determined by some quality of the child, rather than determining the later development of schizophrenia in the child. Indeed, Nameche, Waring, and Ricks (1964) found that these children were often in need of special care, had been felt to be sickly and weak, or seemed to require special treatment by their mothers. This agrees with the findings of several other studies reviewed above (Kasanin et al., 1934; Gerard and Siegel, 1950; Lidz, 1967; Alanen, 1966; Pollin and Stabenau, 1968). There does not seem to be anything specific about the effect of these pre-schizophrenic children on their parents, because similar attitudes have been described in the parents of children with a variety of conditions such as school refusal (Hersov, 1960), anorexia nervosa (King, 1963), and cerebral palsy (Margolies *et al.*, 1956). Evidence for the influence that a child's characteristics may have on parental attitudes has been comprehensively reviewed by Bell (1968), and Brown *et al.* (1972) have shown that in parent–child relationships there may be an interaction in both directions.

Another method of avoiding retrospective bias in assessment has been employed by Mednick and Schulsinger (1968) and Mednick (1966). They have begun a prospective study, planned to run for 20 years, of 207 persons with a high risk of developing schizophrenia because they were born to mothers severely affected by schizophrenia. A group of 100 subjects whose mothers were free of schizophrenia were chosen as controls. The authors are collecting physiological and psychological data as well as information about their family life and social adjustment. On the basis of previous genetic studies, they expect thirty of their high risk subjects to develop schizophrenia during the follow-up period. The results reported for the first 5 years show that the high risk subjects differ from the control group in having had more prolonged births and a higher proportion with an abnormal placenta. On the G.S.R. they show a significantly shorter reponse latency with larger amplitude responses and a quicker recovery. In a blind evaluation it was found that more of the high risk subjects had a disturbed home life and more of them were reported by their schoolteachers to get upset easily. So far only one parental measure has been found to be significant, namely, the relationship between the duration of mother's absence from home and the degree of disturbance in the child when seen for the initial evaluation. In every case in which separation occurred it was on account of the psychiatric hospitalization of the mother.

This kind of study does not separate the effects of environmental and genetic factors. Two interesting recent studies hold the genetic factor constant for both the index and control groups and examine the influence of different environments on the incidence of schizophrenia. Lindelius (1970) studied all admissions from 1900 to 1910 to a Swedish mental hospital, employing as the environmental variable the loss of a parent from death, divorce, illegitimacy or other causes before the child was 15 years old. Only those schizophrenics currently in good mental health were included as index cases and 1,516 siblings of these patients were followed up. All these siblings presumably had a similar risk of developing schizophrenia on a hereditary basis, but 263 of them came from broken homes while the remaining 1,253 came from intact homes. The proportion who developed schizophrenia was actually slightly less in the group coming from broken homes, suggesting that this environmental factor is not of aetiological importance.

The other study is that of Fischer (1971), who compared the incidence of schizophrenia among two cohorts of the children of monozygotic twins, discordant for schizophrenia. One cohort comprised the offspring of the schizophrenic twin and the other cohort the offspring of the non-schizophrenic twin. Both cohorts had the same genetic risk of developing schizophrenia but one was brought up in the disturbing environment provided by a schizophrenic parent. In fact the proportion developing schizophrenia was slightly less for those raised by the schizophrenic parent (9·4 per cent) than for those raised by the non-schizophrenic co-twin (12·3 per cent). Female offspring were more frequently affected (19·7 per cent) than male (3·2 per cent).

Another group of studies attempts to separate the effects of environmental and genetic factors by examining schizophrenic patients who have been separated from their biological parents at an early age. Wender et al. (1968) compared three groups of parents. One group consisted of 11 sets of parents who had adopted children before the age of one year who later developed acute, chronic or borderline schizophrenia. A second group consisted of parents who reared their own schizophrenic children, while the third group comprised adoptive parents of normal subjects. The three groups of parents were matched on a number of demographic variables. This was not possible with socio-economic status because Class IV and V adoptive parents of normal children were unwilling to participate in the study. Unfortunately, the schizophrenic adoptees are unlikely to be a representative sample as they make up only 2 per cent of the expected number of such patients in the area from which they were drawn. The interviewer knew which experimental group each subject belonged to, but the data were also assessed by a rater who did not know the diagnoses and the agreement between the two was high ($r = 0·81$).

The authors found that the biological parents who had reared schizophrenic offspring were significantly more disturbed than the parents who had adopted children who became schizophrenic ($p < 0·005$). The prevalence of schizophrenia among the relatives of the biological parents was significantly higher than among those of the adoptive parents ($p < 0·07$). On the other hand, the parents who adopted children who became schizophrenic were significantly more disturbed than those who adopted normal children ($p < 0·05$). There was a significant correlation ($p < 0·05$) between the severity of disorder in the schizophrenic offspring and their biological parents. This correlation was not significant between children and their adoptive parents.

This evidence supports the hypothesis that a significant part of the increased disturbance found among the immediate relatives of schizophrenics is due to a common biological inheritance. That the sick child may also exert a disturbing effect on the parents is suggested by the greater amount of illness found among the adoptive parents of schizophrenics than among the adoptive parents of normal children. However, as Wender et al. (1971) suggest, this could be due to situational factors in the interview, such as a sense of unease at having brought up a child who has become ill, or could imply the possibility that schizophrenia is more likely to develop in children who are adopted by abnormal parents.

This study is open to the criticism that the criteria for the diagnostic categories were loosely defined, and that a questionable assumption is made that 'schizoid' and 'borderline' disorders lie along the same dimension. Furthermore, as mentioned above, the possibility of bias affecting the information-gathering process was not adequately controlled for. The limitations of this study have largely been overcome by other work on adoptees which made use of national registers. Kety *et al.* (1968) studied both the biological and adoptive parents of adoptees who later became schizophrenic. From the records of all adoptions in Denmark from 1917 to 1947, 33 schizophrenic index cases were identified. Controls, matched for sex, age, age of adoption, and socio-economic status of the adoptive family, were selected from the adoptees who were psychiatrically well. Ninety-two per cent of the biological and adoptive parents were interviewed and information was checked against public records. American diagnostic practices were employed and subjects were rated as acute or chronic schizophrenia, borderline state, or personality disorder. All these diagnoses were included under the rubric 'schizophrenic spectrum disorder' (S.S.D.).

The schizophrenic index cases were found to have a significantly greater number of biological relatives (8·7 per cent) with S.S.D. than the control subjects (1·6 per cent, p<0·01). When schizophrenia alone was looked at, the difference between the groups was still significant. The difference in the proportions with S.S.D was largely accounted for by a high prevalence (10 per cent) among the biological half-siblings of the schizophrenics, whereas the half-siblings of the controls showed no psychiatric illness. The biological parents of the index and control cases did not differ in the prevalence of S.S.D. It is interesting that no S.S.D. occurred among the relatives of patients with acute schizophrenia, only among the relatives of chronic and borderline schizophrenics. This is in accord with the findings of Waring and Ricks (1965). It was also found that more of the adoptive parents of the index cases suffered from other psychiatric disorders than of the controls. When the biological and adoptive parents of each subject were compared, more S.S.D. was found among the former.

The 10 per cent prevalence of schizophrenia among the biological relatives of schizophrenics reared in adoptive homes is considered as evidence for a genetically transmitted factor. The fact that S.S.D. was as prevalent among the relatives of borderline schizophrenics as of chronic schizophrenics is interpreted as supporting the validity of the concept of a spectrum of schizophrenic disorder. On the other hand, the greater amount of other psychiatric disorders among the adoptive parents of index cases than among those of controls argues for an environmental effect, acting either from adoptee to adoptive parent or vice versa.

In another study using the Danish Register, Rosenthal *et al.* (1968, 1971) investigated the incidence of schizophrenia among adoptees whose biological parents had developed schizophrenia. A carefully matched control group consisted of adoptees whose biological parents were free of psychiatric illness.

The diagnoses were made from case abstracts prepared by workers unaware of the purpose or design of the study. These abstracts were rated blind by two to four raters, who then came to an agreement.

It was found that 31·6 per cent of the index cases were given a diagnosis of schizophrenic spectrum disorder compared with 17·8 per cent of control adoptees (p<0·05). The index cases showed more severe disorders. The authors point out that these results are qualified by the fact that it was not known for certain that the parents of the controls were free of psychiatric illness, only that they had not contacted a psychiatric facility. However, this possible bias would tend to diminish the difference found between the index and control groups. These results support the hypothesis of a genetic factor operating in schizophrenia, but do not, of course, rule out an additional effect of environmental factors in the adoptive family.

Of all the adoption studies, the findings of Heston are perhaps the most striking (Heston, 1966; Heston and Denny, 1968). The study concerned 97 children permanently separated from their parents by the age of 2 weeks. Forty-seven of these had been born to mothers who developed schizophrenia during the pregnancy, while the remaining 50, who formed a control group, were born to mothers who had no known psychiatric disorder. Half the subjects in each group had been reared in foundling homes and eventually adopted, while the other half were fostered, usually by relatives. Some children born to schizophrenic mothers had been fostered by their fathers. The diagnosis of schizophrenia in the mothers was biased towards severe chronic disorder. Only children who had no contact with their mothers were included in the study. Controls were found by using the records of the same foundling homes, and were matched individually for sex, type of eventual placement, and length of time in the child care institution. Psychiatric illness in the control mothers was excluded by a search of state hospital records.

The children were followed up by an extensive search of public records in three states, and 72 of the 97 were interviewed. Adequate information was obtained for the remaining 25. The diagnosis of schizophrenia was used conservatively.

The findings are striking. Both groups had the same experience of rearing, yet the offspring of the schizophrenic mothers were significantly more disordered on each of six indices of psychiatric disorder: a mental health rating scale (p<0·0006), the number of mental defectives (p<0·05), the number of schizophrenics (five in the experimental group, none in the controls, p<0·024), the number of sociopaths (p<0·02), the number of neurotics (p<0·05), and the number of persons who had spent at least 2 years in jail (p<0·006). Three other findings support the hypothesis that the form of rearing is not an important determinant of schizophrenia. First, there was no difference in the incidence of schizophrenia or in the mental health ratings whether the children were reared in foster homes, foundling homes, or adoptive homes, and whether they were reared by the relative of a schizophrenic mother or not.

Secondly, there was no consistent relationship between the social class of the home of rearing and the child's mental health rating. Thirdly, the age-corrected rate for schizophrenia among the adopted offspring of schizophrenics was 16·6 per cent. This is almost identical to the rate of 16·9 per cent found by Kallman for children raised by their schizophrenic mothers. Had the family environment been a significant factor, the incidence of schizophrenia in children reared apart from their schizophrenic mothers should have been lower than in those reared by their biological mothers. Thus Heston's work established that the incidence of schizophrenia in the children of schizophrenic mothers is not affected by their being reared apart from their biological families.

The studies reviewed above provide such strong evidence that there can be little doubt that there is a genetic factor which predisposes to schizophrenia. It is also clear that some of the individual morbidity and marital disturbance which has been reported among the parents of schizophrenics can be ascribed to a genetic factor which is common to one or both parents and the child. However, the findings discussed do not rule out environmental factors, and some of the studies indicate their importance (Wender et al., 1971; Rosenthal et al., 1968).

Another group of studies sheds a different light on the way in which the attitudes and behaviour of parents may influence the development of schizophrenia. Brown and his colleagues (1962) carried out a carefully planned study of the effect of the schizophrenic patient's emotional relationship with his family on the course of his illness. This work differs in aim from all that has been discussed above in that it focuses on patients in whom schizophrenia has already become evident and examines the role of the family in precipitating a further breakdown. The concern with precipitating rather than predisposing factors can still lead, by inference, to a greater understanding of the aetiology of illness.

These workers interviewed the relatives of male schizophrenics being discharged to an address in London, excluding hostels. The patient's mental state and social behaviour on the ward were evaluated just before discharge and at readmission. If the patient remained in the community for a year then his mental state was re-evaluated at the end of that time. The interviews with the relatives were conducted at the time of discharge and 2 weeks later. They took place in the presence of the patient and lasted 2–3 hours. Ratings were made on the degree of emotion, hostility, and dominance expressed by the key relative to the patient, and on the amount of emotion and hostility shown by the patient to the relative. In 16 pilot interviews there was only 7 per cent disagreement between investigators on the 96 items rated. At follow-up a time budget of the patient's activities was drawn up to determine the amount of contact with his relatives.

Clinical deterioration was only recorded if marked. Fifty-two per cent of the cohort deteriorated or relapsed within 9 months. Deterioration was significantly related to the severity of symptoms at discharge and to a number of pre-discharge measures, including the amount of disturbed behaviour before admission, the decline in occupational level, and whether the patient had been unemployed for more than 2 years.

For the 97 patients who had returned to their families on discharge, the degree of deterioration was significantly related to the amount of expressed emotion and hostility in the household. When the scales were combined, 76 per cent of patients returning to 'high emotion' homes and 28 per cent of those returning to 'low emotion' homes deteriorated (p<0·001). These findings held even when mental state at discharge was controlled for, and were applicable whether the patient returned to parents, wife, or other kin. In the high risk group, patients who spent less than 35 hours in contact with their relatives showed significantly less deterioration than those who spent more time in contact. This was not true of the low emotional involvement group.

Subsequently, Rutter and Brown (1966) showed that they could achieve a high reliability on measures of family relationships by recording spontaneous expressions of emotion in the interview situation itself. On ratings of observed warmth of a subject towards his spouse, the number of critical comments made in the interview, the frequency of reported irritability, participation in household chores, and a global judgement of the marital relationship, they achieved an inter-rater reliability of 0·60–0.91. The reliability between self report and reporting by the spouse was above 0·67 for all measures. Great care was taken in these studies, for example, interviews took from 6 to 8 hours and were scored from tape recordings. The measures developed by Rutter and Brown were employed subsequently by Brown, Birley, and Wing (1972) in a study of a representative sample of 101 patients with a new episode of schizophrenia who lived in the Camberwell area. A minimum of eight interviews by psychiatrists and sociologists was carried out for each patient. An over-all index of emotional response (E.R.) of relatives was developed from the measures used, the most important factor being the number of critical comments made by the relative about the patient. The findings of the previous study (Brown et al., 1962) were confirmed, as a significantly higher proportion of patients returning to a high E.R. home relapsed in the subsequent 9 months compared with those returning to a low E.R. home. When the patient's behaviour at discharge was controlled for, the relationship held true, so that one cannot argue that both relapse and relative's attitude are a consequence of the patient's degree of disturbance. Rather it appears that the patient's relapse is directly related to the relative's critical attitude. In this study but not in their previous one (Brown et al., 1962) it was found that living with relatives resulted in a higher relapse rate than living with a spouse. It was confirmed that patients returning to a high E.R. home had a significantly lower risk of relapse if they spent less than 35 hours per week in contact with other members of the household.

The studies of Brown and his co-workers provide strong evidence that the way parents react to offspring with a known vulnerability to schizophrenia significantly affects the likelihood of their developing a further schizophrenic breakdown. It seems likely that a similar relationship exists between parental attitudes and the first onset of schizophrenia. This work also demonstrates that emotional relationships can be measured in a reliable and reproducible way.

In considering research into schizophrenia a final point about the reliability of diagnosis needs to be emphasized. This is of fundamental importance and applies to almost all the studies we have reviewed, with a few exceptions such as the work by Brown and his colleagues. Researchers in the field have paid scant attention to the criteria for making a diagnosis of schizophrenia. Most workers have relied on the clinician's diagnosis, or the diagnosis in the case records, but both practices are open to criticism. Kendell, Cooper, and their colleagues (Kendell et al., 1971; Cooper et al., 1972) have shown that there are marked discrepancies between diagnostic practices in the United States and Great Britain. In New York, nearly twice as many patients admitted to psychiatric hospitals are labelled schizophrenic as in London. These workers found that it was largely attributable to the much broader concept of schizophrenia held by the American psychiatrists. This finding has been confirmed in the International Pilot Study of Schizophrenia (World Health Organization, 1973), a cross-national study of diagnosis in nine countries.

We can therefore assume that many of the patients included in American studies as schizophrenic would be excluded from British studies. The problem is magnified by the failure of research workers to state their criteria for schizophrenia and to establish, either by interview or by a careful review of the case records, whether the 'schizophrenics' they have included meet these criteria. A further complication is that several of the studies reviewed here included childhood schizophrenics among their index cases. It was not made clear whether these were adult type schizophrenics with onset in adolescence, or even before puberty, a rare condition (Kolvin, 1972a and b), or were patients who had presented originally with Kanner's infantile autism. There is ample evidence for regarding infantile autism as completely unrelated to adult schizophrenia (Rutter and Bartak, 1971; Wing, 1966).

In view of the fact that the question of reliability of diagnosis has been hardly touched on in most of the studies reviewed here, we have had to accept the authors' contention that they were studying schizophrenics, while entertaining reservations about the results of any study in which the criteria for the diagnosis have not been stipulated. At least we can assume that among any group of so-called schizophrenics there is certain to be a sizeable core of patients who would be accepted as schizophrenic by workers in most countries (World Health Organization, 1973).

CHAPTER II

QUESTIONNAIRE STUDIES

In this chapter we consider studies which use questionnaires to measure ways in which the attitudes of parents of schizophrenics differ from other parents. The studies to be reviewed in this and succeeding chapters do not clarify any further the relationship between abnormal characteristics of parents and the development of schizophrenia in their offspring. Rather they are concerned with identifying more specifically the particular ways in which the parents function abnormally. Once these can be identified it should be possible to carry out further studies to determine how far such traits reflect a genetic and how far an environmental effect, and in which direction the effect is operating.

The first study to use a questionnaire technique in this field was that of Mark (1953), which is frequently quoted and which has influenced much of the later work. He gave a questionnaire to 100 mothers of hospitalized schizophrenics and 100 mothers of medical patients, not all of whom were in hospital. The groups were matched for age, religion, education and socio-economic status, as well as for the age and number of offspring. The mothers of schizophrenics were found to differ from the controls on 67 of the 139 items. The results were interpreted to mean that the mothers of schizophrenics were significantly more restrictive and controlling in their attitudes to child-rearing than the control mothers. On some items they were judged to be more devoted and on other items more detached than the control group. The author points out that this apparent ambivalence may be an important feature of the mothers of schizophrenics, but alternatively it could reflect a lack of consistency and reliability in the test items.

Despite the painstaking way in which this study was carried out it has many methodological flaws. The test-retest reliability of the questionnaire was never assessed, nor was its validity. One possible check on the validity would be to obtain reports from relatives on the mother's attitudes to her children. A further check, which Mark himself suggests, would be to apply the questionnaire to another sample. The items were chosen to reveal attitudes towards child-rearing, but in practice most parents' attitudes vary with their different children. This is particularly likely to be true of a mother's attitudes to her schizophrenic child as opposed to her normal children, and Mark's study did not allow for this distinction. The control group in this study was more appropriate than in any other of the questionnaire studies reviewed because the controls were the mothers of patients, but they were medical patients, not all of whom were in hospital. In the previous chapter we pointed out that if the circumstances of testing are not the same for all the groups under study then critical differences in response bias may result. This point has been emphasized by others (Mishler and Waxler, 1968a; Schopler and Loftin, 1969; Zuckerman et al., 1958). The last-named authors reported on a Ph.D. thesis by Toms, who tested 30 mothers of schizophrenics and 30 control mothers with the M.M.P.I. He found that the mothers of schizophrenics scored significantly higher on the two scales measuring defensiveness (L and K). Zuckerman and his colleagues stress the importance of controlling for social desirability and suppression of response when using attitude scales.

Yet another weakness shown by Mark's study is that the conclusions depended on the interpretation four judges put on the classification of the items. We do not know to what extent the judges shared the same point of view; their grouping of the items into categories labelled 'devotion', 'detachment', etc., may only reflect a common professional training and theoretical background.

We have made extensive criticisms of Mark's study because it provides a yardstick by which we can measure the succeeding ones. Our criticisms are to some extent vindicated by McFarland's attempt to replicate Mark's study. Using the same items he failed to find a significant number of questions which distinguished mothers of schizophrenics from normal controls (personal communication reported by Zuckerman et al., 1958). As far as we know, none of the other questionnaires discussed below has been validated on a second sample, although some have been used in part by later workers. This gives rise to a further difficulty in reviewing questionnaire studies, namely the problem of comparing results from studies which have used different questionnaires. In the 16 reports reviewed here, seven different questionnaires were employed. The problem is exemplified by the study of Freeman and Grayson (1955) who compared mothers of schizophrenics and normals using the Shoben parent–child attitude survey (Shoben, 1949). No difference was found between the groups on the dominance scales, but altogether 14 of the 85 items differentiated between the groups. Inspection of these suggested that the mothers of schizophrenics were over-protective towards their children and showed 'subtle domination'. It is difficult to compare these workers' findings of over-protection and 'subtle domination' with Mark's characterization of the mothers as 'more restrictive', and to know whether these terms refer to similar things or not.

Freeman and Grayson estimated the reliability of their instrument by calculating the split-half reliability (it was 0·92). However, the value of their findings is diminished by the unsuitability of their controls. Their control mothers were tested at home by lay interviewers, whereas the experimental group was tested at hospital by the authors. Furthermore, the control group was contacted through friends of university students, which suggests that they may have had a different social background and response set from the experimental group. The importance of controlling for social class was shown by Freeman et al. (1959), who constructed a questionnaire by inserting items from the Shoben scale into another schedule. They found a significant inverse correlation between the 'possessiveness' rating of their questionnaire and education, rent, and income, suggesting that any index of social class would be similarly associated.

The Schafer and Bell Parent Attitude Research Instrument (PARI) was a further development based on the questionnaires of Mark and Shoben. It includes 23 subscales theoretically related to personality development in children. A factor analysis of normative data was used to derive three weighted scales labelled (A) Authoritarian Controlling Factor, (B) Hostility-Rejection Factor, and (C) Democratic Attitude Factor. Zuckerman et al. (1958) used the PARI to compare 42 mothers of schizophrenic patients with 42 mothers of controls, collected at community functions and matched with the experimental group for mother's age and education. An attempt to check the validity of the hospital's diagnosis was made by comparing it with independent ratings of severity of illness in 30 cases. A significant correlation was found between these two indices. An analysis of variance between the groups, using the three factors plus 20 individual subscales, did not reveal any significant differences which could not have occurred by chance. Across the groups, however, there was a significant inverse correlation between education and the Authoritarian Controlling Factor, once more demonstrating the importance of controlling for social class and education. This correlation was significantly higher for mothers of schizophrenics than for mothers of normals. These workers concluded that they had failed to substantiate the hypothesis that the mothers of schizophrenics are more controlling and rejecting than the mothers of normals.

Klebanoff (1959) used the PARI to discriminate between the attitudes of different groups of mothers who were currently raising ill children. He gave the PARI to 15 mothers of hospitalized autistic children, 15 mothers of hospitalized mentally retarded and brain-damaged children, and 26 mothers of normals. The groups were matched for age and socio-economic status, but not for education. Mothers of both groups of ill children showed more extreme attitudes than mothers of normals, but more abnormal attitudes were shown by the mothers of brain-damaged and retarded children than by mothers of autistic children. The author suggests that the results may be understood as reflecting the degree of strain suffered by the parents in raising their children. Only three of the autistic children had shown symptoms before the age of three, whereas 13 of the organic group had done so. The effectiveness of the PARI in discriminating between the groups in this study may be due to the fact that the attitudes being tested related to ongoing behaviour and interactions concurrent with the period of research. When the questionnaire method is used to assess the child-rearing attitudes of parents to their children after they have grown up and perhaps have left home, it is less likely to be effective and any differences found may be only distantly related to what actually went on when the children were being reared.

The PARI was also used by Horowitz and Lovell (1960) to compare a sample of 30 mothers of female schizophrenics with 30 mothers of normal girls. Only two of 19 subscales (Fostering Dependency and Being Secluded) differentiated significantly between the groups. A further analysis of the data showed that the younger control mothers had significantly more deviant scores than the younger mothers of schizophrenics. This finding of more deviant responses in the normal mothers, if corroborated, would cast serious doubt on the validity of the PARI as a research instrument.

Four studies can be mentioned which have paid greater attention to methodology in an attempt to overcome some of the problems outlined above. McGhie (1961a and b) tried to control factors affecting the subject's response set by using a group of non-schizophrenic psychiatric patients. He compared 20 mothers of schizophrenics with 20 mothers of neurotic patients and 20 mothers of offspring who had no psychiatric history. The groups were matched for parents' age, age of offspring and social class. However, since the schizophrenics were hospitalized while the neurotic patients were not, factors affecting response set were not adequately controlled for. McGhie used the Child Rearing Questionnaire, which consists largely of items which Mark (1953) found to differentiate between the mothers of schizophrenic and non-psychiatric patients. McGhie found that the mothers of schizophrenics scored significantly higher over-all than the mothers of neurotic and normal children, whose scores were very similar. Examination of the content of the eleven most highly discriminating items suggested that the mothers of schizophrenics tended to be more restrictive and more preoccupied with the possible adverse effects of sex on their children than the mothers of the two comparison groups. This result is very important as it confirms some of Mark's original findings and hence strengthens the validity of the questionnaire.

Sharp et al. (1964), working in a United States Naval Hospital, noticed that parents of schizophrenics interacted more vigorously with their sons than parents of sociopaths. They compared the parents of 20 schizophrenics with the parents of 20 sociopaths who had a history of criminal behaviour but no psychiatric illness. The groups were matched for age, history, race, religion, and social class. However, eight sociopaths came from broken homes compared with only two schizophrenics. The Social Service Questionnaire was sent by post to the parents. The mothers of schizophrenics were found to be significantly more concerned with conventional values and how their children's behaviour reflected on them than the mothers of sociopaths. Half of the parents of sociopaths were rejecting towards their sons whereas only 10 per cent of the parents of schizophrenics were. During the period of study 80 per cent of the schizophrenics had visits from their families compared with 50 per cent of the sociopaths ($p < 0.001$) and significantly more parents of schizophrenics wanted their sons to return home. Despite interesting aspects of the experimental design, it is difficult to see how these findings enlarge our knowledge of the parents of schizophrenics since they can be entirely explained by postulating a more rejecting attitude on the part of the parents of sociopaths.

Guertin (1961) carried out one of the earlier studies, which examined the possible relationship between the form of the schizophrenic illness and parental attitudes. He differentiated 49 male schizophrenics by a factor analysis of their symptoms into 5 subgroups; catatonic, over-expressive, paranoid, resistive isolated, and anxious dysphoric. The patients' mothers completed the PARI and significant correlations were found between their responses and the diagnostic subgroups. However, the majority of the correlations were with the anxious dysphoric subgroup of neurotic symptoms and very few were with the more characteristically schizophrenic subgroups. The design of the study automatically controls for the effect on parents' attitudes of having a child in hospital with a chronic psychiatric illness. It demonstrates an association between parents' attitudes and various clinical symptoms, but does not attempt to answer the question of whether the parents' attitudes influence the form of the child's illness or vice versa. The results suggest that any relationship between the two is stronger for neurotic than for schizophrenic symptoms.

Farina and Holzberg (1967) conducted one of the most rigorous studies in the field using the Child Rearing Attitude Scale derived from Mark's work. This questionnaire was administered to the parents of 24 non-schizophrenic psychiatric patients, 26 schizophrenics with a good premorbid personality, and 24 schizophrenics with a poor premorbid personality. The personality assessment was made using the Phillips scale (Phillips, 1953). Five judges, who achieved a high inter-rater reliability, identified 27 items in the questionnaire as reflecting Dominance, 25 as reflecting Over-protection, and the remaining 11 as not relevant to either. Independent measures of Dominance were developed to validate the questionnaire. Testing was conducted blindly and included the administration of the questionnaire to the offspring of the three groups of parents. A three-way analysis of variance was carried out involving groups of parents versus informant (parent or offspring) versus attitude scales. The groups did not differ significantly on the attitude scales or on the extent of agreement with their offspring. The agreement between the attitude scores of parents and those attributed to them by their offspring was high, but the offspring of all three groups saw their mothers as having significantly more extreme attitudes than the mothers ascribed to themselves. Heilbrun (1960a) found this to be true of schizophrenic women in regard to their mothers but not of normal women.

Farina and Holzberg found no consistent relationship between observed dominance behaviour as defined by specific criteria of interaction and the scores on Dominance derived from the questionnaire. The correlation between these two measures was negative for parents of controls and schizophrenics with a good premorbid personality, but positive for parents of schizophrenics with a poor premorbid personality. Hence the content validity of the questionnaire was not confirmed by the other independent measures used in this study.

Baxter *et al.* (1966) also tried to control for differences in response bias by using the parents of non-schizophrenic psychiatric patients for comparison, and by taking account of the socio-economic characteristics of their subjects. Unfortunately their samples were small, consisting of 6 neurotic patients and 16 schizophrenics, 8 with good (Goods) and 8 with poor (Poors) premorbid personalities. All the cases were in hospital at the time of the study. Interviews with parents were conducted using the Mark-Shoben questionnaire to determine their attitudes to their children and the Marlowe-Crowe questionnaire to test for the social desirability of their responses and to give a lie score. The tests were administered and scored blindly and the raters were ignorant of the hypotheses being tested.

In addition to the questionnaires, the parents were given a fantasy test consisting of 10 cards, each depicting a child-rearing problem. The parent was asked to say how he or she would have handled the situation if the child in the picture had been their son at age 8–10 years. Raters were asked to rate the transcript of each subject on the likelihood of whether he or she would employ the same strategy. Transcripts were in random order and all were rated for one category of discipline before rating the next. The agreement between raters for all nine categories was 96·2 per cent. No differences were found between parental groups in respect of social class or the social desirability of the answers. Results from the Child Rearing Questionnaire showed that both parents of Poors had significantly more deviant attitudes than the parents of the neurotic patients, while only the fathers of Goods were more deviant. The mothers of Goods were found to have the least deviant attitudes of all. Parents of the controls were intermediate between the parents of Goods and parents of Poors on the number of extreme ratings made. This inconsistent finding casts doubt on the validity of the questionnaire.

The fantasy of handling child-rearing problems did not in general reveal any significant differences between the parental groups. The one exception to this was that the parents of Poors subscribed less to physical discipline than the parents of Goods or controls.

This study was carefully designed and well controlled but the number in each group was small. The findings were too inconsistent to draw any firm conclusions. In particular the results from the questionnaire were not confirmed by the fantasy task, so that the authors were unsuccessful in their attempt at validation. It is also possible that the differences found related more to the premorbid personality of the patients than to the illness which later emerged. This interpretation is supported by the fact that differences were found between the parents of schizophrenics according to whether their children had good or poor premorbid personalities. This finding raises the question of whether retrospective studies of this kind are likely to shed any light at all on the aetiology of schizophrenia.

There remains a small group of questionnaire studies which all direct themselves at the patient's view of his parents' attitudes rather than sampling the parents' attitudes directly. Not only are these studies liable to the short-comings discussed above but they suffer from the limitations that the information comes second-hand from an observer who is likely to be biased, subject to falsification of memory, and affected by other distortions stemming from his or her illness.

Heilbrun (1960a) gave the PARI to 25 hospitalized schizophrenic women and 22 normal women and asked them to respond as they thought their mothers would. She found that the patients attributed much more deviant responses to their mothers than the control subjects. However, when the mothers themselves completed the questionnaire there was no significant difference between the two groups. In view of this finding one can attach little aetiological significance to the findings of Garmezy et al. (1961), who showed that schizophrenics with good premorbid personalities reported more maternal dominance than normal controls, while schizophrenics with poor premorbid personalities reported more paternal dominance. Horner (1964) matched 20 schizophrenic in-patients with 20 normal people on a number of variables and interviewed them with the Pascal–Jenkins Behaviour Scale. This aims to elicit retrospective information from the respondents about their parents' attitudes during the respondents' first *ten* years of life! It almost goes without saying that such information is likely to be influenced by prevailing social attitudes and psychiatric theories about the aetiology of mental illness popular at the time which have filtered through to the lay public. The findings of Heilbrun's study, reported above, make it incumbent on all succeeding workers to show that such factors are not significantly affecting patients' assessments of their parents, or the attitudes of the parents themselves.

Lane and Singer (1959) carried out a carefully designed study which emphasizes the complexity of factors that determine patients' responses to such questionnaires and the interpretation of the results. They set out to examine the interaction between status as a schizophrenic patient and social class in determining patients' attitudes towards their parents. The subjects consisted of 24 middle class schizophrenics, 24 lower class schizophrenics, and 48 surgical patients free of psychiatric illness, also divided evenly between the same two social classes. All subjects were in hospital at the time of the study. The groups were carefully matched on nine different demographic variables including the length of education. The diagnostic criteria were specified, an unusual feature among these studies. All the schizophrenics had a history of delusions and/or hallucinations and were literate and co-operative, while all the surgical patients had a Cornell Medical Index score of less than 10. Subjects were tested with the Elias Family Opinion Survey (EFOS) and the Family Attitude Survey (FAS), the latter being a projective test in which the subject rates on a five-point scale how far the given description of a picture applies. Among the numerous detailed results reported, the most salient and consistent finding was that most of the results were attributable to the difference between the middle class normal subjects, who scored closest to the judges' ratings for normality, and the other three groups, whose scores were similar. The greatest differences were between the middle class normal subjects, who scored highest, and the middle class schizophrenics, who scored lowest. These findings are closely paralleled by those of Kohn and Clausen (1956) [see p. 9] and underline the importance of controlling for social class when examining attitudes.

Other significant findings which emerged from Lane and Singer's work concerned the patient's attitude to and his perception of his parents. Schizophrenics expressed greater dependence on their parents, especially their mothers, than normal subjects. They also showed more hostility towards their parents, perceived more inter-parental friction, and felt more rejected. Over-protection by the mother was related more to social class than diagnostic group. This study shows that not only does social background influence the subject's responses, but also the rater's evaluation of these responses.

Apperson (1965) and Apperson and Adoo (1965) published the results of a questionnaire study of the parents of schizophrenics, in which a group of alcoholics and a group of non-schizophrenic psychiatric patients were used as controls. Once more the aim was to obtain the subjects' view of their parents attitudes. Becker and Siefkes (1969), and Magaro and Hanson (1969) gave a questionnaire to schizophrenic patients and normal controls for the same purposes, while Kayton and Biller (1971) asked their subjects to match their parents with a set of descriptive paragraphs, and Nathanson (1967) used both verbal descriptions and photographs for matching. These studies are open to the same objections as the other similar work reviewed.

We conclude that the body of work which uses questionnaires to identify characteristic attitudes of the parents of schizophrenics is heterogeneous and confusing because of the lack of continuity between the various studies. Workers using questionnaires have been more systematic in developing the research instruments than workers using the more clinically orientated methods reviewed in the previous chapter. In some cases the questionnaires were developed using normal populations first and tests of reliability, and susceptibility to response acquiescence, were carried out. Unfortunately there was often insufficient awareness of the special circumstances created when patients suffering from severe mental illness became the focus of study. It is therefore not surprising that the great majority of studies failed to show significant differences between the attitudes of the parents of schizophrenics and of normal subjects. There were only two formal attempts to repeat the few positive results found, one being successful (McGhie, 1961 *a* and *b*) and the other unsuccessful (McFarland, reported by Zuckerman, 1958).

There has been a tendency for each author to use a different questionnaire, developed by selecting parts of previous ones but adding something of his or her own. The only instrument to be used in the same form by several authors, the PARI, gave paradoxical results in that the parents of normal subjects were rated as more deviant than the parents of schizophrenics (Horowitz and Lovell, 1960). Not only has there been a failure to replicate findings but there has been little overlap in the kinds of attitudes being studied. No attempt has been made to reach agreement on the operational definitions of the concepts being studied.

If there is a consistent finding from this work, it is that there are numerous factors affecting attitudes which must be taken into account if this kind of research is to have any chance of success. The importance of education and social class has been repeatedly demonstrated, and the many factors affecting the premorbid characteristics of index subjects as well as the response of those being tested have been shown to be of great relevance.

Apart from these considerations, which can be taken into account in the design of a study, there are more fundamental problems inherent in the questionaire approach. The view that the assessment of current attitudes of the parents of schizophrenics throws light on the aetiology of schizophrenia involves too many assumptions for comfort. The assumptions are that current attitudes are related to attitudes some time in the past, that self-reported attitudes reflect actual behaviour, and that attitudes are stable and do not differ from day to day, in different environments, according to the prevailing mood, or in relation to one child rather than another. Certainly there is plenty of scope for the development of more precisely controlled and replicable studies, but the results of this work to date do not suggest to us that it is an approach which will elucidate significant factors in the aetiology of schizophrenia. The most consistent finding to emerge from this body of work is that the mothers of schizophrenics are more restrictive and controlling than the mothers of normal subjects. However, this finding has to be viewed in the light of the observation of Zuckerman *et al.* (1958) that authoritarian controlling attitudes are inversely related to the subject's level of education.

CHAPTER III

SMALL GROUP INTERACTION STUDIES OF PARENTS OF SCHIZOPHRENICS USING TECHNIQUES DERIVED FROM SOCIAL PSYCHOLOGY

INTRODUCTION AND BACKGROUND

THE studies discussed in this chapter are all based on methods developed by social psychologists for the detailed analysis of the behaviour of small groups. Workers in this area, such as Bales and Parsons, developed their methods of studying the interaction of two or more people at a time when neo-Freudian psychoanalysts in the United States, such as Fromm, Horney, and Sullivan, were shifting their emphasis away from libido theory towards the role of social and interpersonal factors in the genesis of mental illness. Sullivan, particularly, focused on schizophrenia, which he viewed as being a form of personality distortion resulting from disturbed interpersonal relationships. This view was shared by more recent psychoanalytic theorists, such as Lidz, Bateson and Wynne,* who have stressed the importance of the early family environment in the aetiology of schizophrenia. For certain psychoanalysts the findings of anthropologists, sociologists and social psychologists produced a shift in interest from the individual to interactions occurring in dyadic and triadic family groups. It was assumed that if particular patterns of interaction characterized the family and involved the child, then they could be expected to have specific effects on the child. Thus Lidz and his co-workers claimed that it was not just the effect of cold, rejecting, excessively dominant mothers that was important, but this effect in combination with a weak, passive father. A female child exposed to this pattern of interaction was believed to be particularly at risk of developing schizophrenia (Lidz *et al.*, 1957 *a* and *b*; Lidz, 1967). Although Lidz, Wynne and others had begun to conceptualize schizophrenia as the outcome of abnormal social interaction patterns, their approach was essentially clinical and descriptive and did not easily lead to experimental verification. However, the techniques developed by two social psychologists, Bales (1950*a* and *b*) and Strodtbeck (1951, 1954) seemed particularly suited to the scientific study of these theories. A brief introduction to the nature and rationale of these techniques is apposite to a discussion of the individual studies reviewed in this chapter as they form the basis of almost every one. Because the techniques used are so similar we will discuss the

* The theories and work of these authors are discussed in CHAPTER I, page 14, and CHAPTER V, page 72.

strengths and weaknesses common to most of them before considering them individually.

BALES' CATEGORIES OF BEHAVIOUR

Social– Emotional Area: Positive	1. Shows solidarity 2. Shows tension release 3. Agrees
Task Area: Neutral	4. Gives suggestion 5. Gives opinion 6. Gives orientation 7. Asks for orientation 8. Asks for opinion 9. Asks for suggestion
Social– Emotional Area: Negative	10. Disagrees 11. Shows tension 12. Shows antagonism

The technique developed by Bales, called Interaction Process Analysis (I.P.A.), provides a perfect example of what is named micro-analysis in sociology. Bales developed a method of classifying behaviour act by act as it occurs in small groups of people interacting with each other. He set out twelve categories of behaviour which are used to describe group processes and, by inference, the factors influencing these processes. The categories, each of which is intended to delimit the smallest definable unit of behaviour, are listed above. It should be noted that the observer must *interpret* each item of behaviour as falling into one or more of these categories by taking into account the content of what is being said, the context in which it occurs, and the inferred intent of the speaker. The twelve categories are further classified as either Expressive or Instrumental in character, and each pair of categories is related to a continuum of 'interlocking functional problems', namely, problems of orientation, evaluation, control, decision, tension management, and integration.

Behaviour is scored from direct observations or recorded interviews by a rater who labels who did what and which category of behaviour took place. Different authors have modified the I.P.A. and employed various methods of calculating the indices and variables scored according to their own purposes. The technique is capable of being adapted to a wide variety of groups. It is not necessary to go into further detail of each author's method of abstracting the data but the relevant information can be obtained from the individual papers.

The I.P.A. provides a basis for the analysis of behaviour in groups but does not offer any particular experimental framework. Strodtbeck (1951, 1954) developed the Revealed Difference Technique which is a method of stimulating interactions within small groups which can then be scored using the I.P.A. The basis of Strodtbeck's method is the administration of an attitude questionnaire to individual family members which requires them to commit themselves to particular attitudes on a number of issues. For example, they would be asked to indicate whether they agreed or disagreed with the statement that 'teenage girls should be able to stay out as late as they wish'. The individual family members are then brought together and asked to discuss certain questions on which they disagreed in order to reach some common agreement. The family discussion is recorded and the interaction is coded by raters who can be kept in ignorance of the index offspring's diagnosis. This technique does not require the presence of the investigator, who could influence the transaction. The transcripts can be rated by more than one rater, allowing the inter-rater reliability to be determined. Thus it provides a controlled experimental situation in which free discussion and interaction can readily take place and the interest of the subjects be maintained.

The basic method can be altered to suit various purposes, for example the measurement of dominance, yielding behaviour, and the amount of over-all group conflict. These measures can be defined in operational terms and can be taken by raters who are ignorant of clinical information about the family. As the technique also avoids informant bias and retrospective reporting, it has many attractions as a scientific method of studying behaviour in small groups. However, as we have indicated before (CHAPTER I, p. 11), because researchers are confined to the study of families *after* a member has become schizophrenic and because all the studies to date using social-psychological techniques have been limited to families in which the biological parents have reared the child, this body of work cannot separate genetic and environmental influences or distinguish parent-to-child effects from child-to-parent ones. These studies can only help us to discern whether there are certain characteristic patterns of family structure and interaction which are associated with the presence of schizophrenia in a family member. Our interest in this review will therefore be focused on the degree to which family interaction studies reveal reliable and valid differences between the families of schizophrenics and other families.

With a few exceptions, the studies of social interaction discussed here are characterized by a high standard of methodological rigour. Ancillary variables such as the subject's age, education, and social class are almost invariably controlled for. The reliability of the scoring method generally reaches satisfactorily high levels. However, a number of questions arise regarding the extent to which the findings can be generalized. Do measures taken on one day relate to how the family will perform on another day under the same or somewhat different circumstances? Does what is measured in these highly structured experimental situations relate very clearly to the way the families behave in their everyday lives? Winter and Ferreira (1967) discuss this point and refer to a study by Borgatta (1964), who used the I.P.A. to observe a number of groups of college students. Although he found some consistency between the behaviour observed in five-person discussion groups at university one semester and the behaviour of the same students in three-person groups the following semester, the test-retest correlations were disappointingly low, ranging from −0·2 to +0·67. Correlations between their behaviour in five-person discussion groups and their behaviour in a different sort of group situation, namely role-playing, were even lower (−0·12 to +0·23). When the situational task was changed radically, the behaviour of the subjects also changed and could not be predicted from their previous behaviour. Borgatta's findings relating to the behaviour of university students with their peers cannot readily be generalized to family groups, where we would expect a clearer demarcation of different roles, and interactions which are more stable over time. Mishler and Waxler (1968a and b) examined how much change over intervals of time parents showed on I.P.A. measures, and found some to be stable and others not, depending on the person with whom a subject was interacting. The relevance of the stability of interaction patterns over time depends of course on what is being tested. If parents were found to act the same with the well sibling as the sick one, this would weigh against a specific effect of parental behaviour in the transmission of schizophrenia.

Another general criticism has to be considered regarding the interpretation of the studies reviewed here. The majority of these studies are concerned with issues such as conflict, dominance, hostility, harmony, etc., and in most cases these terms are operationally defined. However, the definitions differ from author to author, so that it is difficult to compare the findings of the various studies. Moreover, as discussed above, it is questionable whether dominance defined in terms of, say, the length and number of times a person speaks in an experimental situation is related to dominance in making decisions in the everyday life of the family.

We have begun this chapter with a more extensive introduction than other chapters because the methods discussed here are unlikely to be familiar to persons working in psychiatry and yet appear to have considerable relevance to many research problems in this field. Having discussed some of the strengths and weaknesses of these methods we now go on to review the relevant studies in greater detail.

RESEARCH FINDINGS

Farina and his colleagues have conducted a number of investigations into the relationship between the sex of the dominant parent and the premorbid sexual and social adjustment of the patient. The parents of patients suffering from tuberculosis were used as controls. The schizophrenics were divided into those with good and poor premorbid personalities (Goods and Poors respectively) on the basis of their score on the Phillips scale (1953). The parents of 12 male subjects from each group, Goods, Poors and Controls, were tested. Dominance was determined by who spoke first, last and the most, and by the number of times one parent yielded to the other on a matter of opinion. Parental conflict was measured by the frequency of disagreement and the number of aggressive remarks made by one parent to the other. Using these measures Farina (1960) and Farina and Dunham (1963) found that parents of Poors had the highest scores, differing significantly from parents of Goods and normals. The interaction of parents of Poors was characterized by maternal dominance, and there were significantly more disagreements and aggressive remarks shown by these parents than by the other groups. The interaction of parents of schizophrenics taken as a whole was more hostile and contentious than that of parents of normals.

In a subsequent study also employing male index cases, Farina and Holzberg (1967, 1968) used similar measures in blindly conducted interviews and failed to confirm the previous finding of more maternal dominance in the parents of Poors. The groups, which were matched for I.Q., consisted of the parents of 26 Goods, 24 Poors, and 24 non-schizophrenic patients from a state psychiatric hospital. In this study, the only differences to reach significance were in the area of family conflict. The families of Poors had a significantly higher number of failures to reach agreement, and they recorded a significantly greater number of disagreements and aggressive remarks.

The same measures of conflict and dominance that were used by Farina were employed by Becker and Siefkes (1969) in a careful study of *female* schizophrenics. The parents of 15 Goods, 15 Poors and 15 non-psychiatric controls were tested with the Phillips scale and the Revealed Differences technique. Although the groups differed on I.Q. and education, these differences could be adjusted for by a co-variant analysis. These workers found that the fathers of Poors tended to be more dominant than the fathers of the other two groups. The parents of Goods did not differ from the control parents. Differences between the groups on measures of conflict failed to reach significance. There was a trend on all indices for paternal dominance to be most marked in the group of Poors. The pattern emerging from these three studies is an association between poor premorbid personality in the patient and dominance of one parent by the parent of the opposite sex to the patient. Unfortunately, Becker and Siefkes did not separate the control group into those with good and poor personalities, so that the positive finding could relate as much to personality characteristics as to schizophrenia. This consideration is particularly important in view of the differing diagnostic habits of American and British psychiatrists. As discussed earlier, many patients diagnosed as personality disorder by a British psychiatrist would be called schizophrenic by an American psychiatrist.

Further evidence on the significance of parental dominance and conflict comes from an excellent study by Caputo (1963). He compared the parents of 23 male chronic schizophrenics (in hospital 2 or more years) with the parents of 20 normal subjects obtained from the Veterans' Organization. The groups were matched on age, social status, and education. The interactions were scored by two observers using Bales' I.P.A., and Osgood's Semantic Differential (Osgood *et al.*, 1957) was used to determine in which direction the strongest bonds of identification lay.

The scores from the I.P.A. did not confirm the author's prediction of maternal dominance based on the theories of Lidz and Fromm–Reichman. In fact the fathers won the majority of decisions in the experimental group, while these were shared equally between mothers and fathers in the control group. These observational findings were supported by the results from the Semantic Differential. Mothers of schizophrenics did not rate themselves as more potent or dominant than control mothers, nor did they rate their husbands lower in potency. Similarly fathers of schizophrenics did not rate themselves lower in potency than control fathers and they thought more highly of themselves, but the findings are somewhat equivocal as they also rated themselves significantly higher on submissiveness (versus dominance).

The findings of this group of studies comprise strong evidence against theories which require male schizophrenics to have been exposed to a passive father plus a dominant and restrictive mother. However, previous findings regarding parental hostility receive confirmation from Caputo's work. The results he obtained from the I.P.A. showed that the parents of the schizophrenics expressed significantly more hostile feelings towards each other than the parents of the normal subjects. For example, 54 per cent of mothers of schizophrenics made negative comments about their husbands compared to 29 per cent of the controls. There was also a significantly greater incidence of inability to reach an agreement in the experimental group (p<0·001). As an aside, it is interesting to note that both mothers and fathers of schizophrenics differed significantly from controls in having more deviant attitudes as measured by the Parent Attitude Inventory.

Stabenau et al. (1965) used the Revealed Differences technique with the families of 5 schizophrenics, 5 delinquents and 5 normals. The groups contained the same proportion of males and females but were not matched for education, age and social class. A further criticism is that the workers who carried out the experiment and scored the interactions were aware of the groups to which the subjects belonged. No differences were found between the groups on any of the objective measures, such as total interaction time, interruptions per minute, etc, but this result should not be given too much weight in view of the small numbers of subjects and the defects in the methodology.

Lerner (1965, 1967) used the Revealed Differences technique to compare methods of resolving disagreements. He tested 24 parents of male schizophrenics and 12 parents of non-psychiatric male hospital patients, the groups being matched carefully for the subject's age, the length of time the patients had spent in hospital, and their socio-economic class. He scored the interactions for compromise, predominance of yielding by one parent, failure to reach agreement, and failure to reach agreement while acting as if it had been reached. Lidz contends that the last item of behaviour is the early basis for learning symbolic distortion as a means of coping. A high degree of reliability was achieved in scoring these items.

Lerner's results, which are consistent with the findings of other workers, were that the control parents resolved their differences by compromise significantly more often than the parents of schizophrenics. The latter group was given the Rorschach test and scored using Becker's genetic level rating for thought disorder. Those with scores indicating the most thought disorder had significantly more disagreements with distortion than the control parents. This subgroup of schizophrenics' parents also showed significantly more masking, a form of yielding in which a partner takes up a position of agreeing without acknowledging that this contradicts a previously expressed opinion. These results were significantly at a probability level of less than I per cent.

In a further analysis of results from this same group of patients, Lerner divided the schizophrenics according to whether they scored high or low on the Zigler and Phillips (1960) scale which measures premorbid social functioning. Resolution of differences by the father yielding to the mother was found to occur significantly more often in the group of low-scoring schizophrenics, while the opposite situation was found more commonly in the high-scoring group. This result is comparable with that of Farina (1960), since the Zigler and Phillips scale employs some of the same measures used by Farina to distinguish Good and Poor premorbid personalities. Both these studies can be seen, therefore, as indicating paternal dominance in male schizophrenics with good premorbid functioning and maternal dominance in those with poor premorbid functioning. However, it must be remembered that dominance is measured in these studies by yielding behaviour in a highly artificial situation while under observation.

Cheek (1964a and b, 1965a and b, 1966) has carried out an extensive investigation with comparatively large samples including both male and female index cases and controls. She used a modified form of the Revealed Differences technique and scored the sessions according to the Interaction Process Analysis. The families of 47 female and 27 male schizophrenics, interviewed just before discharge and at one week and one year after discharge, were compared with 56 normal families who volunteered for the study. Both samples were skewed towards social classes IV and V, and any differences between the groups were adjusted for by a partial correlation analysis. The stability of the interaction patterns of the families over the various experimental sessions was tested for by an analysis of variance. This showed no significant difference between sessions, but this is not an appropriate measure of stability as there may have been considerable within-test variation of the items scored occurring randomly. A more informative procedure would have been to calculate the correlation coefficients between the indices for the various testing occasions.

Considering the over-all activity derived from all the scoring categories, the mothers of schizophrenics were significantly less active than the control mothers. The parents of schizophrenics had significantly lower scores on positive social-emotional behaviour than the control parents. However, the fathers of schizophrenics differed from the control fathers on only two of the twenty-one interaction variables, and these two do not appear to be relevant findings in themselves. There was no evidence of any association between dominance of either parent and the sex of the patient or the diagnosis. In fact, on the attitude questionnaire which was administered, the mothers of schizophrenics were significantly more permissive than the control mothers. The author interprets the finding that schizophrenics' mothers show low activity as an indication of withdrawal. They also scored highly for protectiveness on the questionnaire, and Lerner interprets these two findings as supporting Alanen's (1956) characterization of such mothers as 'inimically protective'. An interpretation of this kind needs to be regarded with great caution since neither the testing of the subjects nor the scoring was carried out blindly and both could be influenced by bias.

Doubt is cast on the validity of the questionnaire by the finding that for the fathers in both groups there were no positive correlations between the responses to the questionnaire and the interaction data (Cheek, 1965a). Cheek (1965b) also examined the amount of spontaneous agreement between dyads (Mother–Father, Mother–Patient, Father–Patient) when subjects completed the questionnaire separately. Cheek's studies showed significantly less spontaneous agreement between the parents of schizophrenics than between the parents of controls. In addition, the fathers of schizophrenics showed significantly less spontaneous agreement with their offspring than the control fathers. Cheek's interpretation of this is that the father is more peripheral in the families of schizophrenics than in normal families.

Cheek (1965a) also examined the relationship between the measures she used and the outcome assessed at interview 3 months and one year after the patient's discharge. A product-moment correlation matrix was constructed between all 158 variables, including questionnaire items, interaction codes, interview notes, demographic characteristics and outcome. Poor outcome (not defined but apparently not equivalent to relapse) was associated with tense, highly active fathers and tense, hostile mothers. Dominance itself did not affect outcome. These results are compatible with the findings of Brown et al. (1962, 1972) that schizophrenics have a higher risk of relapse if they return to families with a high level of emotional involvement than to those with a low level. In Cheek's study, patients whose parents employed positive rather than negative sanctions and showed a more permissive attitude had a better outcome.

Winter and Ferreira (1967) have pointed out that since there were significant differences between the groups in the amount of total interaction shown both by the offspring and by their mothers, the raw scores on all Cheek's variables should be corrected correspondingly. One way would be to use the ratio of the raw score for each I.P.A. category to the over-all amount of interaction. It is possible, as we have shown elsewhere (Hirsch and Leff, 1971), that simply talking more leads to higher scores for some or all of the categories. Although this criticism raises a serious methodological doubt about Cheek's results, they are consistent with the findings from the bulk of studies discussed in this chapter.

Cheek's contention that the fathers of schizophrenics are more peripheral appears to find support in a study by Lennard, Beaulieu, and Embrey (1965). They compared the parents of 10 schizophrenic children aged 9–14 with a group of normal volunteer families. They found that father–son interaction and father's over-all activity in experimental sessions were significantly less in the schizophrenic group than among the normals. On the other hand, the mother–son interaction was found to be greater. However, no diagnostic criteria were given for these schizophrenics, who are unusually young. Furthermore the reliability of the measures and their stability were never determined and the groups were not shown to match on demographic variables. This study has too many shortcomings for the findings to be given any weight.

Ferreira, later joined by his colleague Winter, has carried out a series of careful and important studies using social interaction techniques to compare triadic interactions in families with a schizophrenic with those in other families. Initially an exploratory study was carried out in which 10 families with a schizophrenic offspring aged 10 or older were compared with 25 families with a normal offspring and 15 families in which one of the members, usually the child, had a non-schizophrenic psychiatric condition. Spontaneous Agreement (S.A.) was defined as the amount of agreement between family members (mother, father and offspring) when they each independently completed a 16 item forced-choice questionnaire. Ferreira (1963) found significantly less S.A. in families of abnormals than in the normal families, and the families containing a schizophrenic showed significantly less S.A. than families with a non-schizophrenic abnormal member.

As in the other studies we have considered, the experimental design then required families to fill in the questionnaire jointly. In all groups the choice arrived at more often represented the preference of the father or of both parents than of the mother or the mother plus the child. The dominance ranking was thus father>mother>child (P<0·001) for all groups. This finding provides evidence against theories which postulate abnormal dominance patterns in the families of schizophrenics.

Ferreira and Winter (1965) next conducted an ambitious investigation of 126 families using a number of testing and scoring procedures. Index offspring with a mean age of 16 years were tested with both their parents. The first report concerned 15 families with a schizophrenic offspring, 16 with a delinquent, 44 with a neurotic or maladjusted child, and 50 normals. The groups did not differ on father's occupational and educational level, or on parent's and offspring's age. In this study a questionnaire describing a number of made-up but possible situations was to be completed by family members first individually and then as a group, indicating the solutions they liked or disliked. The authors recognize a bias inherent in the design, namely that the families containing abnormal children viewed the testing procedure as a step towards the determination of their abnormality while this was, of course, not applicable in the normal families.

The reliability of S.A. between family dyads was measured by a split-half reliability correlation and was found to be 0·50. Normals showed significantly more S.A. than Abnormals for all three dyads (father–mother, father–child, mother–child). This finding was not specific to schizophrenic families, who did not differ from the two other abnormal groups on this measure. In families of Normals but not Abnormals the child had a significantly greater S.A. with the parent of the same sex. These findings are in accord with those of Cheek (1965b, above), who found less S.A. between parents of schizophrenics than between normal parents. However, Winter and Ferreira's use of other abnormal groups enabled them to show that this finding was a non-specific one. In addition they showed that there was no better agreement between the mother and child than between the father and child, hence controverting theories of mother–child symbiosis as a special feature of families containing a schizophrenic.

Choice Fulfilment (C.F.) was defined as the degree to which the choice of the individual members separately coincided with the joint family decision. It bears some resemblance to measures of 'yielding' employed by other workers as an index of dominance. Choice fulfilment may also indicate the degree of satisfaction family members derive from joint decision making in so far as it reflects the extent to which family decisions fulfil the wishes and needs of individual members. There was significantly less C.F. in Abnormals compared to Normals, and families containing a schizophrenic had the lowest C.F. score, even after an adjustment by co-variance for a high correlation between C.F. and S.A. ($r = +0·76$). This finding was entirely accounted for by the low C.F. score of the schizophrenic offspring.

These workers used another measure called Chaotic Responses, which they defined as the percentage of joint decisions which differed completely from the decisions of the individual family members. The percentage of Chaotic Responses was significantly higher for Abnormals than for Normals, and families with schizophrenics showed a significantly higher percentage (11·2 per cent) than families with delinquent or neurotic members (4·6 per cent). There were no differences between the groups in the percentage of 'dictatorial' family decisions, in which the individual decision of one member outweighed that of the other two, nor in the percentage of two-member coalitions determining the joint decision.

Thus, abnormal families experienced greater problems in making decisions than normal families, and those with a schizophrenic member were the most affected of the three groups, having the lowest S.A. and C.F.

Using essentially the same group of subjects, Ferreira, Winter, and Poindexter (1966) conducted another study in a different experimental situation. The families were given cards from the Thematic Apperception Test (T.A.T.) and instructed to decide who would tell the story. Abnormal families took significantly longer to come to a decision than normal families, but there was no difference between the three groups of abnormal families. Measures which other workers have used as an index of dominance, such as who spoke first, who spoke most or least, and the number of overlaps (interruptions), did not distinguish between different family members, with the single exception that the patients spoke significantly less than the other members. Thus, these results provide no support for abnormal dominance patterns in these families.

Examining family interactions further in the same groups, Winter and Ferreira (1967) used the I.P.A. to score what happened during the 5 minutes the families were given to make up a story which would link three T.A.T. cards in a given order. The procedure was repeated three times to enable each family member to act as spokesman once. The speaker's remarks were tape-recorded and scored with the I.P.A. The inter-rater reliability, judged by the percentage agreement between two raters on 500 statements from five subjects was 67 per cent. Because of the limited contribution of the index child, schizophrenic and, to a lesser degree, delinquent families had the lowest total interaction scores. To adjust for this, scores on specific I.P.A. indices were expressed as ratios of the total interaction scores.

In terms of interaction variables the I.P.A. provided only a minimal distinction between diagnostic groups. Schizophrenic families were found to interact less, to spend more time asking questions, and to ask for opinions and suggestions in a dependent manner. A similar finding was reported by Lennard et al. (1965). However, since the differences found depended mostly on the interaction between parents and their children the results cannot be taken to indicate parental abnormality per se. Winter and Ferreira criticize the I.P.A. for what they consider to be an unacceptably low reliability and the high order of inference required to classify items because the I.P.A categories are multi-dimensional in meaning. Although we would not be so disparaging about the reliability levels, we would agree that the use of the I.P.A. by these workers in a careful way has provided disappointingly few positive findings.

Ferreira and Winter's work deserves fuller comment. Their methodology was more exact in that they examined the reliability of their measures (split-half reliability on the Spontaneous Agreement score) as well as the inter-rater reliability. The correlation between variables was measured and when necessary an analysis of co-variance was conducted, allowing a more specific interpretation of the findings to be made. This refinement, plus the use of a variety of psychiatric groups for comparison, enabled the differences found to be carefully assessed. Thus, though like Cheek, they found Spontaneous Agreement to be significantly lower in schizophrenic than in normal families, the implication of this finding was modified by the fact that the schizophrenic families were not significantly worse than the families with neurotic and delinquent members.

The study of Fisher *et al.* (1959) deserves further mention here, because in these workers' comprehensive evaluation of parents of schizophrenics, neurotics and non-psychiatric hospitalized patients, they examined aspects of parental interaction while the parents were discussing their son's assets and faults and while they were jointly formulating T.A.T. responses. Parents of schizophrenics were more often in definite disagreement than the other groups of parents, were more ambiguous in the exchange of opinion, and communicated with each other less over-all. The groups were not matched for educational differences but nevertheless the findings are consistent with those from other studies.

Sharan (1966) has made an interesting contribution by testing three principal hypotheses bearing on the ways in which parents might engender schizophrenia in their offspring. The basic assumption is that if parents have a specific aetiological influence on the pre-schizophrenic child then there should be demonstrable differences between the way they interact with their ill child and a healthy one. Sharan studied 12 families with a schizophrenic son and 12 with a schizophrenic daughter, each group containing six non-schizophrenic siblings of the same sex and six of the opposite sex. All the patients were acutely ill with symptoms for less than one year. Both the patients and their siblings were currently living at home.

Each family member completed the Wechsler-Bellevue Intelligence Test for comprehension and similarities. Then the parents formed triads with the ill child and then with the healthy child and re-did the questionnaire, using an alternative form on each occasion. Tape-recordings of the sessions were scored for 'dominance' according to which parent's individual answer most often became the family group decision. 'Support' was assessed by taking into account the number of supportive and non-supportive remarks directed by one member towards another. A ratio score was employed to eliminate differences in responsiveness. In a pilot study two blind raters achieved 92 per cent agreement using the material from 10 groups.

Sharan argued that if communication in the families of schizophrenics is of little use in dealing with the environment (Haley, 1959a and b) or impairs problem solving then the parents–patient triad should be less efficient at solving problems than the parents–sibling triad. 'Efficiency' in this study was calculated as $1-(\text{Maximum Score}-\text{Actual Score}/\text{Maximum Score})$. All family groups achieved approximately the same efficiency score of about 85 per cent and there was no difference in the frequency with which the patient's response or the sibling's response emerged as the joint family response. Thus the first hypothesis was not supported.

Next, Sharan tested Lidz's claim (Lidz *et al.*, 1957b, 1958) that the interactions of schizophrenics' families are characterized by chronic conflict such that the parents do not co-operate in the solving of problems. He reasoned that if this is true and has bearing on why one sibling has schizophrenia and not the other, then the parents should be less supportive of the patient than of his well sibling. He found no consistent differences between parental support of the patient compared with his sibling.

Finally, he endeavoured to test the concepts of role-reversal and break-down of the sex-generation boundaries that are the cornerstones of the theories of Lidz and his school (Lidz *et al.*, 1957a and b, 1958, 1965) [see p. 17]. Two hypotheses that can be derived from their theories are: (1) that the patient and the dominant parent should be of the opposite sex; and (2) that the opposite-sexed parent should have a more mutually supportive re-lationship with the patient than the same-sexed parent. The first hypothesis was not supported in this work because the father's individual response tended to appear as the group response more often than the mother's re-gardless of the sex of the child or whether the patient or the sibling was present. Furthermore, the activity of the parents did not vary according to the sex of the patient or sibling who was present. The second hypothesis received equivocal support. The fathers of female patients were more sup-portive than the mothers, as predicted, and were also more supportive than the fathers of male patients. Unfortunately, no comparison was made to test whether these fathers of female patients treated the well sibling with less support, as confirmation of the hypothesis would require. The one unequivo-cal result which was found was that parents were significantly less supportive and more critical of each other in the presence of the ill child than in the presence of the healthy one. This study comes as close as any to testing some of the influential theoretical formulations in this field and the results are negative.

Most of the studies we have considered in this chapter show that under experimental conditions the parents of schizophrenics exhibit more conflict and have more difficulty in reaching agreement on decisions than the parents of neurotics or normal subjects. The question arises as to whether it is the parents who have affected the child, or vice versa. Sharan's work suggests that parental conflict is more evident in the presence of the ill rather than the well child. If confirmed, this finding would support the theory that the direction of the disturbing effect is from the ill child to its parents.

A very detailed analysis of family interactions has been carried out by Mishler and Waxler (1968a and b), taking into account a wide range of role combinations. The parents of 17 Good and 17 Poor premorbid personality schizophrenics were compared with a group of normal subjects using the Revealed Difference Technique. The groups did not differ on occupational and educational variables or on family income and the parents' birthplace. The experimental design allowed comparison on a number of interaction variables including: the presence of a schizophrenic versus a normal offspring, the presence of a Good versus a Poor premorbid personality, the presence of a male versus a female patient, and the presence of a patient versus his or her healthy sibling. The schizophrenic patients included in the study represented 13 per cent of all schizophrenics admitted to the hospital in question, and the hospital diagnosis was accepted. The recording, transcribing, coding and scoring of the interactions required 129 hours of staff time for every hour of interview. A useful feature was that families were seen for two or three sessions, hence allowing for an assessment of the stability of some of the measures over time. A vast number of analyses were performed; consequently the interpretations of results reported as significant at the 0·1 to 0·2 level are very doubtful indeed as they are very likely to have occurred by chance.

Unlike Ferreira and Winter, Sharan, and many other workers, Mishler and Waxler did not make predictions based on specific hypotheses, but rather discussed the relevance of their measures to various prevailing theories. Moreover, in discussing their findings they interpreted trends as indicating gross qualitative distinctions between groups whereas in fact these often represented only marginal quantitative differences. Nevertheless, we will discuss some of their findings to illustrate the complexity and the shortcomings of their approach. One of the measures they used was 'expressiveness'. This was made up of 12 I.P.A. categories including tone of voice and context, tension, release of tension, agreement and antagonism. Expressiveness was found to be stable from session to session as judged by the rank order within each diagnostic group and each family. Parents of normals had the highest score on this measure, parents of Poors the lowest, while parents of Goods scored in between. The affect accompanying expressiveness was almost always positive for normals but consistently negative for Goods, with Poors falling between the two. Mothers of Poors expressed significantly more affect with their schizophrenic than with their well son, but were not more expressive than the fathers. The families of Poors were found to show the most interpersonal expressiveness, particularly negative affect when the schizophrenic as opposed to the normal son was present. In families containing male Goods there was a lack of confrontation with others and of interpersonal antagonism. Instead, negative affect was expressed indirectly and mostly in the presence of the well sibling. Although Poors received the greatest amount of negative affect, this represented a small proportion only (less than 5 per cent) of the family interaction. These results concerning negative affect are consistent with those of Brown et al. (1972) [see CHAPTER I above].

Consideration of the families of female subjects blurs the picture because the pattern is different from that with males. Like the males, Goods were low and Poors were high on expressiveness, but in contrast to males Goods were high on negative affect while Poors were low.

Another measure used by these workers called 'Power' has similarities to measures of dominance employed by Farina and by Ferreira and Winter. Mishler and Waxler did not find any significant difference between the percentage of total family interaction time taken up by either parent. However, they found that Poor sons spoke more than other sons and directed more of their remarks at their mothers than at their fathers. Moreover, they spoke more to their mothers than their fathers did, and conversely they received more attention from their mothers than their fathers did. In fact they received the most attention of the children of all groups. All these results go against the findings of the studies previously described, but support the theory of symbiosis between the patient and the opposite-sexed parent, at least for male schizophrenics. However, for female schizophrenics the findings were quite different and suggest that they were isolated within the family and received little attention.

The most marked and consistent finding in the study concerned 'Acknowledgement'. Normal families tended to be more responsive in general and were highest in their level of acknowledgement (percentage of acknowledging remarks). All comparisons using this measure showed significant differences between the groups, and the rank order of normals>Goods>Poors remained constant throughout all the comparisons for families containing male subjects. Families with daughters did not show this constant rank order pattern. The authors interpreted their findings as indicating that members of a schizophrenic family do not 'listen' to each other and are therefore impervious to the needs and intents expressed by others. This rather imaginative conclusion is at some distance from the actual results.

Mishler and Waxler's findings relating to abnormalities of communication will be discussed in CHAPTER V. Their work is a compendium of meticulous and painstaking analyses and represents a prodigious effort. Because the analyses were so numerous and complex we have only concentrated on the small number of findings that reached statistical significance. However, even these are of dubious value because of the sheer number of comparisons made. One is forced to question the wisdom of such exhaustive efforts (129 hours of processing per hour of recorded interview) when the number of cases was so small. In contrast to all their care in statistical manipulations, these workers gave no detailed clinical information about the patients studied. They have not used their work to test predictive hypotheses, but have interpreted their findings, including many at the 10 per cent and 20 per cent probability level, in an *a posteriori* way which can only be regarded as speculative. Those findings which were significant for families with a male offspring, were not repeated in families with a female offspring. Their omission of a comparison group of non-schizophrenic psychiatric patients, as used in some of the other studies discussed, further reduces the weight of their findings.

The last body of work to be reviewed in this chapter comprises the studies Reiss has conducted of the relationship between family interactions and the thought processes and perceptions of the family members. He set out to answer the questions: '(a) can we demonstrate in the laboratory that family interaction does affect the thought and perception of its individual members? (b) If so, how is this influence effected?' (Reiss, 1967a). He is perhaps the first to develop quantitative experimental methods of determining the relationship between family interaction and individual thinking. His work represents a definite departure from the other social psychological studies we have reviewed, all of which have concentrated on the verbal interactions which occur when family members attempt to resolve their individual differences. In contrast, Reiss has focused on the individual's problem-solving processes in the family setting.

Reiss has described four experiments in which he attempted to relate individual to family processes and to distinguish between them, using both verbal and non-verbal measures. The same 15 families participated in these experiments and comprised five with two normal offspring, five with one schizophrenic and one normal offspring, and five with one personality disordered and one normal offspring. All the patients had been hospitalized within the previous year. The schizophrenics were described as having shown substantial thought disorder (hallucinations, delusions, autistic and incoherent speech), a gradual onset of social withdrawal for several years, and less than 2 years' total hospitalization. Four of the five were paranoid.

The experimental methods employed by Reiss are complex and it would require an undue amount of space to describe each adequately. Readers who are interested in the details are referred to the original articles. We will attempt to convey the essence of his approach.

In his first experiment family members were isolated in separate booths but could communicate with each other by passing written messages to the experimenter, who in turn handed them on to every other family member. The task of members was to learn the correct sequence of triangles and circles which would turn on a flashing light in their booth. They were given an example of the kind of sequence that would work and were instructed to write down another sequence and pass it to the experimenter. These attempts at constructing sequences were regarded by Reiss as hypotheses. If a sequence was correct a light would flash as a signal to all the subjects. Each hypothesis, whether correct or not, was passed round so that others could learn from it. When any individual thought he had exhausted all the possible solutions he turned on a finishing light. Thereafter, he or she had to continue to provide solutions but without receiving confirmation of their correctness. This process continued until all the finishing lights were on.

In order to measure the way in which the pattern concept of each individual was influenced by the others, subjects were required at the start and conclusion of each problem to indicate on a list of twenty possible solutions those which they thought to be correct. Using a record of the hypotheses circulated, Reiss measured three aspects of family interaction: (1) the focus of hypothesis construction (whether family members used information from others or acted totally individually); (2) risk taking (whether members only copied previous hypotheses if they had been confirmed); and (3) the dynamics of stopping (order, timing with respect to what had been achieved, etc.).

Ratios were calculated of the number of acts in a specific category to the number of acts in all categories. In the first experiment (Reiss, 1967*b*) only measures of focus and risk taking were calculated. The experiment was carried out twice using a more difficult problem the second time. Some marginally significant differences between groups appeared in the second experiment which did not appear in the first. Reiss postulated that this might be a result of the greater difficulty of the second problem, but did not test this idea further. An alternative explanation is that the measures used may not have been reliable.

In discussing the results of this study, Reiss states that 'the most significant finding was that families of schizophrenics showed deterioration of pattern concepts in the course of the task, whereas families of normals showed improved pattern concepts'. Although small differences of this kind were found between families no tests of significance were reported and the differences seem too slight to bear the interpretation Reiss puts on them.

Similarly, the data on the nature of an individual's hypothesis testing and his use of information from other family members yielded no clear-cut positive findings. Differences did appear between the groups of offspring, in that schizophrenics took significantly fewer risks, in the author's terms, than the other groups of offspring. However, the fathers of schizophrenics actually exhibited the opposite tendency, taking significantly more risks than the other groups of fathers. Despite this finding, Reiss states that 'families of normals tested a diversity of hypotheses and appeared willing to assume the risk of constructing incorrect hypotheses. Families of schizophrenics tested a narrower range of hypotheses, very much like their initial example, and were less willing to take a risk.'

In his second experiment (Reiss, 1968) subjects were asked to solve problems which involved devising means of sorting cards held by individual members. No significant differences were found between groups on success in the sorting procedure, although the families of normals did marginally better than the other groups. Reiss also studied the verbal interaction of family members using measures similar to those of Mishler and Waxler, Bales, and Strodtbeck. His finding that no family member occupied significantly more interaction time than any other within or between groups is in accord with that of Mishler and Waxler, but contradicts the findings of the other studies reported in this chapter. Like Mishler and Waxler, he found that normal families showed the most interruptions, families of schizophrenics were next, while families of personality disordered offspring showed the least interruptions. Families did not differ on the number of disruptions, hesitancies, or fragmented or incomplete sentences.

In the third experiment with these subjects (Reiss, 1969), the problem was to discover the missing letters in a complex pattern of letters. The parents of schizophrenics were not found to differ in any important way from the parents of normals and Reiss concluded that 'in tasks in which success depends on evaluating cues from within the family, families of schizophrenics did well'.

Following on these results, Reiss predicted that the family of a schizophrenic would work together closely in exploring the environment ('synchrony'), but at the same time would seek a rapid conclusion when working on a problem and would be less effective in finding a solution. Reiss (1971) makes the explicit assumption here that 'our laboratory for testing families, including its procedures, puzzles, and personnel, is a working replica of the family's everyday environment'. The puzzle in this study again involved the sorting of cards in the correct way.

The three groups did not differ significantly in their effectiveness in solving the problems, and, furthermore, the families of schizophrenics had a lower level of co-ordination than the normal families ($p < 0.1$) and did not differ significantly in this respect from the families of delinquents. We can conclude that the results failed to support the hypotheses that Reiss had elaborated on the basis of his earlier work. However, in the discussion of his results, Reiss states 'we can reasonably assert that the findings support our *a priori* notions'.

It is disappointing that work involving a high degree of methodological sophistication should be undermined by major weaknesses. In some cases, tests of significance are omitted altogether, while in others the generally accepted level of 5 per cent is arbitrarily raised to 20 per cent. Findings which tell against his hypotheses are ignored in his conclusions and the results are generally interpreted at far too high a level of abstraction.

CONCLUSIONS

The application of social-psychological techniques developed in the study of small groups has enabled experimenters in the field of family interaction to collect data free from the bias inherent in the retrospective gathering of information. The method does not avoid the limitations involved in collecting information after schizophrenia has appeared, so that it is impossible to determine the direction in which influences are acting even when an association has been shown. Yet we must not be over-ambitious in our expectations at this stage when there is such a profound lack of objective data, and positive results which cannot be explained away are only just beginning to emerge.

These studies provide experimental evidence bearing on the more popular hypothesis put forward regarding family influences in producing schizophrenia. The early findings of Farina (1960), and others (Becker and Siefkes, 1969; Lerner, 1967) indicated maternal dominance in the families of schizophrenics with poor premorbid personalities. However, several excellent studies in which demographic variables were better controlled failed to support this finding or produced results which contradicted it (Caputo, 1963; Cheek, 1965a and b, 1966; Ferreira, 1963; Ferreira and Winter, 1965; Mishler and Waxler a and b, 1968; Reiss, 1969). Similarly Lidz's (Lidz, Fleck et al., 1965) concepts of role reversal and breakdown of the sex and generation boundaries were supported by Farina and Dunham's (1963) results for poor premorbid personality schizophrenics, and also by the study of Lennard et al. (1965). But they were contradicted by further work (Ferreira and Winter, 1965; Sharan, 1966; Mishler and Waxler, 1968a and b; Reiss, 1968), in particular the better controlled study with larger samples conducted by Caputo (1963).

The findings relating to marital and family harmony and the effectiveness of family endeavour in experimental situations did suggest that parents of schizophrenics do not do as well as parents of normals, although there is much evidence suggesting that this is true of parents of other types of abnormal offspring as well.

Several studies showed that there was less agreement between the individual answers of the parents of schizophrenics when completing an attitude questionnaire than between those of control parents (Cheek, 1965b; Ferreira, 1963; Ferreira and Winter, 1965).

Experiments measuring disharmony, difficulties in reaching agreement, hostility and open aggression between the parents of schizophrenics gave the most definite and consistent results. Seven of the nine studies in question yielded similar findings (Farina, 1960; Farina and Holzberg, 1967, 1968; Caputo, 1963; Fisher et al., 1959; Sharan, 1966; Mishler and Waxler, 1968a and b). Of the two studies which failed to confirm these findings, that of Stabenau et al. (1965) was poorly controlled and used small numbers of subjects, while that of Becker et al. (1969) showed a trend in the right direction which did not reach significance. The latter study was on the parents of female schizophrenics and many workers achieved less impressive results for this group than for the parents of male schizophrenics on a number of measures. This general statement of a positive result needs qualification, in that parental disagreement and conflict was mostly seen with schizophrenics of poor premorbid personality (Farina, 1960; Farina and Holzberg, 1967, 1968) or with male schizophrenics who were chronically hospitalized (Caputo, 1963). This association with premorbid personality and chronicity of illness (which itself might be dependent on personality factors) raises the question of whether the link with schizophrenia is secondary to these other characteristics. While many of the studies demonstrating this association used double-blind techniques with large well-matched samples, in no case were the different diagnostic groups controlled for premorbid personality. This would be necessary to determine whether the association was with poor premorbid personality regardless of the nature of the illness.

The other problem concerns the differing diagnostic habits of British and American psychiatrists. All these studies are American and in none are the diagnostic criteria described in sufficient detail to decide what proportion of the patients would conform to the narrower Anglo-European concept of schizophrenia (Kendell et al., 1971). In most of the investigations reviewed in this chapter it was the rule for the researchers simply to accept the hospital diagnosis of the patients studied.

An important point which may apply to all the studies considered here was made by Kohn (1968). He stated that up to that time there had not been a single well-controlled study that demonstrated any substantial difference between the family relationships of schizophrenics and those of normal people from social classes IV and V. While the studies reviewed have matched groups for social class variables, they have not examined whether the results hold true in the lower socio-economic groups. This is a further deficiency which needs to be remedied before the importance of the findings can be fully determined.

CHAPTER IV

PSYCHOLOGICAL TESTS OF ABNORMAL THOUGHT PROCESSES IN THE PARENTS OF SCHIZOPHRENICS

IN this chapter we examine evidence, based on standard methods of psychological testing, that parents of schizophrenics have abnormal thought processes. None of the work we have reviewed so far has included objective measures of the individual psychological functioning of parents. It is important to investigate possible links between thought disorder in the schizophrenic and ambiguous, unclear, or peculiar modes of speech in his parents which may reflect an underlying disturbance of thinking. This chapter includes all the studies to date which employ formal psychological tests in a systematic attempt to investigate the thought processes of parents.

Although thought disorder has been extensively studied in the past 50 years (for reviews see Payne, 1960; Buss and Lang, 1965; McGhie, 1967; Rosenberg et al., 1968), McConaghy (1959) was the first to test the parents of schizophrenic patients. He used the Object Sorting Test (O.S.T.), first devised by Rapaport (1945), and later modified by Lovibond (1954). Lovibond found that the O.S.T. could discriminate at a high level of significance (p<0·001) between patients judged on clinical grounds to show thought disorder and normal subjects, although 9 per cent of the normals scored within the abnormal range. In Lovibond's modification, the subject is shown 33 common objects displayed on a tray. In the first part of the test the subject is presented with one object at a time in a standard sequence and is asked to select from the remaining objects those that belong with the test object. On each occasion he is asked 'why do these all belong together?' In the second part of the test the subject is shown the objects sorted into 12 standard groups, each having some common characteristic, and is asked why the objects in the group belong together. The protocols are rated blindly for the degree to which the subject's explanation of the grouping applies equally to objects not included in the group. The higher the score, the greater the degree of irrelevant, over-inclusive thinking.

McConaghy chose this test because he had noticed that when the grosser aspects of thought disorder had disappeared, schizophrenic patients continued to show over-generalized, irrelevant expressions when encouraged to discuss abstract issues such as the nature and significance of their illness. McConaghy (1959) later called this mode of thought, typified by abnormal responses on the O.S.T., 'allusive thinking'. He believed that 'allusive thinking' is related to schizoid personality traits which reflect a predisposition to schizophrenia, and that the same quality of thinking that was apparent in his patients in remission could be detected in their parents.

In his first attempt to test this (McConaghy, 1959) he studied the parents of 10 chronic hospitalized schizophrenics and found that 60 per cent of them scored seven or higher on the O.S.T. compared with 10 per cent of 65 normal controls (p<0·001). The patients had been in hospital from 1 to 7 years and all had high scores on the O.S.T. He found that at least one parent of each patient had a score in the abnormal range and interpreted this as indicating that thought disorder is transmitted by a dominant gene. The study represents an interesting beginning in this field of inquiry but has a number of defects. The tests were not administered blind, and the control group was not comparable with the experimental group on a number of characteristics, including I.Q. This failure to match the groups on I.Q. is a serious limitation in view of the findings of other workers that performance on tests of concrete and abstract thinking is significantly correlated with I.Q. (Payne, 1960; Forrest et al., 1969). Equally important is the fact that the controls were not randomly selected and unlike the experimental group were not the parents of hospitalized psychiatric patients, a characteristic which may well influence the test scores (see Schopler and Loftin, 1969, reviewed below).

Lidz and his colleagues at Yale (Lidz, Wild et al., 1963) repeated this work again using normal subjects as a comparison group, but taking greater care to match the groups on other variables. The parents of 10 normal subjects were matched with the parents of 21 thought-disordered schizophrenics on the number of years of their education and their performance on a vocabulary test. The scoring of protocols was blind and a high inter-rater reliability was achieved (r=0·90). Using the same scoring criteria and cut-off point between high and low scores as did McConaghy, these workers found no significant difference between the groups. However, when the scoring procedure was modified and the cut-off point was lowered from seven to five a difference did emerge which was significant at the 0·02 level. Using this point, a very large proportion of normal parents (38 per cent) scored in the 'allusive thinking' range. However, adjusting the cut-off point to achieve a significant result is a dubious procedure.

A further replication of this work was attempted by the same group at Yale. Rosman and his colleagues (1964) blindly administered the O.S.T. to 115 control subjects, including 49 pairs of parents, and the parents of 34 thought-disordered schizophrenics. This study does not represent an independent replication of the previous work because a substantial proportion of the subjects were the same (29 per cent of the experimental group and 27 per cent of the control group). Nevertheless, this modified version of the experiment is of interest. Two raters scored all the protocols with good agreement (r=0·90). With the increased number of subjects, moderately significant differences appeared between the groups. Using McConaghy's cut-off score of seven, there was a trend at the 0·05 level for more patients to have at least one high-scoring parent than normal subjects. This difference was almost entirely accounted for by the greater number of mothers of schizophrenics with high scores. The authors noted that in the control but not the experimental group there was a significant correlation between the O.S.T. score and I.Q. (r = − 0·23), and occupation (r = − 0·20). They therefore divided the subjects into high and low level groups for I.Q., education, and occupation. When this was done the difference in O.S.T. scores between parents in the low groups was not significant, but the difference was significant between parents of schizophrenics and controls in the high intelligence, education, and occupation groups. However, in view of the finding that 56 per cent of parents of schizophrenics compared with 32 per cent of parents of normals had high O.S.T. scores the results cannot be considered very impressive since such a high proportion of normal parents scored in the 'allusive thinking' range.

Though these findings from the O.S.T. are less impressive than those from other studies, the work is better controlled and more reliable. They still leave unanswered the question whether parents of schizophrenics differ from parents of offspring with other types of psychiatric disorder. Stabenau and his co-workers (1965) approached this question by testing the parents and one sibling of five schizophrenics, five delinquent and five normal subjects. Using the scoring methods employed by previous investigators, they were unable to show any significant difference between these groups. This study deals with numbers too small to draw anything but tentative conclusions, but it does emphasize the importance of using a control group of parents of patients with non-schizophrenic psychiatric disorders.

McConaghy's (1960) contention that allusive thinking is a normal mode of conceptualization was given support by the finding of Rosman et al. (1964) that over a third of their control subjects achieved high scores on the O.S.T. To confirm this result McConaghy gave the O.S.T. to 101 university students. He picked out the 16 students with the highest scores and the 10 with the lowest and tested their parents in the same way (McConaghy and Clancy, 1968). There was a significant tendency for students with a high score to have at least one high-scoring parent compared with students with a low score. The sex of the parent was not linked with the scores achieved. Allusive thinking was not related to schizophrenic pathology as measured by the F scale of M.M.P.I., nor to poor performance in examinations.

McConaghy (1971) has recently reported some preliminary findings linking allusive thinking on the O.S.T. with measures of arousal, conditioning, and inhibition, and an ophthalmic measure termed the 'angle alpha'. This is an index of the difference between the optic and visual axes, i.e. the apparent and true lines of vision (see Lyle and Wybar, 1967). Results from 60 subjects assessed blindly and independently by a psychologist using the O.S.T., and an ophthalmologist measuring the angle alpha, showed an association between allusive thinking on the one hand and slow conditioning and weak inhibition of delay on the other. Such evidence suggests there may be a physiological basis for allusive thinking. McConaghy views allusive thinking as an inherited normal mode of thinking associated with a predisposition to schizophrenia, and considers that the angle alpha may be a genetic marker for this trait. His ideas are imaginative and stimulating but as yet rest on tenuous evidence.

Phillips, Jacobson, and Turner (1965) also found evidence of a familial factor in relatives of schizophrenics. Twenty-four parents and 24 siblings of 30 female schizophrenics were given four psychological tests and their scores were compared with those of 45 controls, who were young hospital employees. The statistical analysis of the data, including an analysis of co-variance for indices such as age and education, was exhaustive, but other aspects of their method render their results difficult to interpret. For example, this is one of the few papers to specify the criteria used for a diagnosis of schizophrenia. However, they include 'pansexuality' and 'inability to explain self and symptoms to a thoughtful, compassionate and informed person', and few British psychiatrists would find these acceptable. A further criticism is that they excluded from the original control group of 48, three subjects who scored in the abnormal range; two because they were subsequently thought to be 'ambulatory schizophrenics' and one who was termed a practical joker. They found a significant difference between controls and relatives of schizophrenics (siblings and parents combined) on the Pa scale of the Payne Object Classification Test and the Conceptual Quotient of the Shipley Institute of Living scale. The Benjamin Proverbs Test and the Epstein Test did not differentiate between the groups.

The need for a careful experimental design with an effort to control all relevant variables is shown by two more recent studies. Romney (1969 a and b) noted the failure in most studies employing the O.S.T. to control adequately for differences between groups on I.Q. He studied 30 nuclear schizophrenics, 20 neurotics, and 20 non-psychotic surgical patients and a sample of their first degree relatives. Subjects were given the O.S.T., Bannister Grid, Mill Hill Vocabulary Test, and Raven's Matrices. The effect of I.Q. was partialled out by a two-way analysis of co-variance. The differences between relatives of schizophrenics, neurotics, and normals on the tests of thought disorder did not reach significance, although by combining the two control groups a trend appeared approaching the 0·05 level. Mothers, fathers, and siblings did not show significant differences. By contrast with their relatives, the schizophrenic patients did differ significantly from the neurotic and normal subjects. We are not given the correlations between O.S.T. scores and I.Q. in the different groups, nor are we told whether there would have been significant differences had I.Q. not been partialled out Consequently it is difficult to compare these results with those of other studies in which I.Q. was not taken into account.

Muntz and Power (1970) have criticized Romney because he tested relatives of any schizophrenic, regardless of whether or not thought disorder was a feature. This criticism is valid if the aim is to investigate the causes of thought disorder *per se*, but not if it is to investigate the causes of schizophrenia, of which thought disorder is but one manifestation. Muntz and Power gave the Bannister Grid to the parents of 32 thought-disordered schizophrenics and 30 non-thought-disordered schizophrenics. The groups were matched for age, social class, and Mill Hill Vocabulary Test scores. They found a significant relationship between parental high scores on the Bannister Grid and the presence of clinical thought disorder in their offspring. It should be noted, however, that some workers question whether the Bannister Grid is a valid test of thought disorder (Frith and Lillie, 1972).

A further study that measured allusive thinking was that by Wender and his colleagues (1971). (This study is described in fuller detail from the point of view of the clinical findings on page 28 of CHAPTER I.) These workers compared three groups of parents on clinical and psychological measures. The groups comprised 10 couples who had adopted a child who later became schizophrenic, 10 couples who had reared their own child who had developed schizophrenia, and 10 couples who had reared an adopted child who had not manifested any psychiatric illness. Using the T.A.T., O.S.T., and Proverb Interpretation Test they found no significant difference between any of the groups of parents. The authors criticize their own study for a lack of systematic sampling, and for the use of non-blind interviewing which could have introduced a bias. They have recently confirmed their results in a new study with a consecutive sample interviewed blindly (personal communication).

The importance of factors in the interview situation which could influence the results obtained with the O.S.T. was demonstrated conclusively by Schopler and Loftin. In a preliminary study administering the O.S.T. to the parents of child psychotics, they were surprised to find that the scores were similar to those reported for adult schizophrenics. They therefore designed a study to investigate whether a significant variable affecting parents' scores was the parents' psychological attitude in the testing situation (Schopler and Loftin, 1969). They studied couples who were parents of child psychotics (by Creak's criteria, 1961) and compared them to parents of retarded children (11 pairs) and normals (21 pairs). Ten of the parents of psychotics were not in treatment at the place of testing; these were first questioned extensively as to how they were able to be so successful in bringing up other children normally in the face of the difficulties of having a psychotic child. Their advice was sought. Finally they were given the O.S.T. The other 17 parents of psychotic children had been in treatment with their psychotic offspring at the clinic where they were tested and were told that the tests were for research purposes. All parents were in social classes I–III. The scores of the parents of psychotic children who were tested in a setting where they were viewed as experts in successful child-rearing did not differ significantly from those of controls. The parents tested in the clinic where they were being treated with their child scored significantly higher on the O.S.T.; 71 per cent of couples in the second group had at least one high-scoring parent compared to 29 per cent of parents of normals (p<0·01). Most of the difference was attributable to the mothers in these groups.

This study stresses the importance of what Mishler and Waxler (1968a and b) called 'situation effects', i.e. the circumstances of the interview. It may be that the O.S.T. is sensitive to anxiety factors which impair conceptual thinking only secondarily. The differences found between parents of schizophrenics and normals in the previous studies on the O.S.T. (McConaghy, 1959, Lidz, Wild et al., 1963, Rosman et al., 1964) may have been the result of situational effects, because all these studies used normal subjects or parents of normals for their controls. This would also explain the findings of Stabenau et al. (1965) [p. 48] who were unable to find differences between parents of schizophrenics and delinquents but found that parents of normals scored significantly lower than the parents of patients.

Reiss and Elstein (1971) gave a number of psychological tests to the parents of eight paranoid schizophrenics, eight non-paranoid schizophrenics, and eight patients with neurotic disorders. The groups were matched for age, education, and vocabulary test scores. The results of the test were subjected to a discriminant function analysis. The linear functions which were produced distinguished clearly between all three groups, misclassifying only three of the 24 families using parental scores alone (p<0·001). The authors make wide generalizations from their findings, but are cautious enough to add that the linear functions discriminating between the groups of families are difficult to interpret in psychological terms and that the study needs replication.

THE WORD ASSOCIATION TEST

Closely related to the Object Sorting Test is the Kent–Rosanoff Word Association Test, for which there are norms on 1,000 American college students. Ciarlo et al. (1967) studied the parents of 10 schizophrenics, 10 non-psychotic psychiatric patients, and 10 normals, all with high I.Q.'s. Each subject was asked to give three associations to words on a standard list. Their responses were compared with the norms for the college students, and the degree of originality and of irrelevancy of the associations was assessed by two raters, who achieved an inter-rater reliability of r = 0·82. From the ratings an idiosyncrasy score was calculated. There was no appreciable difference between the parents of schizophrenic and non-psychotic patients, but both of these groups differed significantly from the parents of normals. The authors offer the interpretation either that there is a common factor affecting word association in the parents of psychiatric patients, regardless of diagnosis, or that the parents of both patient groups are more susceptible than the control parents to the kind of situational effects discussed above.

A companion study to that of Wender *et al.* (1971) considered above is that of Zahn (1968) on the same sample of subjects using the Word Association Test. He found that parents whose biological offspring had schizophrenia gave significantly more original and irrelevant responses than parents whose adoptive offspring had schizophrenia. This finding supports the hypothesis that there is a genetically transmitted factor in schizophrenia which is related to thought disorder.

THE RORSCHACH TEST

Most workers have used the Rorschach Test in a qualitative way to assess personality characteristics. However, various quantitative measures have been developed from it, and a few studies of the parents of schizophrenics have been carried out using these. Winder and Kantor (1958) gave the Rorschach test to the mothers of 25 young adult male schizophrenics and compared their responses with those of the mothers of 23 normal people in the community. The protocols were rated for the level of maturity of the personality, and the two judges involved achieved an inter-rater reliability of $r=0.83$. The mean ratings of the two judges were used and it was found that the mothers of the schizophrenics were rated as significantly more immature than the normal mothers ($p<0.01$). However, there was a considerable overlap in scores for the two groups, and since they were ethnically different, in that one-third of the experimental group was foreign-born, the findings could be due to cultural factors. These could conceivably have an important effect in modifying the Rorschach responses, as English was probably not the first language of the foreign-born mothers.

Baxter and his colleagues (1963) also used the Rorschach test to assess the degree of maturity of their subjects, but in terms of the kinds of defences used. Type I defences, denial and projection, were considered to be less mature than Type II defences, displacement, undoing, and isolation. The subjects were the parents of 10 schizophrenics with good premorbid personalities (as assessed by the Phillips scale), 10 with poor premorbid personalities, and 10 neurotics. There were five male and five female patients in each group. Two raters assessing some practice transcripts achieved an inter-rater reliability of $r=0.86$. It was found that there was a significant inter-correlation between age, I.Q., total number of responses, and Defence score. A multiple regression analysis was carried out so that these variables would be partialled out. The adjusted Defence scores were found to distinguish significantly between the parents of Goods and the parents of Poors. The parents of neurotics scored in between the other two groups and did not differ significantly from either. This indicates that the association was between parents' maturity, as judged by the Rorschach response, and the premorbid personality of their children, regardless of diagnosis. This is not a surprising finding and throws no light on the aetiology of schizophrenia

Fisher and his colleagues (1959) used three scales derived from the Rorschach Test: the Fisher Maladjustment Score, the Fisher Rigidity Score, and a score for Definiteness of Body-Image Boundaries. None of these scales differentiated between the parents of 20 schizophrenics and the parents of 20 neurotics. Similarly, Singer (1967) failed to distinguish between the parents of schizophrenics and neurotics using a measure of the percentage of popular responses given to the Rorschach test ('Beck populars'), and a measure of the degree of differentation of each response as a percept ('genetic level score').

SUMMARY

The studies using psychological tests of thought disorder which are reviewed in this chapter are interrelated to a degree unusual in the field dealt with in this book. The workers concerned have endeavoured to link their studies with previous work and in particular to overcome the evident methodological weaknesses of earlier studies. As a result, we have not had to deal with a multiplicity of methods but have largely been able to concentrate on one, the Object Sorting Test. The original finding with this test (McConaghy, 1959) of 'allusive thinking' in at least one member of all pairs of parents of schizophrenics studied was striking. However, important variables were not controlled, and the sample of patients consisted of chronically hospitalized schizophrenics. When subsequent studies were carried out with more rigorous methodology, an increasing proportion of the control parents exhibited allusive thinking (up to 44 per cent), while the proportion of parents of schizophrenics with abnormally high scores decreased. Rosman and his colleagues (1964), using the largest number of subjects reported, found that differences between parents of schizophrenics and controls on the O.S.T. were limited to those of higher education, occupation, or I.Q. This is reminiscent of the findings of Kohn and Clausen (1956) who found a similar association when their results from parental attitude studies were analysed by the education and occupational level of their subjects [see CHAPTER I]. More recently, a number of carefully conducted investigations have produced conflicting, marginal, or negative results (Romney, 1969 a and b; Wender et al., 1971). McConaghy and Clancy (1968) have provided rather strong evidence for the genetic transmission of an allusive thinking factor. However, the O.S.T. has been shown to be very sensitive to the circumstances of testing (Schopler and Loftin, 1969) so that it is imperative to include among the controls, parents of non-schizophrenic psychiatric patients. Only two of the studies reviewed here have taken this precaution (Stabenau et al. 1965; Romney, 1969), and both reported negative results. Allowing for these criticisms, it may be concluded that the bulk of these studies point towards a link between allusive thinking in parents and in their children. McConaghy's work suggests a possible association between allusive thinking and physical features such as the angle alpha, but otherwise there is no reason to favour a genetic over an environmental explanation for this phenomenon. There are no reliable results to date from work using conventional Rorschach testing to discriminate between parental groups.

CHAPTER V

ABNORMALITIES OF COMMUNICATION AND LANGUAGE IN PARENTS OF SCHIZOPHRENICS

IN this chapter we review the work which acted as the immediate impetus for our own study. At the centre of it is the work of Margaret Singer and Lyman Wynne, who were until recently at the National Institute of Mental Health, Bethesda. During the past decade they have carried out a programme of research which has aimed at evaluating their theories and previous findings in increasingly more precise quantifiable terms. This chapter focuses on their work and includes the relevant contributions of other workers. At the end of the chapter we review additional studies which deal with communication from different theoretical bases, and in particular those relating to the 'double-bind' hypothesis.

In order to appreciate the investigations and findings discussed below, it will be helpful to understand something of the theoretical point of view of Singer and Wynne. They believe that there are learned aspects of schizophrenia and that the peculiarities of the schizophrenic patient are in part determined by abnormalities which occur during interactions between family members (Singer and Wynne, 1964, 1966a). They are quite willing to accept that a genetic predisposition is also necessary in at least one, if not all, cases for the development of the condition, and that other aetiological factors may be relevant as well (Wynne, 1967, 1971). However, the essential features on which they focus are aspects of interaction which they believe can be identified in communication among family members, or between family members and some other person such as a research psychologist or psychotherapist (Morris and Wynne, 1965).

In their papers they emphasize that abnormalities which are important are identified by attending to the communication which occurs in a transaction. This requires attention both to the nature of the language used by the speaker, and to the effect of the communication on the listener. They hypothesize that the features of abnormal communication which they identify can be expected to induce difficulties in the listener's ability to focus attention on and handle the meaning of what is being said (Wynne, 1968). Stated in another way, the style of speech of parents which is characterized by disruptions, vagueness, irrelevance, and lack of closure, etc., impairs the ability of offspring to focus attention on the meaning of what is being said. This is believed to have enduring consequences on the child's thought processes and may predispose to, rather than precipitate schizophrenia (Wynne, 1968). The core of the disordered communication is believed to be the inability of parents to direct and restrict a focus of awareness in a sustained, goal-directed way so that what they mean becomes clear. Thus Singer and Wynne believe this 'attentional' aspect of abnormal thought and communication to be a feature of parents which is transmitted to the child. The ability to share a focus of attention is thought to be essential before an individual can validate his concepts against those of others and would therefore be a prerequisite for the interpretation and testing of reality (Singer and Wynne, 1964). It might be inferred from this that abnormality of these processes underlies the pathogenesis of delusions and hallucinations, but this is never stated explicitly.

The authors characterize four varieties of abnormal experience and expression in schizophrenics: (1) *amorphous*, in which there is a 'drift towards subjective experience', as evidenced by an emptiness of ideas, thought blockage and skidding from one thought to another without a unifying goal in the over-all expression of thought; (2) *fragmented*, in which there is greater over-all coherence and purpose to the thought, but disturbing ideas, impulses, and affects disrupt the communication so that it becomes chaotic and difficult to follow; (3) a mixed form of the above; and (4) a stably constricted form which characterizes patients who speak coherently but split off aspects of reality, such as paranoid patients (Wynne and Singer, 1963).

In one of the first attempts to confirm their hypothesis Singer and Wynne (1963) reported a study of the parents of 20 childhood schizophrenics (infantile autism), 20 young adult schizophrenics, 10 withdrawn neurotics, and 10 neurotics with conduct disorders. The groups were satisfactorily matched for demographic variables, including the education and occupation of the parents and the age and sex of the child. Singer was furnished with the T.A.T. and Rorschach test responses of each parental pair, but she did not know the diagnosis of the offspring and any reference to this had been deleted from the transcripts. In the first part of the study Singer selected the responses of the 10 parental pairs which she felt she could most confidently assign to either the child schizophrenic or the neurotic group. Her prediction of the patients' diagnosis turned out to be completely accurate ($p<0.004$). Using more detailed criteria which she developed on the basis of these tests, she correctly predicted for 12 of the remaining 15 couples which were parents of psychotic and which parents of neurotic offspring. The likelihood of these predictions being correct by chance is less than 0.5 per cent.

Describing the kinds of characteristics which she thought helped her to identify the groups, Singer stated that the parents of psychotic children were cynical, embittered, and scornful of warmth; that they were passive and apathetic; that they were obsessive and distant. The parents of neurotics were characterized by clear communication, lack of obsessionality, evidence of low mood, and apathy. Another feature she took into account was whether

FAPS

one parent clarified or limited any confusing features in the other's communication.

In the second part of the study two psychologists used the criteria Singer had developed and independently examined the Rorschach responses she had seen previously plus those of the parents of 20 young adult schizophrenics. The protocols were rated for the presence of features related to schizophrenia, particularly disordered thought processes. Singer and Wynne predicted that the group of young adult schizophrenics would have the greatest number of parent pairs in which both parents showed these abnormalities, withdrawn neurotics would have the next highest, autistic children the next, and children with conduct disorders the least. This prediction proved correct. The proportion of parents showing deviances in each of these groups was, respectively: 95, 60, 20, and 0 per cent, which is the order she predicted.

The authors argue that the fact that they can correctly predict the diagnoses of offspring from the transcripts of parents' tests supports their hypothesis that there is a relationship between the content and form of parents' communication and the development of abnormal thought processes in their offspring.

Similar methods were applied by Singer in a series of young adult patients comprised of 20 schizophrenics, 9 borderline patients (undefined), and 6 severe neurotics, all unmarried, with males predominating 3 : 2 (Singer and Wynne, 1965). In this study parents and siblings were given a battery of 8 psychological tests including the T.A.T., Rorschach, W.A.I.S., M.M.P.I., Object Sorting Test, Proverbs, Draw-a-person Test and Sentence Completion. With the transcripts and test data for each family in hand, Singer made the following predictions: (1) whether the diagnosis of the sick offspring was schizophrenia, borderline state, or neurosis; (2) the thinking style of the patient according to their classification of amorphous, mixed, fragmented, and stably constricted; and (3) a rating on a five-point scale for severity of ego disorganization, which would be compared with the rating of independent investigators who had evaluated the patient clinically. In each of these areas, Singer's prediction was correct at a confidence level of 0·1 per cent. For example, from the data of 35 families tested she correctly identified 17 of 20 families with a schizophrenic member, seven of the nine families with a borderline patient, and four of the six families with a neurotic member. After these predictions had been made, the families were divided according to social class into several small groups of two to five families each and Singer undertook the task of matching blindly the patients' tests and transcripts for each group with the correct family within each group. These matchings were accomplished with only six errors in 36 families, an accuracy which would occur by chance with an exact probability of $0·2 \times 10^{-5}$. The predictions were based on judgements as to how abnormalities noted in one family member were likely to fit with those of other family members. Special emphasis was placed on the language and communication styles in the family. The magnitude of Singer's accomplishment in these studies is truly remarkable.

In a less ambitious simulation of these techniques Morris and Wynne (1965) studied excerpts of family therapy interviews in a sample of eight families, four with a schizophrenic member and four with a neurotic. Morris correctly predicted the diagnoses of the ill offspring at a confidence level of 0·05, and he made predictions of the schizophrenic patient's form of thinking disorder within the amorphous-fragmented classification which were 100 per cent correct.

When three colleagues tried to repeat these predictions after learning the criteria set out by Morris and Wynne in their paper the accuracy of their predictions was at the level of random probability (Palombo et al., 1967). Morris then trained these workers in weekly sessions of from 1 to 2 hours for 9 months. Having completed this training they were given transcripts compiled from therapy sessions of six more families with a member in hospital, three schizophrenics and three neurotics. The transcripts were randomly ordered. At this stage their combined predictions were correct at the 0·001 level. The best of the three judges made no errors and the worst was wrong in three out of six cases.

During the period of training it emerged when the judges compared their evaluations that the language of the individual descriptions was not comparable in spite of efforts to use the terms uniformly. This suggests that the schema put forward by Morris and Wynne was initially formulated at too general a level. The effort to evolve a common approach led to a simplification of the original evaluative procedure. Nevertheless, at the end of the study the judges were still not certain that the schema formed a sole or even a necessary basis of their judgement.

Some judges thought that they were guided by the therapist's comments which were included in the excerpts. An attempt was made to control for this by giving the new judges lists of all the therapist's comments extracted from the 12 sets of excerpts previously judged by Morris. The judges were asked to guess whether the comments were made to an amorphous, fragmented or non-schizophrenic family. No significant level of prediction was achieved. However, it is still possible that other features of the excerpts were leading the judges to predict correctly and we would agree with the statement of Palombo el al. that the basis of the judges' predictions in this study remains an open question.*

One further aspect of this study is worth noting. When a more highly structured interview with parents of two additional patients was recorded, and the full transcript made available, all the judges made *incorrect predictions*

* Wynne (personal communication) emphasizes that 'neither the "guide lines" in the 1965 papers nor the communication deviance manual published in 1966 encompass *all* of the features which can be utilized by a judge in making predictive discriminations. The point is that the schema and scoring manuals are *useful* (but) we still find that the study of entire protocols provides better predictions than the scoring manual.'

for both families. Wynne (personal communication) states that this is because 'individuals can alter how they communicate in different settings and with different tasks, depending on the degree to which the task is structured'. The implication is that parents of schizophrenics can communicate very clearly in a structured setting but fail to do so 'in unstructured home situations'. It is clearly necessary for this body of theory that such situations be shown to pertain during child rearing. As yet there is no experimental evidence on this point.

Beavers et al. (1965) studied the transcripts of nine mothers of hospitalized schizophrenics and nine mothers of hospitalized neurotics who were asked questions under double-blind conditions about their attitudes to their ill offspring in five major areas such as birth, sexuality, etc. Two raters, also ignorant of the diagnosis, reliably counted the number of the mothers' definite responses ($r=0.77$), shifts and disqualifications of meaning ($r=0.82$), and evasions of a definite response. They found that compared to mothers of the neurotic control group, mothers of schizophrenics produced significantly more shifts, more evasions, and less definite responses in each category ($p<0.01$). These categories considerably overlap with the types of abnormality studied by Singer and Wynne and in this respect support their results. Unfortunately, we are not told the diagnostic criteria used, nor given information about the social class, education, or I.Q. of the subjects, which might account for the differences observed. A useful feature of Beavers' study was that the criteria and method for scoring were sufficiently clear and descriptive for other workers to be able to repeat his study without undue difficulty; his positive result needs replicating.

Behrens et al. (1968) used the Loveland Family Rorschach procedure to test Wynne and Singer's concepts in lower class families containing a schizophrenic patient. The 'family' consisted of the principal persons who reared the patient, regardless of their biological relationship. Raters achieved 90 per cent agreement on which unit to score and 82 per cent agreement on the category of score employed, such as clarity of expression, the subject's grasp of what was said, and the co-operation implied in the response. Patients were all in socio-economic groups IV and V (Hollingshead and Redlich, 1958) and included 17 Negro schizophrenics, 11 Negro normal controls and 11 White schizophrenics. Of the families of Negro schizophrenics and controls, 72 per cent were correctly identified using global judgements for the prediction. Blind scoring of the Family Rorschach showed that significantly more families of Negro and White schizophrenics scored above some unstated cut-off point compared to the Negro controls ($p<0.01$). Wynne and Singer infer from this study that their techniques and principles are valid for lower class families of differing racial background, but one would like to have information about other possible sources of variance and the diagnostic criteria. Again, the results need replicating.

Possibly the most convincing study of other workers in support of the validity of Singer and Wynne's approach is that by Wild and her co-workers at Yale (Wild et al., 1965). They studied communication deviances in the parents of a large number of schizophrenic and normal subjects by first constructing a manual for scoring transcripts of parents who had taken the Object Sorting Test. Initially Singer used her predictive technique to correctly identify 21 of 25 transcripts of parents of schizophrenics and normals from an earlier study (Singer and Wynne, 1963). From the notes Singer had made about those transcripts the Yale workers established scoring criteria which employed such concepts as 'fragmented attention', 'inability to maintain a role', 'peculiar verbalization', and vague references'. Comparison with Singer and Wynne's 41-category Rorschach manual shows that these two approaches have much in common (Singer and Wynne, 1966a).

The authors established that two psychologists who evaluated transcripts in the study without any further knowledge of the subject had achieved an inter-rater reliability of $r = 0.91$ (Pearson product-moment correlation). It was also discovered that there was a significant correlation between the subject's score and education ($r = 0.31$), and the score and age ($r = 0.24$). Because of these correlations, 28 of 121 scored protocols were eliminated in order to match parents of schizophrenics with parents of normals on these variables. This left 44 parents of schizophrenics, including 6 parents without a spouse, and 49 parents of normal controls, including 15 without a spouse, for the final analysis.

It was found that 75 per cent of the parents of schizophrenics as compared with 31 per cent of the parents of normals scored above the median score of both groups combined, a significant difference at the 0.0005 confidence level. Looking at the number of parental pairs in which both parents scored above the median, 58 per cent of the schizophrenic parents did so compared to 12 per cent of controls ($p < 0.02$). When the two parents' score was summed an even better discrimination between groups was obtained. Within each group the mother's score did not differ significantly from the father's.

This study represents an advance on previous investigations in the field because less global, more specific criteria which could be assessed quantitatively were used for scoring and the reliability of the technique between raters could be determined.

Subsequently Singer and Wynne have published a detailed manual which provides 41 categories of communication defects and deviances for scoring transcripts from verbatim or recorded sessions of Rorschach testing (Singer and Wynne, 1966a). Studies by Singer and Wynne using this manual have been published for 94 subjects up to November 1969, and similar results with subjects numbering up to 280 have been mentioned summarily in some papers (Wynne, 1968, 1971), with a more detailed account expected soon (personal communication).

The first reports using the detailed scoring manual (Singer and Wynne, 1966b) were based on an analysis of hand-written verbatim transcripts of the

Rorschachs of parents of 19 'unequivocal' male schizophrenics, 20 male neurotics and 20 male normals, 10 of whom were hospitalized for non-psychiatric disorders. This series, referred to as the 'Houston Sample', was collected at another centre as part of a differently conceived study of parents of schizophrenics by other workers (Fisher *et al.*, 1959). Employing the type of analysis which is published in a modified form in their manual, Singer and Wynne showed that a significantly greater proportion of individual parents and parental pairs had a Deviance score above the median for all groups combined (Singer and Wynne, 1966*b*). Of the parental pairs, 78 per cent were correctly classified as having a schizophrenic, neurotic or normal offspring (Wynne, 1967). Comparing parents by sex, the fathers of schizophrenics had significantly higher scores than the fathers of neurotics and normals at the 0·05 level, but the mothers did not differ significantly from mothers of neurotics. The scores of neurotics as a group always fell between the scores of schizophrenics and normals (Singer and Wynne, 1966*b*). Comparable results on the same transcripts were obtained with the use of a more global technique which conceptualizes communication in terms of its 'visualizability', and similar results were obtained on a sample of 35 patients of higher socio-economic class in Wynne's Unit at the National Institute of Mental Health (Singer, 1967). These 35 later became part of his N.I.M.H. sample (Wynne, 1971). When a cut-off point for the Deviance score was defined by the lowest scoring parent of all 19 schizophrenic patients in the Houston Sample, only 42 per cent of the individual parents of neurotics and 22 per cent of normals scored above this point, thereby falling within the schizophrenic range. Moreover, when the mother's and father's scores for each subject were averaged, only 20 per cent of neurotics and 10 per cent of normals scored above the lowest of any pair of parents of schizophrenics ($p < 0.0001$) (Wynne, 1967).

The magnitude of these differences can be contrasted with the results of Fisher *et al.* (1959) who studied the same sample of patients and the same Rorschach tests using a number of other modes of measurement. They were unable to differentiate parents of *schizophrenics* from parents of *neurotics* on the Fisher Maladjustment Score, the Fisher Rigidity Score, or a Barrier Score related to 'body image boundaries', all scored from the Rorschachs. Singer (1967) using other traditional Rorschach measures, such as the Becker Genetic Level Scores and the number of popular responses, also was unable to differentiate between the groups. On one measure, the number of rejected cards, the groups did differ, with parents of neurotics tending more often to reject cards. Singer makes the point that unlike traditional Rorschach scoring, it is the way in which the perceptions of the Rorschach are communicated rather than what is seen that is important in these transcripts, and this is what the manual aims to score (Singer, 1967).

Wynne and Singer have now prepared a more comprehensive and detailed report (to be published) in which they present the results from their N.I.M.H.

sample. They collected 114 index offspring and classified them according to a seven-point severity-of-illness scale ranging from normality, through neurosis, to schizophrenia. With the exception of a small group of normal subjects, the sample was collected over a number of years mainly from neighbouring facilities including psychiatric hospitals and private psychiatrists. The parents of these offspring included 35 pairs whose scores were reported in an earlier paper (Singer, 1967). Apart from acting as experimental subjects, most of the parents participated in psychotherapy as well (personal communication). In contrast to the Houston sample, who were selected from a Veterans' Administration hospital, nearly all of the N.I.M.H. sample were in the upper three socio-economic groups.

The method involved the administration to the parents and their offspring separately of a battery of tests including the standard Rorschach test. The testing was conducted under standardized conditions and the testing psychologists did not have any clinical information about the patient, although they knew which subjects were the parents of normal children. The testers were not aware of the hypothesis being tested nor of the scoring procedures. The tests and results were not available to the clinician who made the diagnoses. The testing sessions were tape-recorded and typescripts were double-checked for accuracy and to eliminate possible clues to the diagnosis of the offspring. Groups of protocols were scored blindly in random order by a psychologist whose only information was the subject's sex and age. Several raters achieved a high level of inter-rater agreement (above 80 per cent) on the presence or absence of deviances scored accordingly to Singer and Wynne's manual.

The results demonstrated a remarkable ability of this technique to differentiate parents according to the severity of illness of their offspring. The mean parental Deviance scores for the various groups were as follows: Normals 0·58, Neurotics 0·66, Borderline 1·32, Psychotics 2·36. The results are presented in a different form in the following table which gives the number of parental pairs in each diagnostic group with scores above and below the median for the whole sample.

When the mid-point between the mother's and father's Deviance score in each parental pair is used the classificatory errors are very small. Only one out of the 89 parental pairs with normal, neurotic and schizophrenic offspring is misclassified on this basis.

Wynne and his colleagues have recently carried out a multivariate analysis of their data, examining the relationship of the severity of illness of the parents and offspring and their Deviance scores.* This represents one of the few attempts in the field to distinguish between genetic and environmental effects. They found that the parents' Deviance scores were more closely related to the offspring's severity of illness than to the offspring's Deviance score. Furthermore the parents' Deviance scores were correlated with the offspring's severity-of-illness score independently of the parents' severity-of-

* We have these results but have not included them at the request of Professor Wynne.

DISTRIBUTION OF DEVIANCE SCORES OF PARENTAL PAIRS

Diagnosis of Index Offspring

(Wynne, personal communication)

	NORMAL (1–2)	NEUROTIC (3)	BORDERLINE (4)	REMITTING SCHIZ. (5)	NON-REMITTING SCHIZ. (6–7)
Mid-point of Deviance Scores for Each Parental Pair					
Above Median (1·30)	1	0	12	24	20
Below Median	19	25	13	0	0
TOTALS	20	25	25	24	20

illness scores. The implication is that the parents' deviant communication has an effect on the offspring's mental state independent of any genetic factor.

COMMENTS AND CRITICISMS

The methods used in these studies are innovatory and the results are striking. Before one can interpret these findings one must look for other possible explanations of such impressive results. Several of these studies involved what Singer and Wynne have called 'predictions' from one set of data to another, such as from transcripts of parents' test response to the diagnosis of their offspring (Singer and Wynne, 1963, 1965). The procedure of matching parents with patients by examining the test materials and transcripts of each certainly reveals Singer's skill in identifying characteristics which parents and patients may have in common, but it is quite possible that these characteristics have nothing to do with schizophrenia. Indeed, this likelihood becomes highly probable when one considers that she could match both neurotic and normal families with their individual offspring as successfully as she could match parents of schizophrenics with theirs. Obviously it could not be the schizophrenic qualities which allow non-schizophrenics to be matched on a one to one basis with their parents.

In their earlier studies, the raters' judgements were global and essentially subjective. Though attempts were made to determine the basis of these judgements, data from their own publications suggest that it was not possible to determine the extent to which the criteria put forward played a part (Palombo et al., 1967, and page 75 of this chapter).

These criticisms are less relevant to later studies which employ objective quantifiable scoring techniques, but they nevertheless remind us of possible unstated factors which may play a part in the later investigations as well. It is a striking feature that there was considerably better agreement between Singer's evaluations of the test material of parents and the clinical evaluations by her co-workers of the patients than has been achieved by several pairs of psychiatrists of similar training, who evaluated and diagnosed patients they were seeing at the same time (Kreitman et al., 1961).

Certain other methodological considerations are also relevant to these studies. There appears to have been preselection of cases in many of these studies such that bias may unwittingly have been introduced in the sample which might in part account for the results reported. On the basis of published material supplemented by personal communications we are unable to rule this out. For example, we do know that Wild and her associates in their study eliminated subjects who had already been tested and scored in order to match groups for age and education but we do not know how it was decided which subjects to eliminate (Wild et al., 1965). Transcripts from the N.I.M.H. sample were disqualified by a blind observer who was instructed to eliminate transcripts in which the tester's technique was considered unsatisfactory (personal communication from Dr. Wynne). It is also quite possible that centres which specialize in the investigation and treatment of families of schizophrenics would get more patients preselected for family abnormalities before referral. (See Discussion, PART II.) However, these criticisms would not apply as strongly to the Houston sample in which all the subjects came from a single Veterans' Administration Hospital.

It is possible that other forms of bias have crept into the material. Consider the Houston study in which transcripts were recorded verbatim by the testing psychologists. Though the testing psychologist would not have realized the way in which these transcripts were eventually to be scored by Singer, it nevertheless seems quite possible that he would have taken greater care to record peculiar nuances of speech for subjects he thought might be parents of schizophrenics than for other groups. The question of whether knowledge of the diagnosis affects the interviewer was raised by Palombo *et al.* (1967).

It is unfortunate that in none of the reports to date is it mentioned that parents were specifically matched for I.Q., or if so whether it was done by deleting families from the study to make groups comparable. The importance of I.Q. was suggested by the studies of Rosman and of Fisher. Rosman and her colleagues (1964) found a Pearson product-moment correlation of -0.31 for parents of neurotics and normals between the Deviance score and education, and of $+0.24$ between the Deviance score and the subjects' age. Fisher provides information on the influence of education in the original Houston study of parents and their analysis of the Rorschachs which were later used as the test material for Singer and Wynne's most carefully controlled investigation (Fisher *et al.*, 1959; Singer and Wynne, 1966*b*). Fisher reports a significant negative correlation between vague responses of a spouse and education at the 0.05 confidence level, and a significant positive correlation with the total number of exchanges between spouses. His maladjustment and rigidity scores on the Rorschach were both negatively correlated with education, and various other measures on the T.A.T. and Rorschach were also significantly correlated with education. Comparing the experimental and control groups in their sample, Fisher reports that parents of normals were significantly higher in education than parents of schizophrenics ($p<0.07$), and significantly higher than parents of neurotics ($p<0.03$), but the neurotic and schizophrenic groups did not significantly differ (Fisher *et al.*, 1959). Singer and Wynne used these same subjects for their Houston sample and some of the correlations between education and 'vagueness', for example, seem particularly relevant to certain of the scoring categories in their manual (Singer and Wynne, 1966*a*).

Mishler and Waxler (1967, 1968*a* and *b*) raised the importance of the circumstances of the interview as a determinant of the experimental results. In connection with this Schopler and Loftin (1969) have shown that the subject's attitude towards the test situation can significantly affect the amount of allusive thinking detected by the Object Sorting Test. Comparisons of parents of severely ill psychiatric patients with those of moderately ill ones or of normal people could well be very sensitive to this effect. Singer and Wynne go some way towards mitigating this possible effect by including hospitalized psychiatric patients with a number of different diagnoses in their Houston and N.I.M.H. samples.

A final criticism, which unfortunately applies to a great deal of psychiatric research, is the failure of investigators to define and describe adequately the nature of the clinical material, particularly the symptoms of the parents studied. The importance of stating diagnostic criteria has been discussed in previous chapters, but needs re-stressing here as the differences in diagnostic practices at different centres can be very great indeed (Kendell *et al.*, 1971). It has been established that the diagnosis of schizophrenia made by American psychiatrists is much broader than that current in the United Kingdom, and may include a substantial proportion of patients who would be classified as personality disordered by British psychiatrists. In the absence of detailed clinical material, one cannot assume that a sample of American schizophrenics is comparable with a sample of British schizophrenics.

It is important to bear in mind that these criticisms amount to no more than a caution that there may be some other explanation for the results of these studies than those offered by the authors. However, when everything is taken into consideration their findings remain remarkable, and demand replication by other workers in different centres, particularly in Great Britain. Further work would need to take account of features of the experimental design which were overlooked in the earlier studies. That is the purpose of the undertaking which is reported in PART II of this monograph.

OTHER STUDIES OF ABNORMAL SPEECH AND COMMUNICATION

A number of workers have studied the communication value of language in the parents of psychiatric patients from standpoints rather different from those of Singer and Wynne. One of the earliest studies was by Mahl (1956). He developed measures of silences and of speech disturbances in patients undergoing psychotherapy. He regarded both these features as due to underlying anxiety in the psychotherapeutic situation. He defined the 'Patient-Silence Quotient' as the ratio of the number of seconds of silence to the number of seconds available to the patient to talk. He categorized seven varieties of speech disturbance, which were developed empirically by noting disturbances that were *sensed* as superfluous or distorting to the communication of content. These categories include 'Sentence Incompletion' and 'Repetition', and almost all of them have their parallels in Singer and Wynne's manual. He defined the 'Speech-Disturbance Ratio' as the ratio of the number of speech disturbances to the number of words spoken by the patient. It is interesting that he took account of the relative verbosity of patients in studying defects in communication, a precaution that was omitted by Singer and Wynne in all their reports except an unpublished analysis of previous data. Mahl tested whether the Silence Quotient and the Speech-Disturbance Ratio were valid measures of anxiety by rating the transcripts of the tapes for anxiety himself. He took the necessary step of eliminating silences, references to silences, and speech disturbances from the transcripts first, but his method of making analytically-based judgements of anxiety from the written word is a dubious procedure. Nevertheless, his attempt to quantify these aspects of speech was a methodological advance.

Farina and Holzberg (1970) employed both the measures developed by Mahl in a study of family interaction. They used a slightly modified version of the Speech-Disturbance Ratio, from which one category was omitted (the interpolation of 'ah' sounds). The inter-rater reliability for both measures was 0·9 or above, however there was no significant correlation between the two measures. This makes it extremely unlikely that they both reflect anxiety. The authors studied three groups used in previous experiments (see p. 38): non-schizophrenic psychiatric patients, and Good and Poor schizophrenics, and the parents of these patients. There were 24 patients in each group. The subjects were given a task which involved resolving six hypothetical problem situations. They were tested in individual and family group sessions. Sound recordings were made of the sessions and were rated blindly.

The scores on both measures decreased from individual to group interviews ($p < 0.05$), and the consistency of subjects from one session to another was low ($r = 0.5$). The family members differed significantly ($0 < 0.05$) in their scores on both measures, the son scoring highest and the mother lowest in each diagnostic group. Among sons, the Poors scored highest and the controls lowest, with the Goods being intermediate. The authors concluded that the Poors were the most anxious of the three groups, and so were their parents. However, both the anxiety of parents and sons as reflected by these measures *decreased* when they were interviewed together rather than alone. This does not fit in with the theory that parents of schizophrenics exacerbate anxiety in their children when interacting with them. It was also found that there was no relationship between these two indices and measures of parental dominance and hostility. The main criticism is that there is little evidence that the two indices are measures of anxiety. At a less inferential level they are clearly a common component of normal speech and may represent an important aspect of communication. However, their significance needs to be clarified before these results can be properly interpreted.

Mahl's Speech-Disturbance Ratio was also used in a study by Becker and Finkel (1969). In addition they used the 'Cloze' procedure, which involves deleting every fifth word in a transcript. Raters have to guess which word is missing. High predictability of the missing words is assumed to be characteristic of normal speech. The parents of Good and Poor schizophrenics, and of non-psychiatric controls were the subjects. There were 15 parental pairs in each of the three groups. The groups did not differ on social class but did differ on age, education, and I.Q. However, as these indices were not significantly correlated with the two measures used, no statistical adjustments were made. Each subject was asked to speak for 4 minutes on each of four areas related to family life—sex, dependency, aggression, and a relatively neutral topic. The transcripts were then scored for the two measures used. For the Cloze procedure the results were contrary to expectation. The parents of Poor schizophrenics had the highest Cloze scores (i.e. were the most predictable), while the control parents had the lowest scores. In terms of Mahl's Speech-Disturbance Ratio there was no relationship between parental scores and the diagnostic groupings. Hence this study fails to support the findings of Farina and Holzberg (1970).

The results with the Cloze procedure, although going against Becker and Finkel's predictions, are actually in accord with the viewpoint of Mishler and Waxler (1968a and b). These workers argue that disruptions in the flow of communication and variation from ordered, complete sentences are more likely to occur in normal families and that these modes of communication allow for greater adaptability to changing situations. They see these interruptions in the flow of speech as providing opportunities for interjecting rewarding or punitive sanctions and for introducing new information. They argue further that family norms which require complete, unbroken sentences and paragraphs put a strain on others who have to wait until the speaker is finished, and limit the introduction and interchange of new information. To test this information they analysed their original data (Mishler and Waxler, 1968 a and b) with two questions in mind: first, do hesitations in the speech of family members serve the function of introducing new information, and secondly, are there differences between normal and schizophrenic families in the function of these speech events (Mishler and Waxler, 1970)? The technique they used derives from information theory. A subject is asked to guess each successive word in a sentence. If he cannot guess the word within a specified time limit, he is told the correct word and proceeds to try to guess the next word in the sentence. With each successive word the task becomes easier. The more difficult it is to guess the correct word, the higher its information value. They hypothesize that hesitations serve to introduce new information and provide choice points for change. Hence, words following a hesitation should be the most difficult to guess.

The sentences used in their study were drawn from their earlier work on family interaction. A random sample of 12 sentences from normal families and 23 sentences from schizophrenic families was obtained. Each sentence had to contain a pause or silence. Contractions were reworded, pronouns substituted for proper names, and all hesitations were removed. The subjects were 35 college student volunteers, each of whom dealt with a different sentence. It was found that it was no harder to guess words immediately following hesitations than those immediately preceding hesitations and that there was no difference in the predictability of words in samples from the normal and schizophrenic families. Hence, neither of their predictions were supported. They point out that in actual conversation many other cues, such as gesture, tone, and context of the discussion, are available to aid anticipation of the next word or phrase, and they question the validity of concentrating on single words rather than larger units of speech.

Two further studies remain to be discussed in this section. One is a characteristically complex piece of work by Reiss (1968), which has already been outlined in CHAPTER III (p. 59). Families of schizophrenics, personality disordered patients, and normal offspring were compared with regard to their performance on a card sorting task. Apart from the measures discussed above, Reiss rated transcripts of the experimental sessions for the frequency of explicit and implicit 'acts'. Acts corresponded to simple English sentences and usually contained one to six words. An explicit act conveys specific information, for example, 'All the ones with T's go together', in contrast to an implicit act, which only *implies* a specific concept in the speaker's mind, for example, 'These two go together'. It was found that the normal group produced fewer implicit acts than the personality disordered or schizophrenic groups, but that the latter two did not differ from each other. The proportions of task-specific acts that were implicit were respectively 0·20, 0·32, and 0·28. If a high proportion of implicit acts does indicate poor communication of specific information, it is clearly not a distinguishing characteristic of families containing a schizophrenic member.

The last study in this section is that of Feinsilver (1970). He utilized Singer and Wynne's concept of a 'shared focus of attention' in analysing transcripts of the speech of family members. His subjects were six volunteer families containing a schizophrenic patient and a normal sibling, and six control families of hospital personnel who also volunteered for the experiment. The schizophrenics had all been in hospital for 3–9 months and had recovered from an episode of illness in which thought disorder had been a symptom. The two groups of families did not differ in terms of social class or I.Q. The task was for each member of the family in turn to describe a series of common objects to another family member who would not be able to see the objects and who would be required to identify them after the description was completed. The descriptions had to contain five separate characteristics of the object. All possible combinations of family pairs were used in each group. The sessions were taped, typescripts were made of each session, and the transactions were scored by independent scorers. The measures scored were: Misidentification, if the first response given by the listener was not exactly correct; Inappropriate Conceptualization, which represented the degree of overly concrete or overly generalized thinking manifested; and Focal Attention Measures, which comprised adaptions of the categories for measuring impaired focal attention which are given by Singer and Wynne in their manual. Inter-rater reliability for the total scores on the measures was 0·84.

No significant differences were found between any of the various pairings within the families of schizophrenics or within the control families. However, the schizophrenic families taken as a whole differed significantly from the normal families by showing a greater number of object misidentifications and a greater degree of qualities which impair focal attention. The latter scores showed no overlapping between the groups at all (p<0·001). The greatest difference between the experimental and control families was in the child–child pair.

The author is rightly cautious in his interpretation of these findings in view of the small number of subjects. He makes the point that it would be necessary to test the families of non-schizophrenic psychiatric patients. This is particularly important as the set of the parents of psychiatric patients may be very different in a testing situation from the set of the parents of normal children. He did not control for verbal responsiveness in this experiment and an increase in this factor, possibly as a result of increased anxiety, could raise the score on Focal Attention Measures.

He also points out that as no pair within the schizophrenic families differed significantly on these measures from any other pair, defective communication is likely to be a function of the total family and not of the patient alone. Furthermore, it cannot account for the patient, rather than his sibling, becoming schizophrenic. This study of dyadic communication in the family and the issues it raises leads us on to a consideration of the Double-Bind Theory.

RESEARCH ON THE DOUBLE-BIND THEORY

This theory, which treats schizophrenia as a specific pattern of communication, has already been discussed in some detail in CHAPTER I (pp. 14–16). Here we will consider the experimental work that has been done to verify the hypotheses formulated by Bateson and his colleagues (1956). It is worth briefly restating the three conditions which were considered essential for the creation of a double-bind situation. First, the individual must be involved in an intense relationship; secondly, he must be caught in a situation in which the other person in the relationship is expressing two orders of message which are contradictory; and thirdly, he must feel constrained not to comment on the contradiction. Almost none of the studies in this area has employed a design which includes all three criteria. Most of the work has concentrated on the contradictory nature of messages.

Beavers et al. (1965) tested the hypothesis that the mothers of schizophrenics communicate feelings in a quantitatively more ambiguous fashion than the mothers of non-schizophrenics. He selected nine schizophrenic and nine non-psychotic patients who were currently in hospital. In all cases the onset of the illness was before 20 years of age, there was no known brain damage, and the diagnosis was agreed upon by all the staff. The mothers of the patients were given a semi-structured interview by interviewers who were unaware of the offspring's diagnosis. The mothers were asked about their feelings in five major areas, such as the patient's birth, childhood, and sexuality. Transcripts of the interviews were scored for the number of definite, clear-cut responses, and the number of evasions and shifts. Subjects could shift to an entirely different emotional state when asked to confirm a previous response, or could repudiate the assumed meaning of the earlier statement.

The findings were that the mothers of schizophrenics produced more shifts (p<0·006), more evasions (p<0·01), and fewer definite responses than the control mothers. Unfortunately, this study was of a small number of cases and omitted to control for the social class, education, or I.Q. of the mothers. These factors may be more influential in determining the mode of expression of feeling than the offspring's diagnosis. Another defect was the omission of the diagnostic criteria used for schizophrenia. Perhaps the most important methodological criticism can be aimed at the assumption that shifts and evasions are equivalent to contradictions. Only one kind of shift categorized here, the repudiation of a previous response, can be considered directly relevant to the explicit double-bind hypothesis.

Another worker who has examined contradictory statements by parents is Berger (1965). He selected four groups of subjects: 20 schizophrenic patients with a history of illogical and fragmented verbalization, 20 non-schizophrenic patients, 20 hospital ward attendants and kitchen staff, and 40 college students. The first three groups were matched for age and parents' education. The students were significantly younger and came from a better social background than the other groups. Berger compiled a list of 30 statements which were judged by psychologists as fulfilling the conditions of the double-bind theory. The subjects were asked to rate the frequency with which their mothers used to make similar statements. The initial finding was that the schizophrenic patients could not be distinguished from the non-schizophrenics or from the hospital staff by their responses. Only the college students stood out as being different from the other groups, and this could be a consequence of their different social background and educational attainment. The author subsequently selected the 12 most discriminating items of the 30 and recalculated his results using these. He was then able to show a significant difference between the schizophrenic and non-schizophrenic patients. However, this is a rather dubious method. Furthermore, a procedure which relies on the retrospective recall of a psychiatrically ill patient is open to serious question.

A different method of obtaining double-bind messages was employed by Ringuette and Kennedy (1966). They used letters written by parents to their children in hospital. Twenty letters were from the parents of schizophrenics and twenty from the parents of non-schizophrenic patients in a state hospital.

In addition, 20 normal volunteers were asked to write letters as if to their children in a state hospital. The letters were blindly assessed by five groups of judges. These comprised a group of experts on the double-bind concept, a group of psychiatric residents trained in the double-bind, clinicians trained in the double-bind, untrained clinicians, and naïve lay people. Each group consisted of three individuals who were asked to rate the letters on a seven-point scale for the degree of double-bind present.

The inter-rater correlations between the judges were very low, reaching only 0·19 in the expert group. The experts included Bateson, Watzlawick and other pioneers of the double-bind hypothesis. The agreement was no better when only the letters from the parents of schizophrenics were considered. It was also found that none of the groups was able to distinguish between the parents of schizophrenics and of non-schizophrenics on the basis of the letters. The only positive finding was that the untrained judges could distinguish between the letters from the normal volunteers and the letters from the parents of patients by using a simple 'like–dislike' scale. The trained groups were unable to achieve this differentiation. The poor agreement between the experts on what constituted double-bind messages is an ominous sign for anyone attempting to do reliable experimental work on this concept. It could be argued, however, that the written word is very different from the spoken word, and that the time for reflection that a letter allows plus the emotional distance it dictates could result in the toning down or elimination of double-bind statements. This objection cannot be made to the study by Haley (1968).

Haley's method involved the giving of instructions over a microphone by parents to their children. The task was for the parental pair to instruct their child to select from 24 Japanese playing cards the eight that the parents had in front of them and to arrange them in the same order. In the first part of the experiment 20 normal children, 12 schizophrenic children, and 12 children suffering from neurosis or exhibiting delinquent behaviour tried to follow the tape-recorded instructions from their own parents. The normal and neurotic children did equally well, placing over 80 per cent of the cards correctly. The schizophrenic children only managed a 45 per cent accuracy in selecting and ordering the cards, a difference significant at the 1 per cent level. In the next part of the experiment the children were allowed to talk back to their parents so that corrections could be made. All groups improved in their scores, but the schizophrenic children improved most, because there was more room for improvement. When this was allowed for, the three groups did not differ in the amount of improvement. These findings left open the question of whether the schizophrenics' poor performance was due to confused instructions from their parents, to their own difficulties in interpreting instructions, or to a combination of the two effects. Haley tackled this question by getting normal children to respond to instructions from the parents of normals and the parents of schizophrenics, both of which groups

GAPS

were strangers to them. He found that there was no difference in the response of normal children to normal parents as compared with the response of normal children to the parents of schizophrenics. This suggests that the main defect in the response of a schizophrenic child to his parents lies in the child himself, and that the parents are not communicating abnormally. Unfortunately, the argument is by no means watertight. Haley did not test out the fourth logical combination, namely of schizophrenic children responding to instructions from normal parents who were strangers to them. In the absence of this experiment, it is not possible to determine whether there is an interactional effect between schizophrenics and their parents. It is possible that it is only in the heightened emotional interaction with their own children that the parents of schizophrenics emit double-bind messages. In the cooler relationship with strange children, the double-bind may no longer be elicited. It must be remembered that one of the original stipulations for a double-bind situation was an intense relationship.

This point is one of the criticisms that can be levelled at the studies of Sojit (1969, 1971). She used the proverb 'A rolling stone gathers no moss' because it has two opposing but equally plausible meanings. This was meant to provide the contradictory aspect of the double-bind situation. Parental pairs were asked to discuss the meaning of the proverb and teach the meaning to their children. The couple's interaction was recorded, and observed by the interviewer through a one-way mirror. Their interaction with the children is not reported in these papers.

A method for scoring dyadic interaction was developed in a pilot study (Sojit, 1969). Each statement made by a parent was considered a message unit, no matter how short or long. Message units were classified in terms of seven categories. The mean inter-rater agreement on all scales used was 85 per cent. The sample consisted of 20 sets of parents of children suffering from ulcerative colitis, eight sets of parents of delinquents, eight sets of parents of adolescent and young adult schizophrenics, nine parental pairs with children suffering from cystic fibrosis, and the parents of nine normal children. Both the delinquents and the schizophrenics were in treatment in a psychiatric facility.

Sojit found that the parents of schizophrenics differed significantly from the normal parents and the parents of children with ulcerative colitis and cystic fibrosis on their scores for three categories of message. The former group more often gave invalid interpretations of the proverb, false abstractions and qualifications, they more often disaffirmed the content of their own or of the other's message, and they made more remarks about the proverb, the interviewer, or the interview situation. However, the parents of schizophrenics could not be distinguished from the parents of delinquents on any of these three measures. Fewer of the parents of schizophrenics remarked that the proverb has two contradictory meanings than did the parents of normal children, delinquent children, and children with cystic fibrosis combined. However, they did not differ from the parents of children with ulcerative colitis on this measure.

It is questionable whether contradictory interpretations of a proverb that has no obvious emotional connotations really simulate a double-bind situation. The author makes much of the emotional involvement of the subjects in the test situation, but it was probably much more intense for the parents of schizophrenic and delinquent children, who were receiving psychiatric treatment, than for the other groups of parents. It is important in this respect that it is just these two groups of parents which were found to differ from the remaining three groups but not from each other. A further criticism relates to the fact that only the parental dyad was tested. The findings might well be quite different in any interaction with the child.

In all the foregoing studies the contradiction in the messages used has invariably been within one order; for example, in the study by Beavers *et al.* (1965) the ambiguity was within the area of expression of feelings, while in Sojit's study it was confined to statements of meaning. Loeff, as reported in the excellent review of this field by Olson (1972), employed conflict between the expression of affect by tone and by content of a statement. He made recordings of happy and unhappy statements and varied the tone so that it was appropriate to the content in some statements, inappropriate in others, and neutral in a third group. The subjects were adolescent girls, 24 of whom suffered from schizophrenia, 24 of whom were delinquents, and 24 normal controls. They were required to rate each statement on a scale indicating the degree of agreement between the tone of voice and the content. Loeff found that all three groups were equally able to discriminate the conflicting messages, but that the delinquents and schizophrenics were more influenced by both the tonal and content aspects of the statements than the control subjects. This latter group placed greater emphasis on the content of the messages than the tone and tended to miss any contradiction between them. A contrary result was obtained by Mehrabian and Wiener (1967) working with normal subjects, who found that when these two aspects of a message were discrepant, the tonal component played by far the most prominent role in the perception of the message.

In considering this group of studies we can see that all of them test limited aspects of the double-bind hypothesis. In none of them are all three of the theoretically essential elements included in the design. The majority of the studies have concentrated on contradictions in parental communications, but some of the investigators such as Beavers *et al.* (1965) and Sojit (1969) have used types of contradiction which seem inappropriate to the original formulation of the double-bind hypothesis. Only two studies, those by Loeff (1966) and Mehrabian and Wiener (1967), employ contradictions between two different orders of the message, in these cases tone and content, and both studies came to opposite conclusions. In many of the studies, the experimental group were not matched for I.Q., social class, or education. This precaution is particularly important in work on aspects of communication. In none of the studies were the criteria for the diagnosis of schizophrenia stipulated. It is possible that all these experimenters are chasing shadows, because even the experts on the double-bind hypothesis were unable to reach even a modicum of agreement on what constituted double-bind statements (Ringuette and Kennedy, 1966). The most valid test of the theory seems to be the study by Haley (1968). His results suggest that any difficulty experienced by schizophrenics in following their parents' instructions is due to some aspect of the patients' pathology. Unfortunately, he failed to carry his work to its logical conclusion to investigate any interactional effect between schizophrenics and their parents. In conclusion, the double-bind hypothesis has not been adequately tested experimentally, but what tentative results there are suggest that double-bind messages are not specific to the parents of schizophrenics. This conclusion was also reached by Sluzki and his colleagues (1967, 1971), who are associated with Bateson's group.

CHAPTER VI
SUMMARY AND CONCLUSIONS

THE preceding chapters have been organized on the basis of the type of methodology used to study the parents of schizophrenic patients. The large number of studies reviewed have provided a mass of contradictory findings. In this chapter we have endeavoured to condense the material and to summarize the experimental evidence for the various concepts and theories about the parents of schizophrenics. We bring together the most important findings from the different experimental areas and give our opinion regarding the present state of knowledge in the field. For a detailed consideration of the studies mentioned here, the bibliography should be consulted for cross reference to earlier chapters.

ARE MOTHERS OF SCHIZOPHRENICS OVER-PROTECTIVE AND INTRUSIVE?

A number of studies have examined this question. Kasanin, Knight, and Sage (1934) in a study of case-notes found evidence of maternal over-protection or rejection in 60 per cent of schizophrenics. However, no control group was used so that the significance of this finding cannot be assessed. Witmer (1934) conducted interviews with the relatives of manic-depressive and schizophrenic patients and found no difference between the two groups in terms of parental over-protection. This study is weakened by its reliance on retrospective recall. The same criticism applies to the studies by Lu (1961, 1962) and Pollin et al. (1966, 1968). Lu found from interviewing mothers that they had been more over-protective to their schizophrenic child in its youth than to its normal sibling, while Pollin et al. found, also from interviews, that mothers had been more concerned about the behaviour of their child who became schizophrenic than about its monozygotic twin who remained psychiatrically well. When the parents were over-protective the child appeared to have been excessively dependent. Gerard and Siegel (1950) avoided the bias of retrospective reporting and concentrated on the current situation. They found a heightened relationship between almost all the schizophrenics they studied and their mothers, whereas this was not found at all in a control group of normals. However, the groups were not matched on age, ethnic group, education, or social class. Mark (1953) took this precaution when he gave a questionnaire to 100 mothers of hospitalized female schizophrenics and 100 mothers of medical patients. He concluded that the results showed mothers of schizophrenics to be more restrictive in the amount of control they wished to exert over the child. Hotchkiss et al. (1955) observed that mothers of male schizophrenics appeared to be over-involved when visiting their sons in hospital, but this is a potentially disturbing situation and demands a control group of non-schizophrenic hospital patients, which was not used in this study. Using two separate samples, Alanen (1958, 1966, 1968) interviewed the mothers of schizophrenics and compared them with the mothers of neurotics and normals. He found that the mothers of schizophrenics were more over-protective than the other two groups. However, the interviewers were aware of the diagnostic groups of the families interviewed and may have been influenced by this knowledge, as they have an expressed bias towards a particular psychoanalytic viewpoint.

Freeman and Grayson (1955) compared the mothers of schizophrenics and normals using the Shoben parent–child attitude survey. They found the mothers of schizophrenics to be more over-protective towards their children, but this result was not replicated by Freeman et al. (1959) who rightly criticized the former study because the groups were not matched on social background and were interviewed in different circumstances. Another study of relevance to this topic was by Mishler and Waxler (1968a and b) who used the Revealed Difference Technique and analysed the interaction of family members. They found that in the setting of a family group, male schizophrenics of poor premorbid personality received more attention from their mothers than did the children of the other experimental and control groups.

Possibly the best design to overcome the problem of retrospective bias was employed by Ricks and his colleagues (Waring and Ricks, 1965; Ricks and Nameche, 1966; Nameche, Waring, and Ricks, 1964), who studied the records of Child Guidance Clinics to obtain material collected about the patients before they became schizophrenic. They compared children who later developed chronic schizophrenia with a matched group of child referrals who were not subsequently hospitalized for schizophrenia. Children who later became schizophrenic were more often over-protected by their family than the controls, as shown by behaviour such as bathing the child even in adolescence, isolating the child from his peers, and not allowing him privacy. However, in this group of studies the case notes were not examined blindly.

Despite methodological shortcomings which allow for alternative interpretations of the findings in every study reviewed, eight of the better designed studies suggest that mothers of schizophrenics are more concerned, protective, and possibly more intrusive than normal control mothers both in the current situation and in their attitudes to the children before they showed signs of schizophrenia (Kasanin et al., 1934; Gerard and Siegel, 1950; Mark, 1953; Hotchkiss et al., 1955; Alanen, 1958, 1966, 1968; Freeman and Grayson, 1955; Nameche, Waring, and Ricks, 1964). However, it is important to appreciate that excessive protectiveness in the mother may well develop as a response to an abnormal child, rather than the reverse. The evidence for this is considered below.

ARE MOTHERS OF SCHIZOPHRENICS ALOOF, COLD, OR REJECTING?

THE SCHIZOPHRENOGENIC MOTHER

Alanen (1958, 1966, 1968) found that the mothers of female schizophrenics were over-protective in a hostile way when compared with the mothers of neurotics and normals. His description came close to the concept of the 'schizophrenogenic mother' coined by Fromm-Reichman (1948). Mark (1953) using a questionnaire technique, found mothers of schizophrenics to be both more devoted and also more detached than the mothers of a control group of medical patients. However, Zuckerman *et al.* (1958) using the Parent Attitude Research Instrument found that the mothers of schizophrenics were no more controlling or rejecting than a group of normal mothers matched on age and education. This otherwise well-conducted study has the defect of concentrating on current attitudes rather than on attitudes before the onset of the child's illness, but this is remedied in Gardner's (1967) analysis of data from the same project as that by Nameche, Waring, and Ricks, reported above. Gardner actually found cold, dominant, threatening mothers more commonly among the control group than in the group of children who later developed schizophrenia. This study provides somewhat stronger evidence against the concept of the cold, aloof, hostile schizophrenogenic mother, for which, surprisingly in view of its popularity, we could not find any reliable supporting evidence. In fact, there is an extreme paucity of scientific work relating to this question, but the two studies by Zuckerman *et al.* and Gardner in our view outweigh the work of Alanen and lead us to conclude that the characterization of these mothers as showing a combination of over-protection and hostile rejection cannot be sustained.

ARE THERE ANY CONCLUSIONS ABOUT THE FATHERS OF SCHIZOPHRENICS?

In attempting to characterize the fathers of fourteen schizophrenics Lidz *et al.* (1957a) described five types of fathers! McGhie (1961a) found that fathers of schizophrenics avoided responsibility at home and lacked ambition but these were non-blind summary impressions. Gerard and Siegel's (1950) questionnaire technique suggested that fathers of schizophrenics were passive and ineffectual, but Cheek (1965b) concluded they were supportive and permissive. In Caputo's (1963) excellent social interaction study fathers of schizophrenics did not differ from fathers of other groups in their interaction roles. Generally, the theorists have shown much less interest in the fathers than in the mothers of schizophrenics and this has been reflected in the dearth of adequate experimental work. The bulk of it tackles the question of whether the fathers are more passive or withdrawn from family interaction than normal fathers, and this will be dealt with in the next section.

DO SCHIZOPHRENIC FAMILIES SHOW ATYPICAL DOMINANCE PATTERNS?

This question immediately raises two further questions: what is meant by dominance, and what are typical dominance patterns? Dominance has been measured in a variety of ways by the workers in this field, so that it is difficult to compare the findings. Witmer (1934) conducted interviews with the relatives of manic-depressive and schizophrenic patients and reported very similar proportions of families showing maternal dominance. Nielsen (1954) also interviewed the relatives of schizophrenics and found that their mothers were no more domineering than a matched sample of normal mothers. However, the information about the controls was obtained from a questionnaire which was not assessed for reliability or validity. Nielsen also found no differences between the fathers in each group. Kohn and Clausen (1956) carefully matched a group of schizophrenics with a control group of normal people. They found from interviews with the subjects that normals and schizophrenics from the lower social classes agreed in seeing their mothers as the authority figure. On the other hand there was disagreement between normals and schizophrenics from the upper social classes, the former seeing their father as the authority figure.

The concept of atypical dominance patterns has its strongest advocacy in the work of Lidz et al. (1957a and b) and Fleck et al. (1963). They developed their concepts of 'marital schism' and 'marital skew' and applied them in a descriptive way to the eight and six families in their respective samples. They themselves did not test these concepts experimentally but other workers have done so by studying the interaction of small groups. Most of the workers in this field have used Bales' (1950a and b) Interaction Process Analysis. Caputo (1963) employed this technique to compare the parents of chronic schizophrenics with the parents of normal subjects. He found that the fathers of the schizophrenics won the majority of decisions, while among the control mothers and fathers decisions were shared equally. Cheek (1964a and b, 1965a and b, 1966) carried out an extensive investigation with comparatively large samples including both sexes and found no association between domination of either parent and either the sex of the patient or whether the diagnosis was schizophrenia or normality. Ferreira (1963) assessed dominance by investigating how often an individual's choice became the choice of the family group. He found that the father was equally dominant in families with a schizophrenic patient, a non-schizophrenic psychiatric patient, and a normal child. Using the same groups but a different experimental situation, Ferreira et al. (1966) found no differences in terms of which parent was dominant. Lennard et al. (1965) found that father–son interaction and father's over-all activity in experimental sessions were significantly less in a group of schizophrenics than in a group of normal controls. However, the schizophrenics were unusually young (age 9–14 years) and no diagnostic criteria were given. Furthermore, the groups were not matched on demographic variables. Sharan (1966) investigated triadic interactions in families containing a schizophrenic and a normal sibling and found that the father's individual response tended to appear as the group response more often than the mother's regardless of the sex of the children or whether the sick child or the healthy sibling was present. Both Mishler and Waxler (1968a and b) and Reiss (1968) found in comparisons of normal with schizophrenic families that there was no significant difference in the percentage of total family interaction time taken up by either parent.

The overwhelming majority of these studies suggest that the parental dominance patterns shown by the families of schizophrenics do not differ from those of normal families. The only notable exception is the study of Kohn and Clausen (1956) which suggested that the fathers of schizophrenics may be abnormally submissive but only within the upper social classes. Unfortunately, no one has attempted to replicate their work.

There is a further group of studies to be considered in this section and these focus on the premorbid personality of the patients. Farina (1960) and Farina and Dunham (1963) found that the parents of male schizophrenics with poor premorbid personalities (Poors) showed significantly more maternal dominance than the parents of schizophrenics with good premorbid personalities (Goods) or the parents of normal controls. Unfortunately, in a subsequent study Farina and Holzberg (1967, 1968) failed to confirm this finding. However, Lerner (1965, 1967) working with male schizophrenics also found that the parents of Poors showed significantly more maternal dominance than the parents of Goods. Becker and Siefkes (1969) in a careful study of female schizophrenics found that the fathers of Poors tended to be more dominant than the fathers of Goods or the fathers of non-psychiatric controls. The pattern that emerges from the three studies with positive findings in this group is an association between poor premorbid personality in the patient and dominance of one parent by the parent of the opposite sex to the patient.

However, the small number of investigations on this point and the restricted terms of the experimental situation do not allow us to reach a firm conclusion about the findings. If confirmed, this association could be explained on a genetic basis, or could be interpreted as a consequence of interpersonal relations, for example, that the child's development is influenced by the weak personality of the same sexed parent. In order to demonstrate a specific association of poor premorbid personality in schizophrenics with dominance of the opposite sexed parent, the comparison group must be controlled for premorbid personality as well. None of the studies in this area have used this strategy. Our conclusion is that a link between schizophrenia and atypical dominance patterns in parents has not been established.

IS THERE MORE CONFLICT OR DISHARMONY AMONG PARENTS OF SCHIZOPHRENICS?

More work has been done on this question than on any other in this field. The studies can be conveniently grouped by the technique used into case-note studies, interviews, and the interaction of small groups. There are three relevant case-note studies. McKeown (1950) found that the parents of schizophrenics were more demanding and antagonistic than the parents of normals, but did not differ in this respect from the parents of neurotics. Costello *et al.* (1968) found an equally high rate of marital discord among parents of schizophrenics and those of non-schizophrenic psychiatric patients. Waring and Ricks (1965) used a different approach and consulted the Child Guidance Clinic notes of children who later became chronic schizophrenics. They were carefully matched with children not subsequently admitted to a psychiatric hospital, and it emerged that the parents of the children who became schizophrenic showed 'emotional divorce' or mutual withdrawal significantly more often than the control parents.

Of the workers employing interview techniques, the well-known clinical descriptions of 'marital schism and skew' (Lidz *et al.*, 1957*b*), 'emotional divorce' (Bowen *et al.*, 1959), and 'pseudo mutuality' (Wynne *et al.*, 1958) are all based on uncontrolled intense observation of a few cases which generated hypotheses but in no way tested them. Witmer (1934) found no difference between schizophrenics and manic-depressives in terms of extreme parental friction, while Prout and White (1950) found no difference in marital disharmony between the parents of schizophrenics and of normal controls. The groups in the latter study showed a disparity in ethnic origin. Poorly matched groups were also used by Gerard and Siegel (1950) who found significantly more discord and mutual hostility in the parents of schizophrenics than in normal parents. Fisher *et al.* (1959) used better controls and found that the parents of schizophrenics verbalized more hostility towards their spouses than the parents of neurotics and normals. Alanen (1958, 1966, 1968) also found greater disturbance in the marriages of the parents of schizophrenics than in those of the parents of neurotics and normals. McGhie (1961*a*) took the precaution of matching the mothers of chronic schizophrenics, neurotics and normals on their social class and education, and found that the former group more often had unhappy marriages with poor sexual relations.

The remainder of the relevant studies in this section used techniques for analysing small group interaction in an experimental situation. In a series of studies Farina and his colleagues (Farina, 1960; Farina and Dunham, 1963; Farina and Holzberg, 1967, 1968) found that the parents of schizophrenics were more hostile and contentious than the parents of tuberculosis patients. Parents of schizophrenics with a poor premorbid personality showed more disagreements and agressive remarks than those of schizophrenics with a good premorbid personality. Caputo's (1963) carefully controlled study using similar measures found more disagreement and bilateral hostility between parents of chronic schizophrenics than normal controls, but in Becker and Siefkes' (1969) similar study group differences on conflict did not reach significance, though parents of poor premorbid personality schizophrenics showed the most conflict.

Lerner (1965, 1967) matched parents of schizophrenics with parents of non-schizophrenic psychiatric patients on socio-economic class and found that the former resolved differences by compromise significantly less often than the latter. One of the preliminaries in the Revealed Difference Technique (Strodtbeck, 1951, 1954), used by many of these workers, is the administration of an attitude questionnaire. Both Cheek (1965b) and Ferreira (1963) found significantly less spontaneous agreement between the parents of schizophrenics who completed the questionnaire than between the parents of normal controls However, Ferreira and Winter (1965) showed that spontaneous agreement was just as poor in the families of delinquents and neurotic and maladjusted children as in the families of schizophrenics. Fisher et al. (1959) examined aspects of the interaction of parents while they were involved in discussion with each other and found that the parents of schizophrenics were more often in definite disagreement than the parents of neurotics and non-psychiatric hospitalized patients. The last study in this section, by Sharan (1966), employed a sophisticated method. He studied the interaction of family triads and found that the parents of schizophrenics were significantly less supportive and more critical of each other in the presence of the ill child than in the presence of a healthy sibling.

In conclusion, there is a consistent finding that parents of schizophrenics show more marital disharmony than normals as indicated by open or tacit conflict, expressed hostility, opposition of spontaneously expressed attitudes, and difficulty in reaching agreement. This emerges regardless of the experimental technique used. Several of the studies failed to show a significant difference between parents of schizophrenics and parents of non-schizophrenic psychiatric controls (McKeown, Costello, Waring and Ricks, Witmer) but others showed such a difference (Fisher, Alanen, McGhie). The bulk of the work using small group interaction techniques indicates that the parents of schizophrenics are more often in open conflict and disagreement than the parents of other psychiatric patients, but with few exceptions these findings pertain to chronic schizophrenics or schizophrenics with a poor premorbid personality (Farina, 1960; Farina and Dunham, 1963; Garmezey et al., 1961; Cheek, 1965a and b; Waring and Ricks, 1965; Caputo, 1963).

ARE THE PARENTS OF SCHIZOPHRENICS PECULIAR PEOPLE ?

Many studies of the genetics of schizophrenia have been carried out and indicate that the incidence of this disease in the parents of schizophrenics is relatively low, only 3–5 per cent in most of the studies (Shields, 1967). We are concerned here with the question of whether the parents of schizophrenics show abnormal personality characteristics over and above frank psychiatric illness.

A large number of papers which we have reviewed in detail in CHAPTER I, for example those by Lidz, Wynne, Bowen and their respective co-workers, have approached this problem by detailed case description of parents of schizophrenics but these do not help us answer this question because they all deal with small unrepresentative, highly selected samples without comparison groups.

Alanen (1958, 1966, 1968) attempted to remedy this defect by comparing the mothers of schizophrenics with the mothers of neurotics and normals. He found that significantly more of the schizophrenics' mothers than the other two groups showed 'schizoid' or 'borderline' features such as 'a limited affective life, poor self-control, and an inability to feel themselves into the inner life of people'. Waring and Ricks (1965) using records from a Child Guidance Clinic found that significantly more mothers of chronically hospitalized schizophrenics showed 'schizoid' or 'borderline' character disorders than mothers of released schizophrenics and non-psychiatric controls. Gardner (1967) used material from the same source and found the mothers of the chronic schizophrenics to be shy, inadequate, withdrawn, vague, worried, fearful, incoherent, unreliable, and suspicious.

Vaziri (1961) found alcoholism to be more common in relatives of schizophrenics than in the general population, but Nielsen (1954) found this condition to be equally as common among the parents of schizophrenics as in the parents of normal controls. However, he used different methods of obtaining information for the two groups, casting doubt on the reliability of his finding.

Two interesting studies have focused on the situation of adoption and have thrown light on the relative contribution of genetic and environmental factors. Wender et al. (1968) found that parents who reared their own schizophrenic children were significantly more disturbed than parents who had adopted children who later became schizophrenic. These parents in turn were significantly more disturbed than parents who had adopted normal children.

Kety et al. (1968) compared the biological and adoptive parents of adoptees who later became schizophrenic, and found no difference in the incidence of what they called 'schizophrenic spectrum disorder'. This comprised acute and chronic schizophrenia, borderline state, and personality disorder. However, more of the adoptive parents of schizophrenics suffered from other psychiatric disorders than the adoptive parents of normal controls.

A number of the studies quoted have focused on the mothers of schizophrenics and have generally shown them to be more schizoid than the mothers of neurotics and normals. The adoption studies suggest that the parents of schizophrenics are more disturbed than the parents of normal children, but that at least part of the disturbance may be ascribed to the effect of bringing up a child with schizophrenia.

IS THERE A LINK BETWEEN SCHIZOPHRENIA AND PARENTAL DEPRIVATION?

There is now quite good evidence linking parental loss with severe depression (Birtchnell, 1970) and suicide (Bunch and Barraclough, 1971). Parental deprivation is easier to define than many of the other possibly aetiological factors in schizophrenia, so that we would expect greater agreement between the findings of the studies on this topic. Lidz and Lidz (1949) and Pollock and Malzberg (1940) each found a high rate of parental loss before the age of 19 for a group of schizophrenic patients and a group of manic-depressives, but as we might expect a higher rate than normal among the manic-depressives this result is equivocal. Kohn and Clausen (1956) remedied this defect by matching a group of schizophrenics with normal controls on age, sex and father's occupation. They found no difference in the frequency of either marital breakup or parental bereavement before the age of 13. Oltman and Friedman (1965) confirmed this result by finding no difference between a large group of schizophrenics and a large group of hospital personnel in terms of parental death or separation before the age of 19. Rogler and Hollingshead (1965) took representative samples of Puerto Rican families of low socio-economic status who had not been in hospital but in half of which the male householder had schizophrenia. The incidence of parental loss by the age of 15 was 50 per cent in both groups.

There are two studies in this field with positive findings. Lucas (1964) closely matched youg adult schizophrenics on admission with their classmates. He found a significant association between schizophrenia and the degree of remoteness of the relationships within the family of rearing, and absence of the father during the first 6 years of life. There was also an association with absence of the mother in the early years, but this was highly correlated with being reared in a bad psychological climate and so may not be an independent factor. Costello et al. (1968) compared schizophrenic with non-schizophrenic patients and found that the fathers of the schizophrenics were more frequently absent while their children were between the ages of 11 and 15, but the numbers in their groups were small.

O'Neal and Robins (1958) used Child Guidance Clinic records to compare children who later developed schizophrenia with controls who remained psychiatrically well. The rate of broken homes was very similar in the two groups. This result was confirmed by Lindelius (1970) who used a different approach and studied the siblings of schizophrenics. He compared the incidence of schizophrenia in those who came from intact homes with its incidence in those who came from broken homes, and found it was actually slightly higher in the former.

Thus all these studies agree in finding no association between parental bereavement and schizophrenia which was not also present in a control group when one was used for comparison. When we come to look at the link between schizophrenia and the absence of a parent during childhood due to causes other than death, the findings are contradictory. However, the weight of the evidence is against such a link, and we can certainly consider the case not proven, even if the matter is not entirely closed.

DO THE PARENTS OF SCHIZOPHRENICS THINK IN PECULIAR WAYS?

All the studies of this topic are collected together in CHAPTER IV and summarized at the end of the chapter. We conclude that although recent carefully conducted investigations have produced conflicting, marginal, or negative results, the work as a whole suggests a link between the presence of allusive thinking in parents and their offspring which is probably genetically based and may be more common in families with a schizophrenic member.

DO THE PARENTS OF SCHIZOPHRENICS COMMUNICATE IN PECULIAR WAYS?

The most convincing work on this question is that by Singer and Wynne (1964, 1966a and b), which strongly suggests that the parents of schizophrenics can be reliably differentiated from the parents of neurotics and normals by certain features of their communication. The second part of this volume contains our attempt to replicate Singer and Wynne's findings, and a full discussion of their significance will be found there.

The other work in this field is not nearly as impressive in its results. Farina and Holzberg, (1970) used Mahl's (1956) Silence Quotient and a slightly modified version of his Speech-Disturbance Ratio. They compared the families of schizophrenics with good and poor premorbid personalities with the families of non-schizophrenic psychiatric patients. They found that the Poor schizophrenics and their parents scored highest of the three groups on these measures. Becker and Finkel (1969) used the same measures and the same diagnostic groups, but found no relationship between parental scores and the diagnoses. They also used the Cloz procedure, which is a measure of the predictability of words, and found, contrary to their expectation, that the parents of Poors were the most predictable and the control parents the least predictable. Mishler and Waxler (1968 a and b) also measured the predictability of words but found no difference between schizophrenic and normal families. Reiss (1968) found that the families of schizophrenics produced more implicit acts than normal families in completing a card sorting task, but that they did not differ from the families of personality disordered patients on this measure. Feinsilver (1970) compared the families of schizophrenics and normals on a task which required each family member to describe a series of common objects to another family member, who had to identify them. No significant differences were found between any of the various pairings within the families of schizophrenics or within the control families. However, the schizophrenics' families taken as a whole differed significantly from the normal families by showing a greater number of object misidentifications and a greater degree of qualities which impair focal attention. This result must be treated with caution as there were only six families in each group, and there was no control group of non-schizophrenic psychiatric patients.

We conclude that, with the exception of Singer and Wynne's studies which we attempt to replicate in Part II, the results of the foregoing studies are either negative or contradictory, or else cannot be given much weight because of methodological defects. Finally, we come to the work on the double-bind hypothesis which is reviewed at the end of Chapter V. We concluded there that this hypothesis has not been adequately tested experimentally, but what tentative results there are suggest that double-bind messages are not more characteristic of parents of schizophrenics than of other groups.

DO PRE-SCHIZOPHRENIC CHILDREN AFFECT THEIR PARENTS ADVERSELY?

Though it was not the purpose of our review to make a comprehensive inquiry into the effects of the child on the parent, a number of studies suggest that the child may play an important role in the development of the parents' attitudes. Kasanin et al. (1934) reported that among their cases of schizophrenia there was an excess of birth injury, malnutrition, physical illness, and poor development, and that over-protective attitudes in the mothers were occasioned by some definite illness or anomaly in the child. Gerard and Siegel (1950) reported excessive mothering and over-protection and found that the child was thought to be in need of special care, protection or treatment, or was considered sickly and weak. Ten of fourteen mothers in Lu's (1962) study reported that their schizophrenic offspring were slower and more passive as children than their non-schizophrenic siblings.

Stronger evidence is provided by the long term follow-up studies of Child Guidance Clinic referrals, in which cases who had subsequently become schizophrenic were compared with matched controls who had not. O'Neal and Robbins (1958) found that 38 per cent of the pre-schizophrenic group compared to 2 per cent of controls were over-dependent on their mother. The pre-schizophrenic group had a previous history of more severe infections, disfigurements, and problems with locomotion, and when they presented to the Child Guidance Clinic were found to have had more eating disorders, sleep disturbances, phobias, tics, and antisocial behaviour. Ricks and Nameche (1966) also studied Child Guidance Clinic records and found that more schizophrenics had histories of traumatic pregnancies, delayed motor development, and poor co-ordination than controls, and more of them were found to have an unusual gait and hyperactive reflexes. There was also a history of late speech development in 25 per cent of the schizophrenics. It should be noted that in both studies the over-all proportion of affected cases was small.

Pollin *et al.* (1966, 1968) compared schizophrenics with their non-schizophrenic identical twins and found that the schizophrenic was more often the second born, weighed less at birth, and had been described as more passive as a child. Klebanoff (1959) found that mothers of autistic children had significantly less deviant attitudes than mothers of brain damaged and re-tarded children, though they were more deviant than mothers of normals. Although not directly applicable to adult schizophrenics, this finding indi-cates the importance of the child's influence on the parent. In their study of children at high risk of developing schizophrenia, Mednick and Schulsinger (1968) found them to differ from a low risk group in terms of physiological measures and behavioural changes. This confirms that changes are present in a high risk group prior to the appearance of schizophrenia. Other studies reviewed by Bell (1968), Thomas, Chess, and Birch (1968), and Mednick (1967) point to increased protectiveness and greater intrusiveness by mothers of children with a variety of conditions which have little in common except that they cause chronic handicap.

Though the evidence is not conclusive it all points in the same direction; that pre-schizophrenic children show themselves to be biologically dis-advantaged at an early age compared with normal children. The mothers of these children are similar to the mothers of children with chronic handicaps in being excessively possessive, intrusive, protective, and controlling as com-pared with the mothers of normal children. There is therefore a strong possibility that the pre-schizophrenic child exerts a formative influence on the mother's attitudes.

WHAT HAS BEEN ESTABLISHED?

In our view the following statements are reasonably supported by the ex-perimental evidence:

1. More parents of schizophrenics are psychiatrically disturbed than parents of normal children, and more of the mothers are 'schizoid'.
2. There is a link between 'allusive thinking' in schizophrenics and their parents, but this is also true of normal people, in whom it occurs less frequently.
3. The parents of schizophrenics show more conflict and disharmony than the parents of other psychiatric patients.
4. The pre-schizophrenic child more frequently manifests physical ill health or mild disability early in life than the normal child.
5. Mothers of schizophrenics show more concern and protectiveness than

mothers of normals, both in the current situation and in their attitudes to the children before they fell ill.

6. The work of Wynne and Singer strongly suggests that parents of schizophrenics communicate abnormally, but their most definitive findings have not been replicated (see Part II).

7. Schizophrenics involved in intense relationships with their relatives or spouses are more likely to relapse than those whose relationships are less intense.

DISCUSSION: DO PARENTS CAUSE SCHIZOPHRENIA IN THEIR CHILDREN?

In our review we have considered the evidence for the 'environmental transmission' of schizophrenia; namely, that parents cause schizophrenia by their effect on the children during their formative years. In the preceding section we listed the assertions that could reasonably be made on the basis of all the studies we reviewed. In addition we consider that a genetic factor in the transmission of schizophrenia has been satisfactorily established. We now attempt to synthesize these findings on the basis of several alternative aetiological theories. In doing so, four questions repeatedly come up.

1. Can the effect of the environment early on in the patient's life be separated from a genetic effect?

2. What is the direction of cause and effect between the parents and the child?

3. Does any parental influence operate remotely, prior to the onset of the illness, or currently, affecting the present course of the illness?

4. Is any relationship between environmental influences and schizophrenia partly spurious, the stronger association being with other factors such as the patient's underlying personality?

These questions are at the moment unanswered and this uncertainty has largely dictated our choice of alternative aetiological models of schizophrenia. In constructing these we have set aside our reservations about the strength of the evidence and have considered the logical possibilities given the data as set out in FIG. 6.1. We present four alternative models.

1. THE STRICT GENETIC MODEL

Given that there is an inherited factor in schizophrenia it follows that one or both parents and the affected offspring have in common genes determining a predisposition to schizophrenia. It is possible to incorporate almost all the observed facts in a purely genetic model which postulates that the parental abnormalities are an expression of the schizophrenic gene operating in a partial or attenuated fashion. The genetic studies of Kety, Rosenthal and their colleagues [see CHAPTER I] which suggest a 'schizophrenic spectrum

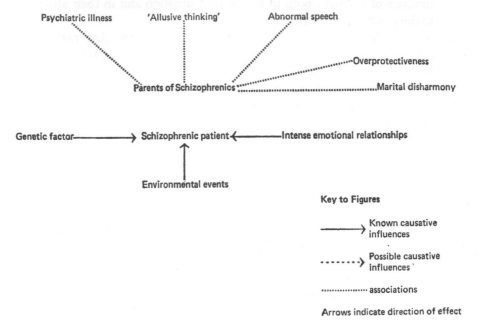

FIG. 6.1. Established facts about schizophrenics and their parents.

disorder' provide the strongest evidence for this hypothesis. 'Allusive thinking', abnormal speech, over-protectiveness, and psychiatric illness in the parents can all be ascribed to their genetic endowment. Marital disharmony would be an expected consequence of the interaction of abnormal personalities. Environmental factors may act on the genetic predisposition, for example stress may aggravate personality disorder, increase hostility, and disturb marital relationships. Similarly, stress may precipitate overt schizophrenia in the vulnerable patient. Thus the theory of social stress as a cause for the increased incidence of schizophrenia in the lowest social classes (Kohn,

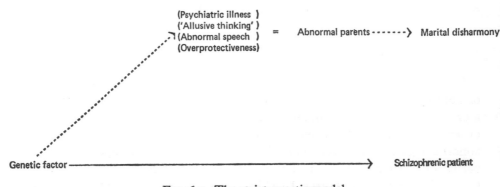

FIG. 6.2. The strict genetic model.

1968) is consistent with this model. By postulating that shared genetic factors operate independently both in the parents and the child, this model accounts for all the observed data without introducing any assumptions about environmental transmission from parent to child.

2. THE CHILD-TO-PARENT MODEL

While this model assumes a genetic endowment in the child, it explains the abnormalities in the parents as the results of rearing an abnormal child. Marital disharmony is seen as arising from the same source. This model is offered for its heuristic value, but is not compatible with the evidence for genetically based schizophrenic spectrum disorder in the biological relatives of schizophrenics [see CHAPTER I]. It also fails to take into account the current effect of relatives in precipitating florid symptoms in the patient. It is supported by the evidence for physical illness or disability in children who later develop schizophrenia.

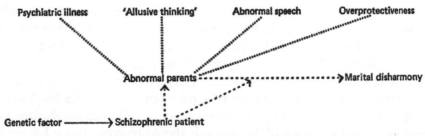

FIG. 6.3. The child-to-parent model.

3. THE EARLY ENVIRONMENT MODEL

The additional assumption introduced in this model is that one or more of the parental abnormalities which have been found in association with schizophrenia in the offspring exert a specific schizophrenogicic effect during the patient's formative years at a time remote from the onset of the illness. Genetic factors contribute the necessary predisposition in both parents and patient. The crucial point here is that no study to date has provided evidence for this additional assumption. Of all the work reviewed, only that of Wynne and Singer has produced findings which bear on this issue. They argue for a specific schizophrenogenic effect of the parents' communication disorder because they found as close an association between communication disorder and schizophrenia in the offspring as between clinical abnormality in the parent and illness in the offspring, and the two factors were independent of

each other. [See CHAPTER V.] These findings, however, have not been replicated [see PART II]; moreover their argument involves a host of further
assumptions which require experimental testing.

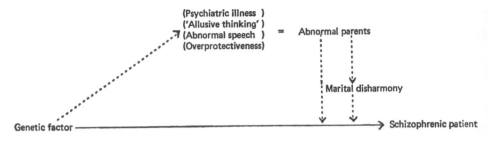

FIG. 6.4. The early environment model.

4. THE RECENT ENVIRONMENT MODEL

While there is little or no evidence for remote causal effects from parent to
child, there is a growing body of evidence (reviewed in CHAPTER I) that the
type of environment the patient returns to after remission of a schizophrenic
illness affects the subsequent course of the illness. Continuous contact with
parents or spouses who are highly involved emotionally at the time patients
are admitted is associated with a high rate of relapse. This effect is modified
by drug therapy (Brown *et al.*, 1972). The recent environment model
treats these influences as current stress factors which precipitate episodes of
florid illness rather than operating at a time remote from the breakdown.
The fact that spouses as well as parents exert an influence emphasizes the
recent or current operation of the stress. It should be noted that it has yet to
be shown that this kind of stress is specifically linked to schizophrenic
breakdowns.

It is likely that the situation is more complex than depicted in any one of
the models described, and that a combination of models would be necessary
to represent it accurately. There is an additional factor not incorporated in
any of the models presented. Patients with a poor premorbid personality may
have a heavier genetic loading for schizophrenia which renders them more
vulnerable to environmental influences at all levels. This would be consistent
with the numerous studies which show that the strongest association between
parental abnormality and schizophrenia occurs in chronic or 'process'
schizophrenia.

At this point we may ask what is the value of the psychoanalytically based
observations which inspired much of the zeal for the research we have reviewed. As general statements applicable to a large proportion of schizophrenics they have not stood up to the test of carefully controlled investigation. Nevertheless, psychotherapists are keen clinical observers and their
reports may be valid descriptions of ways in which abnormal personalities

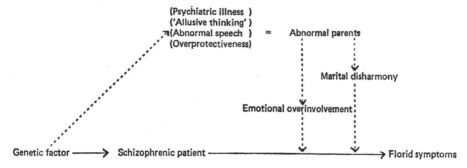

FIG. 6.5. The recent environment model.

present themselves to the observer. Bateson's double-bind may represent one way in which intense, over-involved relationships are manifested, and Wynne's pseudomutuality or Lidz's marital schism and skew may characterize others. There is probably scope for a multitude of theories of this kind, each representing an individual worker's view of how people interact. The evidence to date indicates that these ways of behaving are by no means confined to parents of schizophrenics, but are also shown by parents of neurotics, personality disordered patients, and normal people. It seems likely that the popular theorists are describing ways of behaving which generate high emotion or over-involvement. This is a form of stress which, according to the recent environment model, is likely to precipitate florid schizophrenia in the vulnerable individual.

We have offered these models for their heuristic value, to make explicit the underlying logic which may govern the established associations between parental abnormalities and schizophrenia. The work up to this time has been largely concerned with the discovery of qualities in parents that are related to illness in their offspring. It is clear that the next step must be the determination of the direction of cause and effect in the relationships between schizophrenics and their abnormal parents. The work of Wynne and Singer goes as far as any in attempting to do this. For this reason, we focus on their research in PART II and on our attempt to replicate their work.

PART II

AN INVESTIGATION OF COMMUNICATION DEFECTS AND DEVIANCES

CHAPTER VII

ABNORMALITIES OF SPEECH IN THE PARENTS OF SCHIZOPHRENICS: A REPLICATION STUDY

§ I. INTRODUCTION

FROM our review of the literature there is no longer any doubt that there are transmitted factors in the aetiology of schizophrenia. It may be helpful at this juncture to recapitulate certain points. The evidence that there is a genetic factor seems conclusive but its nature and importance is still far from clear. There is strong evidence that environmental factors are important as precipitants of a schizophrenic breakdown, but the hypothesis of an aetiological environmental factor or, more specifically, parental abnormalities bringing about the predisposition to schizophrenia in the offspring, has little firm support. We know of no studies to date which exclude the possibility that the abnormalities attributed to parents of schizophrenics are due to genetic factors commonly inherited by parent and child. Yet whether one believes that genetic or environmental factors are the more important in the aetiology of schizophrenia, or like Shields (1967) believes that there is an interaction between the two, it is relevant and necessary to discover and identify characteristics of parents of schizophrenics which may distinguish them from parents of other psychiatric patients and the population at large. Once this has been done it will then be possible to carry the research further to decide between genetic and environmental mechanisms and investigate further the pathogenic links involved. The adoptive studies described in CHAPTER I provide one technique by which the nature/nurture issue might be unravelled.

When one looks for studies attempting to measure some aspect of parental function which is related to the appearance of schizophrenia in the offspring, the work of Singer and Wynne which we have described in CHAPTER V stands out in sharp relief from all the rest. These authors have conducted research for over 10 years which has produced results consistently in the same direction using increasingly more objective, quantifiable techniques which lend themselves to replication by other workers. Their recent studies employing a manual for scoring defects and deviances of communication under controlled experimental conditions have produced reliable results in their hands. They have been able to use their technique with such discrimination that no pair of parents of schizophrenics has been found to score within the range of the parents of normals (Wynne, 1971), and taken individually, only 32·5 per cent of parents of non-schizophrenics have scored above the lowest scoring schizophrenic parent (Wynne, 1967). If these results could be independently replicated at another centre with a different sample of patients, they would provide the most promising basis for future work which is yet available.

Unfortunately, there are several aspects of Singer and Wynne's work which have not been adequately reported or may not have been carried out in a sufficiently systematic way to allow for replication. There is very little information about their selection procedures, the demographic characteristics of their samples,* and the detailed clinical characteristics of their patients, including past history and symptoms. Furthermore, they have not published certain of their data in sufficient detail, including quantitative aspects such as the means and variation of their scores.* Other secondary issues remain unanswered as well. How reliable is the 41-category Rorschach manual in the hands of others? Can their techniques be simplified or improved? What is it, in fact, that they are scoring? Can their findings be explained by alternative hypotheses such as a failure to control experimental and comparison groups for I.Q.?

Prompted by the potential importance of Singer and Wynne's findings we decided to try to replicate the essential aspects of their work as closely as possible, while at the same time identifying and controlling more carefully other variables which may have contributed significantly to their results.

In order to be able to reproduce the essential aspect of their study as closely as possible one of us visited their unit on two occasions, the first before drawing up the experimental design of this study and the second after two-thirds of the series had been collected but no transcripts had been scored. The second visit was devoted to learning their techniques of scoring.

It was decided to compare parents of acute schizophrenic patients in hospital with parents of non-psychotic depressed and neurotic patients in the same hospitals. If the deviances Singer and Wynne have found are in some way specific for schizophrenia then a significant difference between these two groups should emerge. This is in one sense a more stringent test of the hypothesis than using parents of normal subjects as controls, since Singer and Wynne consistently find that parents of neurotics score between those of schizophrenics and those of normal subjects (Singer and Wynne, 1966a and b; Wynne, 1968, 1971). On the other hand it is a more valid test in so far as it eliminates the influence which being tested as the parent of a hospitalized psychiatric patient could have on the results by equating the experimental and control groups for this variable (Mishler and Waxler, 1968a and b; Schopler and Loftin, 1969).

Certain aspects of our study differ from theirs because in addition to attempting to replicate their work we were concerned to introduce a more strictly controlled experimental design. Their research was exploratory, opening up a new field, and in the circumstances it is not surprising that

* This information is now available from Professor Wynne and awaiting publication.

criticism can be levelled at some aspects of their methodology. In their published work they do not give adequate details about their subjects with respect to demographic data, nor do they describe what steps were taken to ensure adequate control of certain factors. These include prior knowledge that the testing psychologist may have had of the patient and his or her family, and any bias that may have influenced the selection of subjects. Unpublished work and personal communications from Singer and Wynne partly rectify these deficiencies. For our study we collected a serial sample of patients who were admitted to a group of National Health Service psychiatric hospitals, and who met stipulated criteria. Our groups of schizophrenics and neurotics were matched on a number of demographic variables, and we have allowed for the possible influence of verbal intelligence by testing all subjects for verbal I.Q. and making statistical adjustments for any differences between the groups.

It was part of our original design that both testing and scoring of transcripts were carried out with the investigator blind to the diagnostic group of the subject's offspring. The subjects were unaware of what we were testing. Thus we endeavoured systematically to eliminate experimental bias at these initial stages. Transcripts of testing sessions were scored by both the authors and subsequently by Dr. Singer herself, providing an estimate of the inter-rater reliability of the testing procedure. A number of additional steps were taken to bring our testing and rating procedures, the essential aspects of this investigation, into line with those of Singer and Wynne.

It is perhaps relevant at this point to make a distinction between the context in which Singer and Wynne view their study of speech abnormalities and that in which we view ours. Their hypothesis is that specific varieties of communication defects and deviances shown by parents are important in predisposing otherwise susceptible offspring to develop schizophrenia. We are testing a more limited hypothesis, that parents of schizophrenics show a significantly greater number of communication defects and deviances in their speech when tested under controlled conditions than parents of neurotic patients. The question of the cause and the effects of such deviances, if found, is left for future consideration.

§ II. SELECTION OF SUBJECTS

UNDERLYING PRINCIPLES

The parents of two groups of acute psychiatric inpatients were studied, one schizophrenic and the other neurotic. It was decided to include 20 parental pairs in each group. The principle which governed the selection procedure was to match parents and patients on several demographic variables while having only a minimal overlap of symptomatology in the two patient groups, and no family history of schizophrenic or psychotic illness in the neurotic group. It seemed essential to the hypothesis as formulated by

Wynne and Singer that our testing be limited to those families in which both parents had reared the patient since birth, the principal language of rearing was English, and the parents were not suffering from any specific disorder which would affect their verbal abilities, such as mental deficiency or dementia. It was desirable that the groups be representative within the limits of the criteria employed, and it was considered important that the person who tested the subjects had no information on any variables relating to the subjects or their offspring at the time of testing. The following procedure was therefore employed.

SELECTION PROCEDURES

Stage 1

All admissions to the Bethlem Royal, Maudsley and St. Francis' Hospitals were screened together with all Camberwell patients admitted to Cane Hill Hospital. This was done by a secretary who excluded those patients outside the age limits of 15–55; she included all patients with a preliminary diagnosis of 'depression', 'schizophrenia', 'schizo-affective psychosis', 'manic-depressive psychosis' and 'personality disorder'.

Stage 2

These cases were then screened further by one of us (J.L.) after consulting the case-notes and sometimes talking to the Registrar. At this stage we excluded patients if they had a history of:

1. Severe psychotic symptoms continuously for the past 3 years or more.
2. Total hospitalization of 2 years or more in the past 5 years.
3. Regular abuse of alcohol or other drugs acting on the central nervous system.
4. Mental retardation (I.Q.<70).
5. Any organic basis to the psychosis, including concurrent epilepsy.
6. Difficulties in communication due to hearing defects or poor understanding of English.

These criteria were adopted because we took advantage of the fact that one of us was in the process of screening all admissions to the Joint Hospitals and all admissions from the Camberwell catchment area for another study. As a consequence chronic or doubtful cases are likely to have been excluded from our sample. All patients who were not excluded under any of these categories were included in the study if they satisfied all the following criteria:

7. The patient's clinical diagnosis was either schizophrenia or some form of depression or neurosis. The criteria for these groups are described below.

8. The patient's natural parents were both living, available for testing and less than 66 years of age.

9. The patient was reared to school-leaving age with these parents. An absence of one parent for more than 2 years continuously or 3 years intermittently in the patient's first 7 years of life excluded the family from the study.

10. The patient's language of rearing was English, and culture of rearing British. Patients with non-British parents were included if the culture was European and the principal language during rearing was English.

11. If there was evidence that either parent was of subnormal intelligence or suffered from organic brain disease the case was excluded from the study.

Stage 3

Patients who met these criteria and were thought diagnostically suitable were then seen on the wards and given the Present State Examination (Wing *et al.*, 1967; Wing *et al.*, 1974). This is a semistructured interview schedule in which the interviewer rates the presence or absence of 140 symptoms and signs covered by 640 items for the 4-week period just preceding the interview. We describe below separately the diagnostic criteria used for the schizophrenic and neurotic samples.

The following categories of patients qualified to be included in the study as schizophrenics:

1. Patients with first rank symptoms of schizophrenia as defined in the Present State Examination and adapted from Schneider (1957). These include:
    (i) Voices speaking about patient in third person.
    (ii) Voices giving a running commentary on patient's thoughts or actions.
    (iii) Experiences of thought insertion or substitution.
    (iv) Experiences of thought withdrawal attributed to an external agency.
    (v) Experiences of thought spoken aloud (echo de pensée).
    (vi) Experiences of thought diffusion or broadcasting.
    (vii) Delusion of control by an external agency.
    (viii) Somatic experiences attributed to external influences.

2. Patients with persistent hallucinations, even if voices speak directly to the patient and not in the third person, providing the content is not depressive and not thought to be deserved. Hallucinations may be evident from behaviour rather than reported, but they must then be unequivocal.

3. Patients with specific catatonic symptoms such as flexibilitas, stereotypies, echolalia, echopraxis, mitgehen, posturing (but not muteness,

jerky movements, restlessness, excitement, etc. which are not specifically catatonic). Transient symptoms during or following acute excitement followed by manic symptoms do not qualify.

4. Patients with persistent incoherence of speech due to grammatical distortion, lack of logical connection between sentences, neologisms, or a
   rich vein of fantasy resulting in a constant flow of fragmentary delusions, etc.

5. Patients with delusions without hallucinations, not accompanied by
   'first-rank' symptoms, but also with no clearly depressive or manic
   symptoms, e.g. delusions of reference, persecution, religion, science-
   fiction, etc.

6. Patients with symptoms from groups 1–5, but also with a mild admix-
   ture of 'organic' symptoms such as disorientation, clouding of conscious-
   ness, visual hallucinations, etc. which makes the diagnosis less certain.
   If organic symptoms were marked, the patient was of course excluded.

7. Patients who qualify under categories 1–6 above, who also have symptoms of an affective disorder.

Parents with a past history of psychosis were not excluded if well at the
time. In practice only one parent of a schizophrenic patient had been diagnosed as schizophrenic in the past and she had also had a manic episode.

SELECTION OF THE CONTROL GROUP: NEUROTICS AND DEPRESSIVES

We wanted to avoid genetic overlap of the two parental groups so that
none of the control group would have a family history of schizophrenia. The
intention was to maximize the differences between the two parental groups
on this variable. Therefore only patients with an affective or neurotic illness
but without psychotic symptoms or a family history of psychosis were included as controls. Thus patients with a personal history or family history
suggestive of schizo-affective or schizophrenic illness were excluded from the
sample, as were persons with a personal or family history of hallucinations,
delusions, stupor or intense excitement, or bizarre behaviour.

Initially, we only selected patients with an affective illness for our control
sample. However, after more than half the controls had been collected there
was a delay in finding enough subjects because of a dearth of patients with
depressive disorder who satisfied all the criteria. One reason for this seemed
to be the high prevalence of patients who had experienced parental separation
or loss in childhood. As a consequence the criteria were extended to include
patients with a diagnosis of obsessional illness or phobias, in addition to
affective disorder, and these changes were incorporated in Stage 1 of the
selection procedure. Patients nevertheless had to conform to all the other
requirements of the non-psychotic control group.

Throughout the remainder of this monograph the control group, which includes patients with non-psychotic depression, obsessional illness and phobias, will be referred to as 'the neurotic group'. At the time patients were screened and interviewed an item sheet which acted as a check list covering all the categories for excluding patients from the study was filled in. Clinical information, including the findings on the Present State Examination, was also recorded. Demographic information which was based on case notes or information from the patient was confirmed at the interview with the parents after testing was completed.

MATCHING

Initially it was intended that patients from each group would be matched individually for the fathers' occupation. This was the only reliable information one could get prior to seeing the parents which might be helpful in approximating the two groups for social class of the parents and, broadly speaking, the level of verbal abilities. It was found that this plan had to be abandoned, in order to complete the sample in a reasonable amount of time. Consequently, all subjects who satisfied our selection criteria were included in the study. The nature of the sample and demographic differences between groups were then compared to ensure the groups were adequately matched. These comparisons are considered under the results.

§ III. METHODS

PROCEDURES FOR REFERRAL, INTERVIEWING, AND TESTING

Referral

The sample was drawn from consecutive admissions to the Joint Hospitals and from catchment area patients going elsewhere. Parents were contacted shortly after the patient was admitted if, after having been given the Present State Examination by one of us (J.L.), it was found they met our diagnostic criteria. The parents' names and addresses were put on a list which was then passed on to the other researcher (S.R.H.) in random order when eight pairs of parents had been accumulated. This procedure ensured that the second worker remained blind to the offspring's diagnostic grouping. The number of patients in either diagnostic group was not specified and the groups were not necessarily represented equally. This procedure was repeated with lists of subjects in varying numbers but only at the end of the study did any list include less than four sets of parents. At no time was it possible to guess in advance from which diagnostic group the subject came.

Parents were written to, informing them of no more than that we were conducting a study involving a large number of parents of patients at several hospitals and asking if they would kindly come for an interview. A stamped addressed card was enclosed with several alternative appointments and they were asked to check which ones would be convenient. A telephone number was provided should they have any queries and the Social Psychiatry Unit secretaries dealt with any calls. If the subjects did not reply, they were sent a follow-up letter or telephoned asking them to come up at a time of their choosing. If necessary, the home was visited personally and in a few instances the opportunity was taken to complete the testing at the time of the visit. Parents were asked to come to the hospital together.

The Interview

When subjects came for testing it was explained that we were seeing a large number of parents at several hospitals. They were cautioned that it was very important for the work we were doing that they should not reveal any information except in reply to a few questions which would be asked. It was explained that they would be able to ask questions at the end of the interview or learn how they could get their questions answered, but that the investigator knew nothing about their child who was a patient. It was emphasized that it was most important for the research in hand that they should not mention anything about the nature or course of the illness, the diagnosis, or the treatment. In this way it was possible to prevent the subjects revealing any information suggestive of the diagnosis in 79 of 80 subjects tested.

Some subjects among the first few groups felt pressured into co-operating because their child was in hospital but this difficulty was later avoided and their co-operation enlisted when it was explained at the outset that this interview would be of no direct help to them or their ill child whatsoever, but that their generous help and welcomed co-operation was of great importance to the investigator.

After the initial remarks the parents were separated into two rooms. In the first room the father was asked to complete a Mill Hill Adult Vocabulary Scale, Form 2 Senior (Raven, 1948). His task was explained to him and he was taken through the sample and one example under supervision. When the testing was later completed the investigator inspected the vocabulary forms to make sure they were readable. Subjects were encouraged to complete every answer even if this required a blind guess. One subject had a specific dyslexia so the form was read to him.

While the father was completing the vocabulary form, the Rorschach test was administered to the mother in another room. This procedure was tape-recorded. The mother was then asked a list of set questions to confirm that she satisfied all the criteria for inclusion in the study. A number of demographic variables were recorded as well. These included the ages of the subject and the patient, the number of years of separation from the patient during the patient's first 7 years of life, the subject's education and the subject's occupation. If an inadvertent clue to the offspring's diagnosis occurred during the interview a note was made, but only one subject in 80 gave information which even indirectly suggested a diagnosis. This subject made a reference to a sibling of the patient who had been treated for hallucinations. From this it could be deduced that the parents had schizophrenic offspring.

Having completed these procedures, parents then changed places and the mother completed the vocabulary form and the father was given the Rorschach test and was questioned according to the item sheet.

The circumstances of testing were not held constant. Parents were tested in any of a number of rooms at the Maudsley Hospital, at St. Francis' Hospital, or in their own home. Some were tested during a week day, some on a weekend, and some in the evening after supper. In only one instance were the parents seen separately, the father at the hospital and the mother at home, where she had been housebound for 20 years, afraid to go anywhere except to the corner shop.

Testing

Training for Rorschach Testing

The investigator was uninitiated in the techniques of Rorschach interviewing prior to undertaking this investigation. As part of an effort to reproduce the essential aspects of Wynne and Singer's work, their Unit at the National Institute of Mental Health in Bethesda was visited on two occasions. During the first visit a Rorschach interview was observed through a one-way screen and the technique was outlined and explained. Later, after this investigation had begun and eleven sets of parents had been tested, Dr. Singer was sent tape recordings and transcripts of four interviews in order to compare and comment on the testing methods that had been used up to that time. Because of her comments, the technique of administering the Rorschach was modified. This is described below and became an important consideration in the analysis of our results.

Technique of Testing

Subjects were told that they would be shown pictures made originally from ink blots by folding a page with wet ink forward on itself thereby producing an image which was the same on both sides. They were given standard instructions as follows:

'I am going to show you these ink blots, they mean different things to different people. I want you to tell me everything they remind you of, all the things they look like to you or you can see in them. It may be the whole ink blot which reminds you of something or only a tiny little part of it but I would like to know everything they look like to you.'

The subject looks at each card in turn and the investigator waits until the card is handed back to him before going on to the next card. If the subject cannot think of anything or gives less than three responses on any of the first three cards, he is encouraged to hold the card a minute longer and see if anything further comes to mind. The responses of the first viewing are recorded verbatim by the tester, in addition to being tape-recorded.

IAPS

After the subject has responded to the first ten cards he is shown each card in turn again. The tester introduces this 'Enquiry' part of the Rorschach with the following type of instruction.

'Now I want to go over these cards again with you. I'll remind you of what you said you saw in them, and you can tell me how you came to see this, where you saw it and what it was that made the ink blot look like this to you.'

The part of the blot which he uses for his response is recorded by the investigator on a miniaturized chart of the ten ink blots for later reference when scoring.

The first part of the test is called the First Viewing and is thought to involve a process of describing one's perceptions, while the second part of the procedure, called the Enquiry, is thought to involve a process of reasoning and explaining (Singer and Wynne, 1966a).

The Enquiry procedure in the Rorschach is the part that Wynne and Singer have found most susceptible to variation among testers, and they believe least reliable (personal communication). Indeed, when they examined the transcripts of the testing sessions they told us that our technique adhered too closely to traditional Rorschach methods and they suggested certain changes.

It is worth recording at this point for workers who may consider using this method in the future that the method employed for the first 42 subjects was based on that described in a standard text on projective techniques, which seemed to conform to the method demonstrated to one of us at the National Institute of Mental Health by Dr. Winifred Scott. It was modelled after the style used by the testing psychologist on two transcripts of Rorschach sessions that Drs. Singer and Wynne had provided from their study. The subject was instructed to explain how he came to see what he did, but also asked to say where he saw it on the blot, and if it was the shape, the shading, or the colour which influenced his perception, and whether it was the whole blot or just a part of it.

After studying the tapes we sent her, Dr. Singer wrote back:

'In your enquiry, your questions were primarily directed at locating where the idea was to fit, and to get a statement about shape, colour and traditional Rorschach scoring details from the parent. Thus my feeling is that your parents' tests may show some tendency to have less deviance scores occur in the enquiry part of the procedure than our method.'

It was suggested that in the future we adhere less closely to traditional Rorschach methods and be more open-ended in trying to get subjects to convey their reasoning by asking questions like 'can you tell me more about that ?', etc., thus encouraging the subjects to elaborate and reason more about their ideas (letter from Dr. Singer, 4 December 1968).

At the time we received these suggestions, 21 pairs of parents, of 11 schizophrenics and 10 neurotics, had been tested. With the remaining 19 parent couples the technique was altered to conform to the suggestions Dr. Singer had offered. The effect of this change in method is considered with the results in SECTION V, p. 152.

Preparation of Transcripts

During the Rorschach testing the interview was tape-recorded and subsequently transcribed. The typescript was then checked for errors against the tape and a corrected protocol was prepared in duplicate according to procedures used by Drs. Wynne and Singer. References to the subject's name were deleted but it was never necessary to delete any references which could directly suggest the offspring's diagnosis. Each transcript was identified by a code number chosen randomly from 1 to 1,000.

RATING EDUCATION AND SOCIAL CLASS

During the question period after testing, demographic data relating to the family were collected. These included details about the education and occupation of the subject. A seven-point education scale was adapted for use with subjects educated in Great Britain from the Hollingshead–Redlich 2-factor social index (Hollingshead and Redlich, 1958). This is included as APPENDIX 2. The patient's father was placed into one of seven categories of an occupational scale based on the Registrar General's 1960 Classification of Occupations, and he was also rated according to the Hollingshead–Redlich seven-point scale for occupation. These are included as APPENDIX 3.

The subject's social position was then determined by the Hollingshead–Redlich 2-factor index of social position (see APPENDIX 3). This method combines education and occupation by weighting the former by a factor of 4 and the latter by a factor of 7. The social position of subjects in this study could then be compared with studies reported elsewhere which employ the Hollingshead–Redlich 2-factor social index method.

USE AND MODIFICATIONS OF THE 41-CATEGORY RORSCHACH MANUAL

Training Raters

Both authors rated every transcript so we could make our own determination of the inter-rater reliability of Singer and Wynne's 41-category manual. A considerable effort was made to learn to use the manual (Singer and Wynne, 1966a) similarly to Singer and Wynne. Initially the general principles of scoring were discussed with Dr. Wynne. During a subsequent visit to his Unit at the National Institute of Mental Health Dr. Singer spent the better part of 2 days reviewing in detail our first attempts at scoring three manuscripts, and she discussed those categories which had given her co-raters the most difficulty. Dr. Wynne then provided photocopies of 12 protocols of Rorschachs from their study and later sent us copies of those protocols with the specific abnormalities scored and underlined, or copies of score sheets with their ratings. We were subsequently able to score the protocols and compare our results in detail with theirs. Sometimes we did not understand their use of a particular category or we noted a disparity between the way it was defined in the manual and the way they had used it on a transcript. Sometimes we disagreed with their use of a category. Some categories seemed too general and it was difficult to know when to apply them and when not to. Often categories needed redefinition because more than one category seemed to apply to the same type of abnormality. These kind of queries were enumerated and sent to Dr. Singer who was generous and helpful with her detailed explanations which, not uncommonly, incorporated some aspect of our suggestions in her clarification or redefinition of the category in question. We also sent her two transcripts we had scored after initially discussing between ourselves what the best scoring seemed to be; Dr. Singer helpfully criticized these as well.

In all, we scored twelve practice transcripts, some more than once. Careful statistics were not kept of these attempts but some estimate was made of the number of deviances scored by each of the authors and Dr. Singer on each transcript. Comparing the number of deviances scored on a transcript by one rater with that of another, we had an over-all agreement of about 75 per cent, and the agreement of one of us with Dr. Singer's score was about 82 per cent. When agreement on individual items as opposed to the over-all score of the transcript was considered we never achieved much better than 60 per cent between ourselves, or between Dr. Singer and one of us.

Finally, a list of 25 clarifications and redefinitions for the manual were drawn up, with some additional procedural rules for applying some of the categories. These were sent to Dr. Singer for her approval and by and large we accepted the few disagreements she offered. A list of the 41 categories and our 25 addenda to the manual are included as APPENDIXES 4 and 1 respectively.

Procedures

The typed protocols, labelled only with a code number, were randomized in lots of 40, 20, and 20 by a research assistant who thereby determined the order in which they would be scored. There was some cross-over of transcripts between the first and second half of the series. There was no indication whether the subjects were male or female and transcripts of a parent couple were not kept together.

Only the first response to each ink blot was scored. This included the First Viewing of the blot and the Enquiry, at which time the subject explains and elaborates on his initial response. References to the first response in later responses were not included or scored but these were rare. Scoring was done on a separate sheet. Each time a category score was assigned, the abnormal element of speech in the transcript was recorded on the score sheet beside the category.

Calculating the Score

Following the method of Singer and Wynne (1966a), a Deviance Score was calculated by counting the total number of deviances, 'd', and dividing by the number of responses, 'r'. If a subject rejected a card by simply handing it back, for example, this would not be counted as a response, because sufficient words were not spoken. Ten cards are shown in all, giving an opportunity for 20 responses, 10 on the First Viewing and 10 on the Enquiry. Sometimes a card was rejected but the subject said enough in doing so to score a response. Thus the Deviance Score is the ratio of total deviances per number of responses (d/r).

The Mill Hill Vocabulary forms were scored by an assistant in order to avoid any contamination between a knowledge of the I.Q., a recollection of the subject from the interview, and recognition of the subject's transcript. It was, however, very uncommon to recognize a transcript.

It may be worthwhile to point out that although one of us (J.L.) had interviewed the patients clinically and was aware of their diagnoses, he had never seen the parents and had no way to tell which transcripts were which when he scored them because they were only identified by a code number. Thus both raters were unaware of the diagnostic group to which a transcript belonged.

§ IV. RESULTS

THE NATURE OF THE SAMPLE

Default Rate

An attempt was made to contact all the parents of all patients from the Bethlem and Maudsley Hospital, St. Francis' Hospital, and Cane Hill Hospital, who appeared to satisfy the selection criteria. This included parents of 46 patients and covered a period of 11 months before the sample of 20 families in each group was complete. As a matter of chance, no patients from Cane Hill Hospital fulfilled the criteria during this 11 months' period. There were six families who were written to but not included in the study.

TABLE 1

SIX FAMILIES WRITTEN TO BUT NOT INCLUDED IN THE STUDY

	NUMBER
Never replied	1
Moved address, never contacted	1
Excluded before interview: unsuitable	2
Excluded after interview: unsuitable	2
TOTAL	6

One family never replied and one family had moved without leaving a forwarding address. Two were excluded before being interviewed when further information revealed that the mother of one patient had been in hospital with presenile dementia, and the father of another patient was aged 75. Two families were excluded at the time of interview after testing when it was revealed that they did not meet our criteria: the mother in one case had been to a school for educationally subnormal children, and the father in the other case had been separated from the patient for more than 3 of his first 7 years of life. Thus there was only one family who is presumed to have received a request by post to be a subject in the study and was otherwise suitable but did not reply to our letters and was not included, *a default rate of 2·4 per cent.*

One father who was tested revealed his age of 68 in the interview. As this family was suitable from every other point of view they were not excluded from the study, though the father's age was above our original limit of 65.

TABLE 2

AGE DIFFERENCE BETWEEN GROUPS

	NEUROTIC GROUP	SCHIZO-PHRENIC GROUP	t	DEGREES OF FREEDOM	SIGNIFI-CANCE*
Age of patient	24·5 ±6·3	21·6 ±4·7	1·650	38	n.s.
Age of mother	52·5 ±6·8	50·5 ±6·6	0·940	38	n.s.
Age of father	54·6 ±7·6	53·2 ±7·7	0·558	38	n.s.
Age difference between mother and patient	27·9 ±6·3	28·6 ±5·1	0·386	38	n.s.

* All comparisons reported for this study are based on a 2-tailed test. Non-significant (n.s.) is taken as above the 0·05 level.

Comparison of Schizophrenic and Neurotic Samples for Demographic Differences

Age Differences between Groups

There was no statistical difference at the 0·05 level between the schizophrenic and the neurotic sample for the age of the patient at the time of interview, the age of the patient's mother or father, or the difference in age between the mother and patient [see TABLE 2].

Distribution by Sex

There was a trend for male patients to outnumber females among the schizophrenics and females to outnumber males among the neurotics. This difference is significant at the exact probability of p=0·054 [see TABLE 3] and will be taken into account in analysing the results.

TABLE 3
NUMBERS OF MALES AND FEMALES IN EACH GROUP

	MALE	FEMALE	TOTAL
Schizophrenics	15	5	20
Neurotics	8	12	20

p = 0·054

2 × 2 Contingency Table (Finney et al., 1963)

Recent Domicile with Parents

There was little difference between groups for the number of patients who had not been domiciled with their parents within the previous 2 years [see TABLE 4].

TABLE 4
NUMBER OF PATIENTS NOT DOMICILED WITH PARENTS
WITHIN 2 YEARS

YEARS NOT WITH PARENTS	LESS THAN 2 YEARS	2 OR MORE YEARS
Schizophrenics	17	3
Neurotics	14	6

n.s. (Finney et al., 1963)

Parents' Education

There was little difference between groups by parents' education. In TABLES 5 and 6 the mothers' and the fathers' education is assessed independently.

TABLE 5
EDUCATION OF MOTHER

HIGHEST LEVEL OF EDUCATION	MINIMAL LEAVING AGE	GRAMMAR SCHOOL MINIMAL AGE + 1 YEAR	MATRICULATION, OR 'O' LEVEL, 5 OR MORE SUBJECTS	TOTAL
Schizophrenic	13	4	3	20
Neurotic	15	2	3	20

n.s. (Finney et al., 1963)

TABLE 6
EDUCATION OF FATHER

HIGHEST LEVEL OF EDUCATION	MINIMAL LEAVING AGE	GRAMMAR SCHOOL MINIMAL AGE + 1 YEAR	MATRICULATION, OR 'O' LEVEL, 5 OR MORE SUBJECTS	TOTAL
Schizophrenic	14	4	2	20
Neurotic	10	6	4	20

n.s. (Finney et al., 1963)

Parents' Social Class

Considering now the social class of the parents, there was no significant difference between the schizophrenic and the neurotic group when this was evaluated by the Registrar General's 1960 Classification of Occupations [TABLES 7 and 8], or by the Hollingshead–Redlich 2-factor index of social position [TABLE 9]. Failure to find significance at the 0·05 level holds when the classes are amalgamated into manual versus non-manual [TABLE 8] or if any arbitary cut-off point is chosen dividing the groups into any two groupings for social class above and below the line, analysing the difference by Finney's 2 × 2 Contingency Tables (Finney *et al.*, 1963).

TABLE 7

OCCUPATIONS OF FATHERS BY REGISTRAR GENERAL'S
CLASSIFICATION, 1960

CLASS	PRO-FESS:	INTER-MED: PROFESS:/ MANAG:	MANAG:/ OWNER SMALL CONCERN	SKILLED MANUAL	SKILLED NON-MANUAL	SEMI-SKILL: MAN:	UN-SKILL:	TOTAL
	I	2	3	4	5	6	7	
Schizophrenic	2	0	4	8	4	2	0	20
Neurotic	3	4	3	2	I	7	0	20

n.s. (Finney *et al.*, 1963)

TABLE 8

OCCUPATION OF FATHER BY REGISTRAR GENERAL'S
CLASSIFICATION, AMALGAMATING CLASSES

OCCUPATIONAL CLASS	NON-MANUAL	MANUAL	TOTAL
Schizophrenic	10	10	20
Neurotic	11	9	20

n.s. (Finney *et al.*, 1963)

TABLE 9

SOCIAL POSITION OF FATHER ON
HOLLINGSHEAD-REDLICH 2-FACTOR SCALE

SOCIAL POSITION	I & 2	3	4 & 5	TOTAL
Schizophrenic	2	4	14	20
Neurotic	6	4	10	20

n.s. (Finney *et al.*, 1963)

The social position of subjects in TABLE 9 was amalgamated for comparison with the N.I.M.H. sample which is given in TABLE 10.

TABLE 10

N.I.M.H. SAMPLE: SOCIAL POSITION OF FATHER
ON HOLLINGSHEAD-REDLICH SCALE
(Singer and Wynne, 1965)

SOCIAL POSITION	1 & 2	3	4 & 5	TOTAL
Schizophrenic	8	8	4	20
Borderline	7	2	0	9
Non-schizophrenic	4	1	1	6

n.s. (Finney et al., 1963)

The Patients' Personality and Symptoms

Previous Personality (Heterosexual Functioning)

We were unable to find a reliable single measure of previous personality. One of the most often used measures is the Phillips scale (Phillips, 1953) which is heavily weighted for measures of heterosexual functioning. We have not used it but have some limited measures of sexual and interpersonal functioning.

None of the 20 schizophrenics had been married or admitted to having had sexual intercourse in the year previous to interview. Only four had been involved in a prolonged friendship with the opposite sex. Eight of the 20 neurotic patients were married and two had had sexual intercourse in the context of a prolonged relationship, making a total of ten in all. Three additional neurotics who had not married had had a prolonged relationship without sexual intercourse. Thus 7 neurotics compared to 16 schizophrenics had had only brief casual relationships or none at all. These differences are all significant at the 0·01 level or better.

In addition, information from the case-notes was used to make a global rating of whether the premorbid personality was abnormal or not. If traits such as excessive jealousy, obsessional behaviour, or extreme shyness were described the premorbid personality was rated as abnormal. Such an assessment may sound very crude, but has proved useful in predicting prognosis in schizophrenic patients (Leff and Wing, 1971). In terms of premorbid personality 10 of the 20 neurotic patients were rated as normal compared with 7 of the 20 schizophrenics. Six schizophrenics showed a mild abnormality compared with 3 neurotics. None of these differences are significant.

Symptom Profile of Patients

TABLE 11 indicates the principal symptoms of patients in the schizophrenic group. They were all considered definite schizophrenics and no

TABLE 11

PRINCIPAL SYMPTOMS OF SCHIZOPHRENIC PATIENTS[1]

PATIENT'S CODE NUMBER

SYMPTOMS	502†	506†	507*†	512†	518*†	557*†	546	561*	569	573	577	605	612*	619	634	654	657*	658	659	664
P. 1 Voices speaking about patient in 3rd person								x	x			x	x		x					x
P. 2 Voices: running commentary on patient's thoughts	x																	x		
P. 3 Voices: running commentary on patient's actions				x								x			x		x			
P. 4 Thought insertion or substitution		x	x	x					x			x			x		x			
P. 5 Thought withdrawal due to external agency	x												x					x		
P. 6 Thoughts spoken aloud (echo de pensée)			x	x				x	x					x				x		
P. 7 Thought diffusion or broadcasting						x			x		x			x	x			x		
P. 8 Delusions of control by external agency			x	x		x			x					x	x		x	x		
P. 9 Somatic experiences attributed to external influences		x	x																	
P. 10 Delusional mood					x	x											x		x	
Depressive delusions			x												x	x				
Other symptoms							‡Laughing for no reason			‡Thought block ‡Pedantic speech						‡Speech irrelevant and incoherent ‡Fantastic delusions				‡Paranoid delusions of reference ‡Mutism
History							‡Delusions of reference ‡Irrelevance of speech													

[1] M.R.C. Present State Examination, 8th edition.

* Has one parent among lowest six for Deviance score in schizophrenic group.

† Combined parents score among lowest six for couples in schizophrenic group.

‡ Indicates column referring to patient with this symptom.

schizophrenic patient had been diagnosed clinically as neurotic. All but three patients had first rank schizophrenic symptoms. On the basis of information provided in TABLE 11 the diagnosis might be questioned for No. 573 but the history left no doubt as to the diagnosis (see narrative history which follows). Thus all schizophrenic patients can be considered 'typical'.

Among the neurotic patients there were seventeen with non-psychotic depression, two with obsessional illness, and one phobic patient. Patients with a principal diagnosis of personality disorder were excluded. No neurotic patient was thought to be schizophrenic and none had any of the schizophrenic symptoms listed in TABLE 11.

Illustrative Case Histories of Patients

Four case histories are given here, two from each diagnostic group. One of each pair of patients has been selected as being characteristic, the other as being less characteristic or typical.

Number 556. Characteristic neurotic with severe abnormality of premorbid personality. The patient was a single man aged 26 who had been trained in management and real estate but was currently a self-employed writer and publisher. His father was the owner of a wines and spirits business. The patient had been enuretic until age 12 but had received no psychiatric treatment for this. His premorbid personality was described as shy, sensitive, irritable, and jealous. He worried a lot about work and finances. Eighteen months before admission he became emotionally involved with an Iraqi girl. He proposed marriage but she refused. Their relationship became increasingly stormy with frequent rows. He became progressively more depressed and talked of suicide. He also lost weight. Two weeks before admission she told him it was not possible for them to live together. Following this he wept frequently and wandered around London looking for her. For the next few days he roamed about the house calling out her name repeatedly and gazing fixedly out of the window. He was seen as an out-patient several times, then admitted to the Maudsley Hospital.

On examination he sat rather still and spoke in a gloomy tone of voice. He was worried about not seeing his girlfriend and felt tense and restless. He felt very depressed and had occasional suicidal thoughts. He complained of lack of energy and poor concentration. There were no delusions or hallucinations present.

Number 552. Less characteristic neurotic with mild abnormality of premorbid personality. The patient was a married woman age 25 who had no children and worked as a shop assistant. Her father was a machine operator in an engineering works. He had suffered from nervous debility during the last war. The patient had no neurotic symptoms in childhood, but her premorbid personality was described as fastidious and obsessional.

At the age of 17 she weighed 9½ stone. She gradually lost one stone in weight over the next 6 years. In January 1965 her periods ceased. She got married in September 1965 and following this, the weight loss became more rapid. In early 1967 her weight was down to 6½ stone and she was admitted to Hammersmith Hospital for investigation. No physical cause was found and she was then admitted to the Maudsley Hospital. Her mood was found to be labile but her mental state was otherwise normal. She was treated with a special diet and gradually gained weight. She was discharged after 3 months, and given a diagnosis of anorexia nervosa in an obsessional personality.

After discharge her obsessional behaviour persisted. She was seen regularly in out-patients and in June 1968 attended the Emergency Clinic complaining of occasional crying, dread of the day ahead, and ideas of self-blame for about a week. Her obsessional behaviour had been increasing over the past month. She was admitted to the Maudsley Hospital.

On examination she behaved normally and complained of worrying about everything. She felt tense, restless, and anxious. She was slowed down in her thought and movement and was moderately depressed, with morning exacerbation. She had lost a few pounds in weight over the preceding 3 months. She complained of irritability and poor concentration, and had occasional feelings that she was outside herself looking in and that her arms and legs didn't belong to her. She had been spending a lot of time washing and ironing and tidying cupboards. She cleaned the cooker every time she used it. Otherwise there were no obsessional or compulsive symptoms and there was no evidence of delusions or hallucinations.

Number 557. Characteristic schizophrenic with a normal premorbid personality. The patient was a single man age 22 who lived with his parents. He worked as a machine operator in a printing works, while his father was a maintenance electrician. The patient had no neurotic symptoms in childhood and his premorbid personality showed no abnormal traits. He did, however, smoke marihuana at weekends in the company of his friends. There was no family history of mental illness.

The patient left home to live in a flat 2 weeks before Christmas 1967. When he returned home for Christmas he was very quiet and his parents thought he looked ill. His father persuaded him to give up the flat and live at home again. Following this he had a spell of crying, could not sleep, and was afraid of being alone. During January 1968 he had several episodes of peculiar behaviour. He tipped fruit into the middle of the table, went over the table with a blow lamp, and threw all the clothes out of a wardrobe. He said that the foreman at work was making him do things. He felt he was no good and was going to throw himself over the balcony. He was seen by a psychiatrist on a domiciliary visit, who thought he was developing schizophrenia and prescribed chlorpromazine and protriptyline. He improved and the dosage of medication was reduced.

In early June he changed his job but remained symptom-free. In mid-July he began to sleep poorly. He had an argument at work, following which he was dismissed. He then began chain-smoking, woke early in the morning, and one day broke his fishing rod in pieces. He complained about a gang at work. He was seen in the Emergency Clinic where he said he felt like a zombie and heard his colleagues discussing him critically in the third person. He was admitted to the Maudsley Hospital.

On examination he was unkempt and sat rather still. He looked puzzled at times but otherwise showed blunting of affect. His speech was normal. He heard a voice talking to him and possibly commenting on his actions. He identified it as the voice of a work-mate which he thought got to him by hypnotism. He felt it was part of a conspiracy. He believed his thoughts were broadcast to other people, also by hypnotism. He felt he was under the power of the work-mate who controlled his will. He believed he was being victimized by a conspiracy at work. He complained of moderate depression and anxiety but showed no evidence of this.

Number 573. Less characteristic schizophrenic with a normal premorbid personality. The patient was an unmarried man age 19 who was currently a student but had worked in the past as an assistant librarian. His father was a scrap-metal dealer of eccentric habits; he lay in bed till the afternoon every day. The patient had shown no neurotic symptoms in childhood and his premorbid personality appeared to be normal.

He had a prolonged friendship with a girlfriend, but in July 1967 she rejected him. He felt confused for a month then experienced a growing feeling of guilt and suicidal compulsion. In October 1967 he took an overdose of aspirin but vomited most of them and received no treatment. He went to university in October to study geography, but made no friends there.

In January 1968 he became increasingly withdrawn. He neglected his work and lay on his bed most of the day sucking his thumb. He was unable to concentrate and experienced what he called 'mind blanks'. He slept well but his appetite was poor. He moved into lodgings during the vacation in March and became slow in his movements and increasingly anxious. He was frightened of going out in the street and feared he was going insane. He lost his perception of depth for a while. On occasions a particular word would become fixed in his mind. He was referred to a psychiatric clinic by his tutor and admitted to a local psychiatric hospital. In hospital he was continuously but mildly depressed, lacked any motivation, and neglected his hygiene. He was transferred to the Maudsley Hospital in August.

On examination his appearance and behaviour were normal but he showed blunting of affect. He complained of being unable to relax and said he worried about his future, about having heart disease, and about going completely mad. His interests had diminished considerably and he found it difficult to concentrate on anything. He felt unreal and dissociated from his body. He also felt he had changed completely and was 'not in the world of 99 per cent of people'. He experienced his head as having increased in size at the back. There were no hallucinations present. He found that his thoughts were muddled and that sometimes they were repeated over again in his mind. He also experienced 'mind-blanks' which were a cutting-off of his thoughts. He believed that he had been born before his time and belonged at the end of human experience. No other delusions were elicited.

His speech was pedantic and full of pseudoscientific and pseudophilosophical phrases. Some examples follow: 'I had this transcendental experience that is the complete negation of bodily sexual experience. The quantity of gratification derived from it is equivalent to orgasm and is continuous in space and time'. 'My life is ontologically relevant as opposed to ontologically irrelevant.' He thought that he was 'in some sense schizophrenic', and ascribed his state to 'having had the transcendental experience in the first place and having reached a higher intellectual plane'.

INTER-RATER RELIABILITY USING THE 41-CATEGORY RORSCHACH MANUAL

A Spearman rank difference correlation for the Deviance Score (d/r) of all subjects scored by the two raters was rho $=0.89$. Calculating the inter-rater reliability by the Pearson product-moment method, which takes into account the magnitude of the scores as well as their ordinal position, the reliability was $r_p = 0.87$. Because of the close relationship between the two raters' scores, it was decided not to combine scores of the raters. All analyses will be based on the scores of one rater except where specified otherwise.

TESTING THE PRINCIPAL HYPOTHESIS: RESULTS OF PARENTS' DEVIANCE SCORES

The aim of this study was to test if parents of schizophrenics have excessive communication defects and deviances of the sort which Singer and Wynne believe are associated with the development of schizophrenia in their offspring. Having administered the Rorschach under experimental conditions to provide a controlled stimulus for recording samples of speech, and having shown that we can reliably score the transcripts with Singer and Wynne's manual, we can now report our findings.

MEAN DEVIANCE SCORE

The mean Deviance Score for parents of schizophrenics taken as a group was 1.33 ± 0.99, and for parents of neurotics 0.88 ± 0.82. The difference between groups is significant at the 0.05 level ($t = 2.215$, 78 d.f.). The distributions are shown in FIGURE 7.1.

This tends to confirm the findings of Singer and Wynne that parents of schizophrenics have more deviances in speech sampled during Rorschach testing than parents of other groups (Singer and Wynne, 1966b; Wynne,

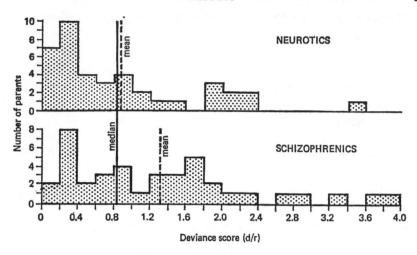

FIG. 7.1. Deviance Score.

1967). However, the considerable overlap of the two groups in this study [FIG. 7.1] differs markedly from the results they have reported more recently. (See TABLE 17 and Wynne, 1968, 1971.) Failure to confirm this aspect of Singer and Wynne's findings has important implications for the 'Transaction' hypothesis they have put forward and will be considered in the conclusion [p. 169].

Visual examination of the distribution of scores shown in FIGURE 7.1 suggests that they are skewed in both groups. If this is true then a t-test is not a valid statistical measure as it depends on the assumption that the distribution of scores around the means is normal.

One technique suitable for dealing with skewed distributions of this sort is to normalize the distributions before applying the t-test by transforming the individual scores into their log values. This was done. The mean log D-Score of parents of schizophrenics was 1·98±0·474. The mean log D-Score of parents of neurotics was 1·728±0·503. These means differ significantly at the 0·05 level (t=2·106, 78 d.f.).

Wynne reports that when the combined averaged scores of the parents of schizophrenic patients are compared with other groups a greater degree of discrimination between the groups is achieved (Wynne, 1967). In this study the mean D-Score of parents' paired scores was 1·35±0·71 for schizophrenics and 0·88±0·61 for neurotics, The difference between groups is significant at the 0·05 confidence level (t=2·140, 39 d.f.) but the level of discrimination remains the same as when parents in each group are taken individually, the only difference being the standard deviations.

The Deviance Scores of fathers and of mothers was also examined separately. The mean D-Score for fathers of schizophrenics was 1·54±1·08, and for fathers of neurotics 0·75±0·61. These means differ significantly at the 0·01 level (t=2·88, 19 d.f.). The mean D-Score for mothers of schizophrenics was $1\cdot26\pm1\cdot07$ and for mothers of controls $1\cdot01\pm0\cdot99$. The difference is not significant ($t=0\cdot767$, 19 d.f.).

Thus most of the difference between parents of schizophrenics and neurotics can be attributed to the difference between fathers. This in fact agrees with the finding of Singer and Wynne (1966b) in their Houston sample where they found a difference between the means of the fathers but not mothers of schizophrenics and neurotics at the 0·05 level.

COMPARISON WITH SINGER AND WYNNE'S FINDINGS, NON-PARAMETRIC ANALYSIS

Previous studies have reported results using non-parametric statistics for the analysis. It is useful to look at the results of this study using these techniques as this allows a more ready comparison with the findings of other workers.

D-Score, All Subjects

Using the median test in which subjects at or below the median for all subjects combined are separated from subjects above the median, there is a tendency for parents of schizophrenics to score above the median and parents of controls to score below; 61 per cent of the individual parents were correctly classified by this method as compared with 50 per cent expected by chance [TABLE 12]. However, a corrected chi-square test, which is appropriate for the number in the sample, indicates that this finding is not significant.

TABLE 12

DISTRIBUTION OF PARENTS ABOVE AND BELOW THE COMMON MEDIAN FOR SCHIZOPHRENICS AND NEUROTICS COMBINED

	EQUAL* OR BELOW THE MEDIAN	ABOVE THE MEDIAN	TOTAL
Schizophrenic	16	24	40
Neurotic	25	15	40
TOTAL	41	39	80

Median Score = 0·85, 61 per cent of parents correctly classified.
Corrected $\chi^2 = 3\cdot2$, n.s.
* There is one subject from each group on the median.

D-Score—Highest Scoring Number

If the Deviance Score was determined by a dominant gene one would predict that the greatest discrimination between groups would be found by looking at the highest scoring parent's score in each group. When this approach was used the difference between groups still did not reach significance and there was no improvement on the degree of discrimination [TABLE 13].

TABLE 13
HIGHEST SCORING PARENT

	BELOW THE MEDIAN	ABOVE THE MEDIAN	TOTAL
Schizophrenic	7	13	20
Neurotic	13	7	20
TOTAL	20	20	40

Median Score = 1·5, 65 per cent of parents correctly classified.
$\chi^2 = 3·6$, n.s.

D-Score of Parents as Pairs

If the parents' scores for each patient are combined and averaged, and the groups of parental pairs are compared, the difference between groups does not reach significance at the 0·05 level [TABLE 14]; 62·5 per cent of parental pairs are correctly classified by this method.

TABLE 14
PARENTS AS PAIRS

	EQUAL* OR BELOW MEDIAN	ABOVE THE MEDIAN	TOTAL
Schizophrenic	8	12	20
Neurotic	13	7	20
TOTAL	21	19	40

Median Score = 2·2, 62·5 per cent of pairs correctly classified.
$\chi^2 = 2·5$, n.s.
* There is one subject from each group on the median.

Separate Comparisons of Fathers and of Mothers

TABLES 15 and 16 readily demonstrate that there is no significant difference between the D-Score of mothers of schizophrenics and mothers of neurotics by the median test, but a comparison of the fathers of both groups shows a significant difference at the 0·02 level.

TABLE 15
D-SCORE OF MOTHERS

	EQUAL* OR BELOW MEDIAN	ABOVE THE MEDIAN	TOTAL
Schizophrenics	9	11	20
Neurotics	12	8	20
TOTAL	21	19	40

Median Score = 0·75.
$\chi^2 = 0·60$, n.s.
* One subject from each group fell on the median.

KAPS

TABLE 16

D-SCORE OF FATHERS

	EQUAL OR BELOW MEDIAN	ABOVE THE MEDIAN	TOTAL
Schizophrenics	6	14	20
Neurotics	14	6	20
TOTAL	20	20	40

Median Score = 0·91.
$\chi^2 = 6·4$, p < 0·02.

TABLE 17

N.I.M.H. SAMPLE, PARENTS AS PAIRS,
41-CATEGORY RORSCHACH SCORING

(Wynne, 1971)

	TYPICAL SCHIZ.	SCHIZO-AFFECTIVE	BORDER-LINE	NEUROTIC	NORMAL	TOTAL
Above median	42	5	10	0	1	58
Below median	0	1	10	28	19	58
TOTAL	42	6	20	28	20	116

From Wynne (personal communication).

It can readily be seen from TABLES 12, 14 and FIGURE 7.1 that a considerable overlap occurred between the scores of parents of neurotics and schizophrenics. TABLE 17 shows the over-all results from Singer and Wynne's N.I.M.H. sample and indicates that they achieved a much higher order of discrimination between groups than the present study. In fact, there was no overlap at all between the typical schizophrenics' parents and typical neurotics' parents such as those included in the present study. Possible explanations for these different findings will be considered in the discussion [p. 156].

WHAT ARE 'VERBAL DEFECTS AND DEVIANCES'? CAN WE IMPROVE ON THE RESULTS BY ANALYSING THE DATA DIFFERENTLY?

On page 134 we reported a high inter-rater reliability, that is to say that the two raters substantially agree when comparing their ratings on the over-all sample as to the ordinal position of patients within the sample and the relative distances apart. This is a valid measure for our purposes because we wished to find out if parents of schizophrenics tend to have an over-all score which is higher than parents of neurotics. Because the score is a composite one reflecting the sum total of all the defects and deviances made during the Rorschach interview, it tells us little about the reliability and validity of the individual 41 categories defined in Singer and Wynne's manual (1966a). It may therefore be useful to consider the manual in further detail, discussing first its face validity as an instrument for testing the hypotheses of Singer and Wynne, and then seeing if a different statistical treatment can enable us to discriminate between groups more effectively.

The 41-Category Rorschach Manual

The scoring categories in the manual were developed as measures of communication defects and deviances, reflecting difficulty in sharing foci of attention with the tester. They are grouped under three headings: closure problems, disruptive behaviour, and peculiar verbalizations. In any scoring procedure it is desirable that the different categories be mutually exclusive. This becomes of prime importance in the procedure used by Singer and Wynne, for if a particular type of Deviance occurs more than once in the same response it is only counted as one Deviance. If categories overlap so that it is possible to assign a deviant communication to more than one category then there is considerable latitude for the scorer to count similar Deviances as repetitions or not. This could affect the Deviance Score considerably.

In our scoring of the pilot transcripts we soon discovered a number of categories in the manual which were overlapping. For instance, category 212 'extraneous questions and remarks' has a lot in common with category 213 'odd, tangential, inappropriate responses to questions'. We were often at a loss whether to score a Deviance as category 181 'contradictory information' or category 183 'incompatible alternatives'. There was also a great deal of overlap between category 193 'remarks implying inability or failure to verify own response', category 194 'retractions and denials', and category 196 'partial disqualifications'. In order to cope with this problem without altering the manual we agreed with Singer on the following rule. When two or more instances of an abnormality appeared within a single response which differed in character from each other, but were nevertheless varieties of the same category, if it seemed possible to assign each of them to one of different but closely related categories, we did so. This ruling clearly tends to increase Deviance scores. However, it does introduce rather arbitrary decisions and we feel a revision of the manual involving condensing of overlapping categories would be preferable.

A similar problem arose with regard to multiple scores, which Singer and Wynne advise can be assigned when appropriate. For instance, category 120 'unintelligible responses and comments' and category 140 'gross indefiniteness and tentativeness' can be applied to passages or phrases which have already been assigned a number of more specific categories of Deviance. The decisions as to when to add these more global categories were difficult.

One further comment is worth recording, namely that some items which seem very important theoretically, for example category 312 'peculiar or quaint, private terms or phrases' and category 317 'cryptic remarks', occur very rarely in practice.

Alternative Statistical Treatments of the Data

In the results reported on pages 134 and 135 above we found a significant difference between the Deviance Scores of parents of schizophrenics and neurotics. This result was based on a replication of Singer and Wynne's methods of scoring transcripts, which is to calculate an individual's Deviance Score as the sum total of the number of deviances scored in the transcript.* Although we found a significant difference between the mean scores of the two groups, there was so much overlap between the groups that the differences which appeared were trivial when compared with Singer and Wynne's results, and do not provide confirmation of their hypotheses. Consequently we carried out a discriminate function analysis to find a set of weights to apply to the 41 categories which would maximally discriminate between composite means for the two groups. This would have the effect of giving increased importance to some of the categories and minimizing others when calculating the scores. If this were successful the transcripts could be re-scored using fewer more highly discriminating categories, or a new sample could be taken eliminating the poorly discriminating categories to confirm that more effective discrimination between groups could thereby be obtained. The discriminate function analysis was carried out but was unsuccessful. We were not able to find a way of weighting the variables which would improve the discrimination between our groups.

It may be that parents of schizophrenics and parents of neurotics exhibit different patterns of communication deviance in addition to differences in the amount of overall deviance. An attempt was made to subdivide the patients into subgroups using methods of cluster analysis, and then to see if the resulting subgroups conformed to parents of schizophrenics and parents of neurotics respectively.

After eliminating all the items which occurred in less than 25 per cent of the sample, a correlation matrix of the remaining 25 items was subjected to a principal components analysis. It was found that three components accounted for the greater part of the variance. These components were subjected to a varimax rotation and the scores on the resulting components were found for each subject. The component scores were then used in a cluster analysis to see if the patients as a whole fell into relatively clear-cut subgroups in the three-dimensional space constructed by using the three principal components as axes. The cluster analysis did produce two relatively clear-cut groups but these were not exclusively composed of parents of schizophrenics and parents of neurotics respectively. The proportion of parents of schizophrenics in the first group was 59·2 per cent ($n = 27$) and in the second group was 45·3 per cent ($n = 53$). Thus we were unable to discriminate parents of schizophrenics from parents of neurotics more sharply by applying these more sophisticated statistical tests to our data.

* Both Singer and Wynne and ourselves only scored the first response on each Rorschach card, but this does not affect the present argument.

§ V. HOW CAN WE ACCOUNT FOR THE DIFFERENCE BETWEEN GROUPS ON THE DEVIANCE SCORE?

We have demonstrated a difference between the mean Deviance Scores of parents of schizophrenics and parents of neurotics and this requires an explanation. It behoves us first of all to search for simple hypotheses stemming from the nature of our data before assuming that the findings represent a true difference which can be related aetiologically to schizophrenia.

VERBAL INTELLIGENCE

Previous authors (Rosman et al., 1964; Fisher et al., 1959) have found that education was significantly correlated with scores of abstract thinking and various other Rorschach measures. It seems an obvious possibility that the number of verbal defects and deviances which someone makes may be related to their verbal intelligence. If D-Score is significantly correlated with I.Q. and the groups being compared are not matched for I.Q. the differences found using the 41-category Rorschach manual between parents of schizophrenics and other groups may simply reflect differences of I.Q. between groups. Previous studies have unfortunately not taken this into account (see CHAPTER V, Abnormalities of Communication and Language).

Verbal Intelligence of Parents, and its Relationship to D-Score

In the sample studied in this investigation there was no significant difference between the Verbal I.Q. of parents of schizophrenics and parents of neurotics at the 5 per cent probability level, as tested by the Mill Hill Vocabulary Scale. The mean I.Q. of parents of schizophrenics was $105 \cdot 1 \pm 13 \cdot 3$ and the mean I.Q. of parents of neurotics was $107 \cdot 5 \pm 11 \cdot 7$ ($t = 0 \cdot 755$, n.s.). These distributions with their means are illustrated in FIGURE 7.2. Further comparisons for mothers and fathers taken separately also failed to show a significant difference between groups.

The relationship between Deviance Score and I.Q. was measured by the Pearson product–moment coefficient, r_p. In TABLE 18 it can be seen that the correlation between I.Q. and D-Score for parents of schizophrenics, $r_p = 0 \cdot 028$, is not significant. However, among parents of neurotics there is a negative correlation of $r_p = -0 \cdot 36$ which is significant at the $0 \cdot 05$ level. It is interesting that this finding is similar to that of Rosman et al. (1964), who found a significant negative correlation between I.Q. and the Object Sorting Test score among normal controls ($r = -0 \cdot 23$) but did not find a significant correlation among parents of schizophrenics.

TABLE 18
CORRELATION OF D-SCORE WITH I.Q.

	PARENTS OF SCHIZOPHRENICS	PARENTS OF NEUROTICS
r_p	$+0 \cdot 028$	$-0 \cdot 36$
Significance	n.s.	$p < 0 \cdot 05$

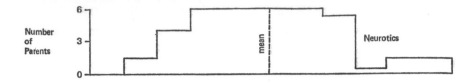

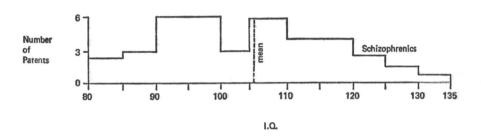

FIG. 7.2. Mill Hill Vocabulary Scale: I.Q.

The meaning of a significant correlation in one group but not the other requires further investigation. However it does suggest there may be an effect from some additional factor in parents of schizophrenics.

An Analysis of Co-variance Comparing the Difference between Groups on D-Score after Taking Out the Effect of I.Q.

An analysis of co-variance was carried out to test whether the regression slope of D-Score on I.Q. was of the same order for parents of schizophrenics as for parents of neurotics, or differed significantly between the groups. Despite the above results, the difference in slopes of the regression lines between the two groups was not significant (F-ratio=2·873, 1 and 76, d.f.). Since the slopes do not differ significantly, it is valid to take out the effect of I.Q. before comparing the difference between groups on the D-Score.

An analysis of co-variance was done in order to compare the difference between groups on D-Score after taking out the effect of I.Q. and see if this would alter the level of significance. TABLE 19 shows that there is little change in the variance after taking out the effect of I.Q. The difference between parents of schizophrenics and parents of neurotics remains significant at the 5 per cent probability level.

TABLE 19

ANALYSIS OF CO-VARIANCE: D-SCORE AFTER TAKING OUT THE
VARIANCE DUE TO I.Q.

	CORRECTED SUMS OF SQUARES	d.f.	CORRECTED SUMS OF SQUARES AFTER TAKING OUT THE EFFECT OF I.Q.	d.f.
Between groups	3·991	I	3·522	I
Within groups	64·028	78	62·711	77
TOTAL	68·019	79	66·233	

F-ratio = 4·325, 1 and 77 d.f.

$p < 0.05$.

One would not in fact expect the difference between groups on the D-Score to be affected appreciably by taking out the contributions of I.Q. because there was almost no difference between the mean I.Q.s of the two groups studied. However, this effect may be important in other studies in which the mean I.Q.s of the experimental and control groups differ considerably. Therefore, this analysis has been included in our results as a model. From these data it seems valid to conclude that parents of schizophrenics make a significantly greater number of communication deviances in a Rorschach interview than parents of neurotics, even after the nature and extent of the distribution is taken into account, and the possible contribution of differences in I.Q. between groups is considered.

SEX OF PATIENT

In TABLE 3 we saw that there were significantly more male than female schizophrenic patients in our experimental group and, correspondingly, fewer males than females in the neurotic group ($p = 0.054$). Since the groups do not match on this variable, it is possible that there is an interaction between the sex of the patient and the Deviance Score of the parent which could affect the outcome when we test for differences in Deviance Score between parental groups. This effect was tested for by an analysis of variance and a significant interaction was not demonstrated, but the small number of subjects makes this test somewhat inconclusive.

THE NUMBER OF WORDS SPOKEN

Since the Deviance Score is a simple ratio of the total number of deviances per number of responses it does not take into account possible differences between subjects in the length of their responses. A likely possibility is that longer responses, measured by the number of words spoken, would be associated with more deviances while brief responses would not give the same opportunity for deviances to occur. This possibility was not considered by Singer and Wynne. To answer this question we first examined the groups to see if they differed in the number of words spoken.

Word Count

It can be seen in TABLE 20 that the mean number of words spoken on the first responses of the Rorschach tests (First Viewing plus Enquiry) is significantly different between parents of schizophrenics and parents of neurotics at the 5 per cent level [see FIG. 7.3]. The difference is mainly due to the significantly greater number of words spoken by the fathers of schizophrenics. The difference between mothers of the two groups was not significant.

TABLE 20

NUMBER OF WORDS USED IN FIRST RESPONSES TO
RORSCHACH CARDS

	SCHIZOPHRENICS	NEUROTICS	t	d.f.	p
Fathers	892·6 ± 489·5	570·0 ± 231·4	2·666	38	<0·02
Mothers	686·3 ± 319·1	654·9 ± 398·1	0·276	38	n.s.
$\dfrac{\text{Fa. and Mo.}}{2}$	789·4 − 421·0	612·2 ± 324·3	2·109	78	<0·05

When the results were recalculated after log transformation to normalize the distributions, the difference was still significant at the 0·05 confidence level.

Correlation of Word Counts with Deviance Score and Analysis of Co-variance to Correct Deviance Score for Differences between Groups in the Number of Words Spoken

Since parents of schizophrenics differ from parents of neurotics on both Deviance Score and the number of words spoken, it is important to see if these variables are correlated. The Pearson product-moment correlation coefficient between Deviance Score and the number of words for parents of schizophrenics is +0·57 and for parents of neurotics +0·76. Both correlations are highly significant (p<0·001), while the difference between them is not (test: Fisher's 'z' transformation) [see FIG. 7.4].

Since the number of words spoken and the Deviance Scores are so highly correlated, the difference between groups on the Deviance Scores may be accounted for simply by differences between groups on the number of words spoken. We may ask the question, if both groups had spoken the same mean number of words, would we expect there to be any difference between their mean Deviance Scores? In other words, what would be the effect on the Deviance Scores if we corrected for differences between groups on word count. We can make an estimation of this by an analysis of co-variance just as we did to adjust the D-Scores for differences in I.Q. In principle we find the regression line which best expresses the relationships between Deviance

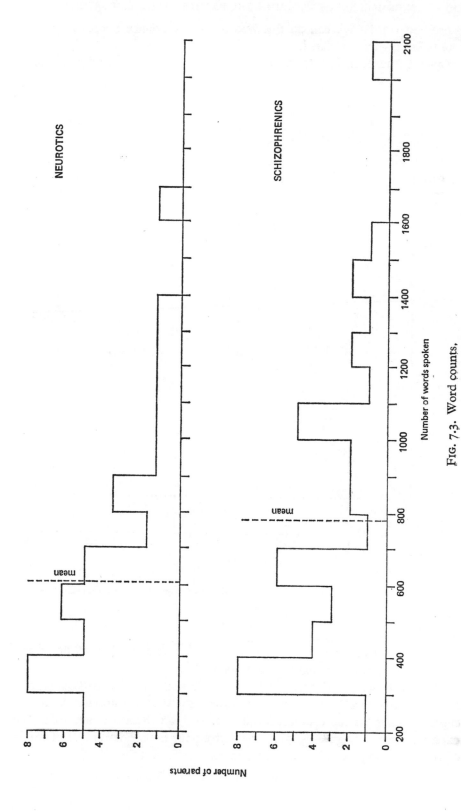

Fig. 7·3. Word counts,

Score and words. We can do this because the Deviance Scores and word counts are highly correlated.

Lines S and N in FIGURE 7.4 represent the regression lines for Deviance

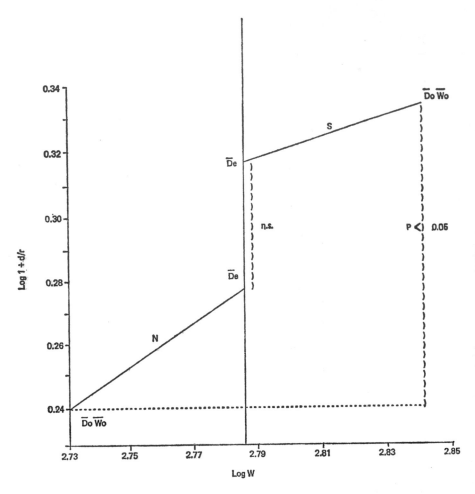

FIG. 7.4. Taking out the effect of the number of words on the Deviance Scores.

Score with words for parents of schizophrenics and parents of neurotics, respectively. The co-ordinates of the points $\overline{Do}$, $\overline{Wo}$ are the observed means for Deviance Score and number of words for each of the two groups. The regression line enables us to predict from a value of the abscissa what the expected value on the ordinate would be. We can therefore determine the expected mean Deviance Score for each group for the mean number of words of the two groups combined.* The mean for the combined groups of the

* The logged values are used here to correct for skewed distributions of d/r and W.

logged number of words is 2·785. $\overline{De}$ is the expected Deviance Score for each group given a regression to this overall mean.

It can be observed from FIGURE 7.4 that when we estimate the Deviance Score expected if both groups are regressed to the same number of words, the difference between groups is reduced considerably to a point where it is no longer significant.

This analysis is done more precisely by an analysis of co-variance which also takes into account the scatter in both groups. The results of such an analysis are given in TABLE 21, which shows that when the variance due to the number of words spoken is taken out, the difference between groups on the Deviance Score becomes negligible.

TABLE 21

ANALYSIS OF CO-VARIANCE TO TAKE OUT THE VARIANCE
DUE TO THE DIFFERENCE BETWEEN GROUPS IN NUMBER OF
WORDS SPOKEN*

	CORRECTED SUMS of SQUARES	d.f.	CORRECTED SUMS OF SQUARES TAKING OUT VARIANCE DUE TO WORDS	d.f.
Between groups	0·166	I	0·021	I
Within groups	2·334	78	1·154	77
TOTAL	2·500		1·175	

F-ratio = 1·419, n.s.

* This analysis is shown for the logged value of D-Scores and words.

While we have given the results of the analysis using the log transformation of the Deviance Scores and word counts to correct for skew, the analysis was also done on the untransformed data and showed an even smaller difference between groups. These results strongly suggest that the difference we observed between the Deviance Scores of parents of schizophrenics and parents of neurotics is due to differences in the number of words spoken. Examination of TABLE 16 and TABLE 20 showed that most of the differences between groups is due to differences between the fathers of schizophrenics, who have the highest D-Score and word counts, and the fathers of neurotics, who have the lowest. There is little difference between the mothers. Thus persons who make longer replies have more opportunity to make communication deviances; persons who speak concisely or have little to say have less opportunity.

Deviance Rate

It is possible that persons who talk more do so because of abnormal thought processes which make their replies more verbose. Thus the amount spoken may be secondary to verbal fluency. For this reason we suggest that the

Deviance Rate, defined as the number of deviances per number of words spoken (d/w × 100), would be a better measure of the deviant quality of speech than the Deviance Score used by Singer and Wynne. Such a measure would clearly be independent of the amount spoken.

In our sample the mean Deviance Rate for parents of schizophrenics was 3.25 ± 2.10 and for parents of neurotics 2.59 ± 1.74. The difference between groups was not significant (t = 1.533, 78 d.f.; n.s.) though a trend was present. After logarithmic transformation of the scores in order to normalize the data the means become Sc. = 1.34 ± 0.481, Neur. = 1.17 ± 0.487, the difference again being non-significant (t = 1.580, 78 d.f.; n.s.).

The Relationship between Deviance Rate and Word Count

We have established that the Deviance Score (d/r) is highly correlated with the word count and we have reported a considerably poorer discrimination between our neurotics and schizophrenics than that found by Singer and Wynne. As we will explain later, Singer and Wynne's neurotics scored in the same range as ours but their schizophrenics have much higher Deviance Scores. It is possible that the relationship between deviances and word count is such that as the word count increases the Deviance Rate rises, resulting in an increasing difference between the two groups. The relationship between Deviance Rates and word count might be linear [Example A, FIG. 7.5] or curvilinear [Example B, FIG. 7.5]. If either case held it would follow that the greatest difference between groups in Deviance Score would be found at the higher levels of word counts, and that the difference between Singer and Wynne's results and ours might be due to the fact that their subjects spoke more. We can test this hypothesis by examining the relationship between Deviance Rate and word count.

An attempt was made to fit the data to a first, second, and third degree equation respectively. The best fit was obtained by the linear regression $d/w = 0.0365 \log w + 2.5010$.

The slopes of the regression lines for the two groups did not differ from each other significantly, nor did they differ significantly from zero. We can draw the conclusion that the Deviance Rate is constant and does not vary with the word count, i.e. that these variables are not correlated. Therefore at higher word counts the number of deviances made by parents of schizophrenics is not likely to be disproportionately higher than that of parents of neurotics.

Multiple Step-wise Regression

A step-wise regression was carried out to see how much of the variance of the D-Score (d/r) was taken up by word count and I.Q. This analysis first examines the prediction from one set of variables (w) to another (d/r), then considers the improvement in prediction achieved by adding another variable

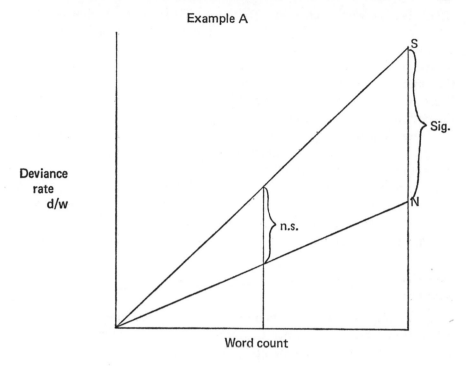

Example A

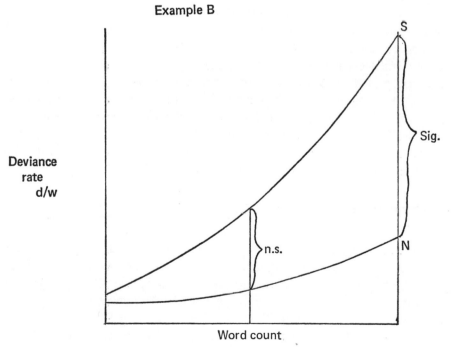

Example B

FIG. 7.5. The relationship between Deviance Rate and word count.

(I.Q.). For the whole sample (n=80) the correlation of d/r with w was 0·665 (r^2=0·44) and for d/r with (w + I.Q.) it was 0·695, a negligible increase of the correlation coefficient. The difference between the residuals of the experimental group and controls was then tested by a t-test. The residual represents the difference between the individual's expected and observed Deviance Scores when his own word count and I.Q. are substituted in the equation for the best fit regression line to obtain the expected score. If the variance about the regression line is significantly greater for the experimental than for the control group because of an unexplained factor, t will be significant. This was not the case and the hypothesis was rejected.

We can conclude from the analyses in this section that the difference between groups on the Deviance Score (d/r) is related to the higher word counts of parents of schizophrenics, particularly the fathers, but we are thus far unable to explain our failure to replicate Singer and Wynne's results.

The Technique of Interview and its Effect on the Over-all Results

Considering the high correlation between Deviance Score and word count (r_p=0·67) we would expect that the Deviance Score would be higher in subjects who talk more, and the results of the preceding section suggest that this effect should be the same for both groups. An unplanned test of these hypotheses occurred during our study. It may be recalled from the section on methods that a slight change was made in the technique of administering the Enquiry part of the Rorschach at the suggestion of Dr. Singer after the parents of 11 schizophrenics and 10 neurotics had been tested. This provided us with an opportunity to examine the effect of this change of technique on the word counts and Deviance Scores by an Analysis of Variance, taking into account the first period of testing involving 42 subjects (Period 1) and the second period of testing involving the remaining 38 (Period 2). In the same analysis it was possible to compare the D-Score on the First Viewing and Enquiry portions of the test as well as the over-all D-Score for the two groups separately. In so doing the portion of the Rorschach test which was most important for detecting differences between groups could be determined.

A Comparison between Groups for the Deviance Score of the First Viewing, Enquiry, and Over-all Test Taken Separately

We were surprised to find that the First Viewing discriminated better between groups than the Enquiry. This was contrary to what Singer and Wynne had found (personal communication). TABLE 22 shows that there was a significant difference between groups on the First Viewing and over-all test but not on the Enquiry. TABLE 23 shows the mean Deviance Scores for groups separately and combined for the period of testing, and TABLE 24 shows the corresponding mean word counts.

TABLE 22

VARIANCE RATIOS (F) AND THEIR SIGNIFICANCE FOR GROUPS AND PERIODS TOGETHER IN ONE ANALYSIS

SOURCE OF VARIATION	d.f.	FIRST VIEWING		ENQUIRY		OVER-ALL DEVIANCE SCORE	
		F	p	F	p	F	p
BETWEEN GROUPS							
Periods combined (schizophrenics *v.* neurotics)	I	6·362	<0·05	2·697	n.s.	5·320	<0·05
BETWEEN PERIODS							
Groups combined	I	<1·0	n.s.	16·970	<0·001	7·336	<0·05
Interactions between group and period	I	<1·0	n.s.	<1·0	n.s.	<1·0	n.s.
Residual	36						

d.f. = degrees of freedom.

TABLE 23

MEAN D-SCORE FOR GROUPS AND PERIODS SEPARATELY AND
COMBINED
A 'FIRST VIEWING' OF RORSCHACH

	PERIOD 1	PERIOD 2	PERIODS COMBINED
Schizophrenic	1·11	1·27	1·18
Neurotic	0·50	0·80	0·65
GROUPS COMBINED	0·82	1·02	

B 'ENQUIRY' OF RORSCHACH

	PERIOD 1	PERIOD 2	PERIODS COMBINED
Schizophrenic	1·08	1·91	1·45
Neurotic	0·63	1·58	1·11
GROUPS COMBINED	0·87	1·74	

C OVER-ALL D-SCORE

	PERIOD 1	PERIOD 2	PERIODS COMBINED
Schizophrenic	1·10	1·59	1·32
Neurotic	0·56	1·19	0·88
GROUPS COMBINED	0·85	1·38	

TABLE 24

A WORD COUNTS—FIRST VIEWING

	PERIOD 1	PERIOD 2	PERIODS COMBINED
Schizophrenic	385	412	797
Neurotic	176	210	386

B WORD COUNTS—ENQUIRY

	PERIOD 1	PERIOD 2	PERIODS COMBINED
Schizophrenic	345	679	1024
Neurotic	267	486	753

*A Comparison between Periods to See if the Changes in Rorschach Technique
Affected the Subjects' Scores*

We introduced the change in method of administering the Rorschach after
testing the first 21 pairs of parents, thereby dividing the sample into 42 and
38 subjects tested during the first and second periods, respectively.

There is a significant increase in the D-Score from Period 1 to Period 2 in the Enquiry, but not in the First Viewing part of the Rorschach [see FIG. 7.6]. This is demonstrated in TABLE 22 for both groups combined, and in TABLE 25 for the groups taken separately. This is what would be expected

TABLE 25

VARIANCE RATIOS (F) AND THEIR SIGNIFICANCE FOR
GROUPS SEPARATELY

SOURCE OF VARIATION	d.f.	F FIRST VIEWING		F ENQUIRY		F OVER-ALL DEVIANCE SCORE	
		Schizo.	Neuro.	Schizo.	Neuro.	Schizo.	Neuro.
Between periods	1	<1·0 n.s.	2·11 n.s.	7·16 p<0·05	10·89 p<0·01	2·39 n.s.	6·89 p<0·05
Residual	18						

d.f. = degrees of freedom.

since it was only the method of administering the Enquiry which changed from Period 1 to Period 2. In addition this analysis shows that a significant difference between periods also occurs on the over-all D-Score, and can be attributed to the between-period difference in the Enquiry.

Since the change in method between periods for the Enquiry appears to have effected a significant change in the D-Score for parents of both schizo-phrenics and neurotics it is important to know if it affected the D-Scores of one significantly more than the other. We can see that it did not because the interaction between the periods and the groups on the D-Score is not signi-ficant in any part of the test [see TABLE 22]. The parallel slopes in FIGURE 7.6 illustrate this point. Moreover, the difference between groups within Period 1 and Period 2 of the Enquiry remained non-significant [see TABLE 26].

This analysis shows that in our hands the First Viewing part of the Ror-schach is more effective in discriminating parents of schizophrenics from neurotics. The Enquiry portion of the Rorschach did not discriminate effectively between groups in either period. When we changed the method of administering the Enquiry and encouraged a longer response there was a significant rise in the word counts of both groups but the groups were not affected differently.

TABLE 24 shows that concurrently with the increase in Deviance Scores there was an increase in the word counts, as we would expect from our previous findings.

Discussion: Interviewing Technique

One interpretation of our findings that the Deviance Score is so highly correlated with the number of words spoken [p. 144], and that by partialling out the word count the difference between groups becomes negligible, is

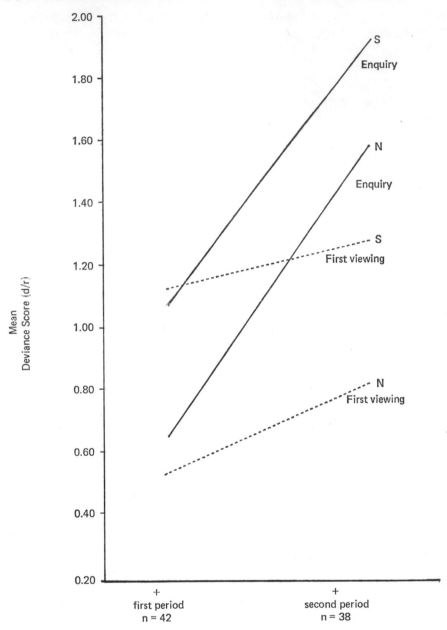

FIG. 7.6. Effect on mean D-Score of change in administering the Enquiry. D-Score increased significantly (p < 0·05) in the second half of the sample when the examiner probed more deeply, but both groups were affected equally. The First Viewing was not administered differently and the D-Scores did not change significantly.

that all differences between groups can be accounted for by differences in verbal responsiveness. Our unplanned experiment shows that parents are very susceptible to the conditions of testing and confirms that altering the

TABLE 26
VARIANCE RATIOS (F) AND THEIR SIGNIFICANCE FOR PERIODS SEPARATELY

SOURCE OF VARIATION	FIRST VIEWING				ENQUIRY				OVER-ALL DEVIANCE SCORE			
	Period 1		*Period 2*		*Period 1*		*Period 2*		*Period 1*		*Period 2*	
	d.f.	F	d.f.	F	d.f.	F	d.f.	F	d.f.	F	d.f.	F
BETWEEN GROUPS												
Schizophrenic v. neurotic	1	3·06 n.s.	1	4·71 $p<0·05$	1	2·47 n.s.	1	1·10 n.s.	1	3·23 n.s.	1	2·89 n.s.
Residual	19		17		19		17		19		17	

d.f. = degrees of freedom.
v.r. = variance ratio.

Rorschach technique can lead subjects to respond more fully and thus increase their Deviance Scores. In a previous publication (Hirsch and Leff, 1971) we pointed out that if the person administering the Rorschach test encouraged one group to respond more fully than another group, the Deviance Scores of the first group could thereby be elevated in comparison to the second. For example, if the testing psychologist suspected which group the subject belonged to and took a greater interest in the responses of say the parents of schizophrenics, she might encourage them to respond more fully. Any number of ancillary factors could similarly influence the psychologist to treat the groups differently, for example, differences between groups in their age, I.Q., social class, education, personality, and so on. For this reason testing must be done blindly, and differences between groups on these other parameters must be controlled or partialled out.

FIGURE 7.6 shows in graphic form that while our subjects showed a significant increase in their Deviance Scores when the technique of testing was altered, they did so equally, as we would expect from the fact that the scoring was done under completely blind conditions. With reference to this point, Wynne has stated (personal communication) that the psychologists administering their tests did not have any clinical knowledge about the subjects. Furthermore, he claims that a multivariate analysis has shown that in addition to word counts, other ancillary variables such as I.Q., social class, etc., do not account for the difference between groups on the Deviance Scores in their sample.

§ VI. COMPARISON OF N.I.M.H. AND UNITED KINGDOM RESULTS—SOME HYPOTHESES WHICH COULD EXPLAIN THE DIFFERENCES

There are some striking differences between the findings of this investigation and those of previous workers. In the present study there was a significant difference between the mean scores for parents of schizophrenics and parents of neurotics but the distribution of scores for the two groups overlaps 97·5 per cent [see FIG. 7.1, p. 135]. This differs considerably from the N.I.M.H. results reported by Wynne and Singer at a recent conference. Wynne stated:

There appears to be almost no overlap between the parents of schizophrenics and parents of neurotics and normals. . . . None of the parental pairs of schizophrenics had low scores, and very few of the parental pairs of neurotics and normals had high scores.

Wynne has written that he and Singer have correctly identified 85–90 per cent of parents in their N.I.M.H. series as parents of schizophrenics, neurotics or normals (Wynne, 1968). TABLE 27 summarizes Wynne and Singer's most recent results for subjects tested to date at the N.I.M.H. and is reproduced below to emphasize how completely the Deviance Scores of their parents of schizophrenics differed from those of parents of neurotics.

In contrast to Singer and Wynne's results we found that 15 parents of schizophrenics, or 8 parental pairs, had very low Deviance Scores, well below the median for the groups combined.

TABLE 27

N.I.M.H. SAMPLE, PARENTS AS PAIRS, 41-CATEGORY
RORSCHACH SCORING

(Wynne, personal communication)

	TYPICAL SCHIZO-PHRENICS	BORDER-LINE	NEUROTIC	NORMAL	TOTAL
Above median	44	12	0	1	57
Below median	0	13	25	19	57
TOTAL	44	25	25	20	114

We must, of course, consider how we obtained such different results from the N.I.M.H. group.

SCORING TRANSCRIPTS

Possibly the first place to look for discrepancies in an attempt at replication is in the scoring of test material. We went to unusual lengths to learn the scoring method. We discussed examples of scoring in person and compared our scoring of transcripts with those of Singer and Wynne for the same protocols. We had the benefit of their criticism of our scoring and after we went through the 41-category Rorschach manual we prepared a list of modifications and classifications [see APPENDIX I] which they approved. Finally, Margaret Singer very generously took the time to score our entire sample. Her results, whether they were based on the scores alone or on a guess based on information we gave her subsequently as to which parents were pairs, were very close to ours.

The comparison of her results with ours is set out in TABLES 28 and 29.

TABLE 28

MEDIAN TEST, UNITED KINGDOM DATA SCORED BY
UNITED STATES AND UNITED KINGDOM RATERS

	NO. OF SUBJECTS SCORING						
	BELOW THE MEDIAN		ABOVE THE MEDIAN				
	Schiz.	Neuro-tics	Schiz.	Neuro-tics	Median score	χ^2	Sig.
Singer's scores	16	24	24	16	0·77	3·20	<0·1
Our scores	16	25	24	15	0·85	4·05	<0·05

TABLE 29

COMPARISON OF GROUPS ON DEVIANCE SCORE, UNITED KINGDOM
DATA SCORED BY UNITED STATES AND UNITED KINGDOM RATERS

| | MEAN DEVIANCE SCORE | | | |
	Schiz.	*Neurotics*	*t*	*Sig.*
Singer's scores	1·14 ±0·74	0·84 ±0·77	1·553	<0·10
Our scores	1·33 ±0·99	0·88 ±0·82	2·214	<0·025

TABLE 30 shows Singer's revised results after we provided her with a
listing showing which protocols belonged together as parental pairs and
giving the sex and age of the subjects. Her first set of predictions was made
on the 80 individual protocols without this information [TABLES 28 and 29].
In 20 cases where one parent had a low score and one parent a high score she
made a prediction of the child's diagnosis based on a consideration of the two
parents' 'over-all communication pattern' without a detailed consideration of
the manual scores. Included in this analysis then were 'features that do not
reach the level of scorability and this also gives an impressionistic weight to
some features as more discriminating than others' (letter from Dr. Wynne).
Singer's results based on a knowledge of which parents were pairs are presented in TABLE 30, which shows that she made 24 correct predictions and 16

TABLE 30

SINGER'S DIAGNOSTIC PREDICTIONS MADE AFTER SCORING
TRANSCRIPTS AND BEING INFORMED OF THE PARENTAL PAIRS

| | PATIENT'S CLINICAL DIAGNOSIS | | |
PREDICTED DIAGNOSIS	*Schizophrenic*	*Neurotic*	*Total*
Schizophrenic	12	9	21
Neurotic	7	12	19
TOTAL	19	21	40

$\chi^2 = 1·726$ n.s.

incorrect ones. This is no better than her results based on a consideration of
parents' scores separately, and is identical to the number of couples we correctly placed above and below the median of the combined couples' scores.
The product-moment correlation between Dr. Singer's scores and ours was
+0·77. This is of the same order as the correlation coefficient for inter-rater
reliability we reported between our own scores (0·87). The correlation coefficient was only negligibly different when we used log transformation or
inter-class correlation coefficients (Dr. Wynne's colleagues kindly computed
this for us).

We can conclude that for the purposes of determining the Deviance Score,
we achieved a satisfactorily high correlation between our scoring and Dr.

Singer's. *The difference between our results therefore cannot be due to our failure to apply their scoring techniques correctly.*

I.Q.

Another possible source of difference between the present study and that of Singer and Wynne is that parents of schizophrenics and neurotics in this series did not differ on I.Q. Wild *et al.* (1965) controlled for I.Q. in their study but they compared parents of schizophrenics with parents of normals. Schopler and Loftin's study (1969), discussed in CHAPTER I, suggests that parents of normals are not suitable as the only control group because of the effect that differences in attitude towards the testing situation have on measures of thought and association. The I.Q.s of subjects were not tested in the Houston sample, or in the N.I.M.H. sample. As discussed in CHAPTER I and CHAPTER V, differences in I.Q. between groups may be important in explaining differences in Deviance Score found in previous studies. The findings of the present study were not sufficient to reach a conclusion on this point.

DIFFERENCE IN TESTING

After examining our protocols and listening to tape recordings of our interviews, Wynne and Singer suggested that our attempt at replication was inadequate because of the way we administered the Rorschach test (Wynne, Dorado Beach High Risk Conference, 18–22 October 1972 and personal communication). He asserted that during the First Period of testing our method put constraints on the patients and inhibited the expression of deviances and defects which might otherwise have occurred. In the Second Period we encouraged the subjects to respond beyond the point of spontaneous expression, again introducing an artefact of distortion. Furthermore, he questioned whether there might be special cultural differences such that people in the United Kingdom are more deferential and inhibited in the presence of authority-figures such as doctors than people in the United States. There seem to be certain assumptions in this point of view. The first is that under the right conditions of testing large differences between groups, not hitherto apparent, would emerge which would not disappear when the effect of word counts was partialled out. From this it must follow that since the two groups in our study were found to have similar distributions of their Deviance Scores then the conditions of testing must be inhibiting the expression of defects and deviances more in one group than the other. One test of this would be to see if altering the condition of testing would affect one group more than the other. But we did just this when we changed our technique from the First Period to the Second. FIGURE 7.6 shows that in our study both groups responded to the change in technique with a significant increase in D-Scores, *but they were both affected to the same extent* (note the lines are parallel). The analysis of variance showed that a significant change took place only in the Enquiry part of the test when the technique was altered, not in the First Viewing [FIG. 7.6]. This supports the view that it was the change of technique which caused the increase in scores. However, Wynne and Singer's hypothesis about the effect of our testing technique requires that the two groups be affected differentially, which was clearly not the case.

We should state at this point that we have analysed Singer and Wynne's data for fathers from their N.I.M.H. sample for their neurotic and schizophrenic groups. We confirmed that the United States data revealed differences between the D-Scores of neurotics' and schizophrenics' parents. We also found high correlations between D-Scores and word counts, but the difference in word counts between their groups did not account for the differences in D-Scores they found.

DETAILED COMPARISON OF THE UNITED STATES AND UNITED KINGDOM DATA

The main differences between the United States (N.I.M.H.) sample and the United Kingdom sample are that there is a higher correlation between d/r and w in the London samples, and that the United States sample has a greater proportion of subjects with high d/r and w scores on each part of the Rorschach test and a greater within-group variance.

We can test the null hypothesis that the groups come from the same population taking any combination of two groups at a time. For this purpose we have chosen the Mann–Whitney U-test because in several cases the variances differed significantly between groups (starred) and therefore the t-test was not applicable. We have only tested the fathers' scores because they discriminated best between schizophrenics and neurotics in both the United States and the United Kingdom samples [TABLE 31].

TABLE 31

t-tests or Mann–Whitney U-tests for differences in means: degrees of freedom for $t = n_i + n_j = 2$ where n_i and n_j are the sample sizes of groups i and j which are compared.

COMPARISON OF WORD COUNTS OF UNITED STATES AND UNITED KINGDOM DIAGNOSTIC GROUPS

FIRST VIEWING WORD COUNT

| | | U.S. | | | U.K. | |
		Dx 3	Dx 5	Dx 6–7	N	S
U.S.	Dx 3		0·62	1·76	0·98	
	Dx 5					0·06
	Dx 6–7					1·16
U.K.	N					1·57
	S					

TABLE 31 (*Cont.*)

ENQUIRY WORD COUNT

	Dx 3	Dx 5	Dx 6–7	N	S
Dx 3		0·36	0·27	1·19	
Dx 5					0·68
Dx 6–7					0·16*
N					0·79
S					

FIRST VIEWING D-SCORE

	Dx 3	Dx 5	Dx 6–7	N	S
Dx 3		4·80*	5·50*	0·44*	
Dx 5					1·78
Dx 6–7					3·81
N					1·87
S					

ENQUIRY D-SCORE

	Dx 3	Dx 5	Dx 6–7	N	S
Dx 3		5·49*	5·31*	1·83*	
Dx 5					2·45
Dx 6–7					3·10
N					1·29
S					

U.S. {
Dx 3 = Neurotics
Dx 5 = Remitting schizophrenics
Dx 6–7 = Non-remitting schizophrenics

U.K. {
N = Neurotic
S = Schizophrenic

Fathers of

Figures underlined —— are significant at the 0·05 level or better, and underlined ══ at the 0·01 level or better.

* Denotes that the variances differ significantly so the t-test is not used. The tables above give the standard normal deviate, z, derived from the Mann–Whitney U-test.

There were no significant differences between the word counts of the United States schizophrenics and the United States neurotics, or between the United States schizophrenics and United Kingdom schizophrenics in the First Viewing or the Enquiry. There were however, significant differences in the Deviance Scores between schizophrenics and neurotics within the United States sample, and between United States schizophrenics (Dx 6–7) and United Kingdom schizophrenics. The exception was the comparison between the United States remitting schizophrenics (Dx 5) and United Kingdom schizophrenics in the First Viewing, where the difference in D-Score was not significant. Incidentally it is worth noting that on this test the difference within the United Kingdom sample between parents of neurotics and schizophrenics on the First Viewing (z = 1·87, p = 0·061) just fails to reach significance because the statistic used is slightly less powerful and therefore more conservative than the t-test used earlier to analyse our results [see p. 134].

TABLE 32 shows the results of an analysis of co-variance between the Deviance scores of the United Kingdom schizophrenics' parents and the United States schizophrenics' parents (Dx 5, 6, 7) in which the contribution of word counts to the variance is taken out. This confirms that the differences

TABLE 32

ANALYSES OF CO-VARIANCE, WHERE WORD COUNT IS THE CO-VARIATE

FIRST VIEWING DEVIANCE SCORE: 2 GROUPS VIZ. U.K. SCHIZO. AND U.S. DX 5–7

Source	SS	d.f.	M.S.	F	
Co-variate	552541·70	1		71·02	p<0·01
Between groups	103696·13	1		13·33	p<0·01
Residual	474555·92	61	7779·61		
TOTAL	1130793·75	63			

ENQUIRY DEVIANCE SCORE: 2 GROUPS AS ABOVE

Source	SS	d.f.	M.S.	F	
Co-variate	625618·58	1		89·37	p<0·01
Between groups	99386·19	1		14·20	p<0·01
Residual	427028·17	61	7000·46		
TOTAL	1152032·94	63			

U.S. Dx 5–7 and U.K. schizophrenics differ significantly in D-Score even after word counts are partialled out.
Hence the difference between United States and United Kingdom schizophrenics' Deviance Scores is not accounted for by differences in word counts.

in the D-Scores remain significant between groups and cannot be accounted for by differences in word counts. TABLE 33 shows comparisons between the Deviance Rates (d/w) of the respective United States and United Kingdom groups. TABLE 34 gives the means and standard deviations of the Deviance Rates for the First Viewing and Enquiry by diagnostic group. It can be seen that in both parts of the Rorschach the ordinal relationship of d/w scores is: United States Dx 3; United Kingdom N; United Kingdom S; United States Dx 5; United States Dx 6–7; with the mean d/w for the United Kingdom schizophrenics' parents falling between United States Dx 3 and Dx 5 for both parts of the test. TABLE 33 shows that the Deviance Rates (d/w) of the United States and United Kingdom samples have different characteristics,

TABLE 33

The distributions of d/w tend to have variances which increase with the mean. The results of significance tests between groups are listed below, and the means and variances are listed for each group for Initial Viewing and Enquiry d/w.

First Viewing   Dx 3 with neurotic $F_{19, 24} = 2 \cdot 16 \ p < 0 \cdot 05$
(i.e. variances different)

             Dx 5 with schizophrenic $t_{42} = 3 \cdot 15 \ p < 0 \cdot 05$
(variances not significantly different, but means different)

             Dx 6–7 with schizophrenic $F_{19, 19} = 3 \cdot 33 \ p < 0 \cdot 05$
(variances different)

Enquiry   Dx 3 with neurotic $t_{43} = 2 \cdot 88 \ p < 0 \cdot 05$
(variances not different, means different)

             Dx 5 with schizophrenic $F_{23, 19} = 3 \cdot 93 \ p < 0 \cdot 05$
(variances different)

             Dx 6–7 with schizophrenic $F_{19, 19} = 13 \cdot 95 \ p < 0 \cdot 001$
(variances different)

TABLE 34

MEANS AND STANDARD DEVIATIONS FOR DEVIANCE RATES OF PARENTS OF UNITED STATES AND UNITED KINGDOM DIAGNOSTIC GROUPS

First Viewing		Dx 3	Dx 5	Dx 6–7	N	S
	$\bar{x}$	0·19	0·53	0·69	0·25	0·32
	s	0·14	0·05	0·17	0·04	0·05
Enquiry						
	$\bar{x}$	0·13	0·58	0·87	0·24	0·31
	s	0·01	0·21	0·74	0·02	0·05
		N.I.M.H.			London	

especially in that the variance of the United States schizophrenics' parents is significantly greater than the variance of the United Kingdom parents of schizophrenics, and the means of the United States groups are greater. These comparisons can be summarized as follows. *The United States data reveal differences between the D-Score of neurotics' and schizophrenics' parents. The United Kingdom data (using this statistic) do not. In both sets of data there are high correlations between D-Score and word count. However, differences in word count between groups from the two centres do not account for differences in D-Score* (see analysis of co-variance).

In a word, the United States parents of schizophrenics score significantly more deviances per words spoken than the United Kingdom parents of schizophrenics. Had the United Kingdom schizophrenics' parents scored as high as the United States ones, the discrimination between the parents of neurotic controls and schizophrenics in the United Kingdom sample would have resembled the United States findings.

From a further analysis we carried out on the United States data (not given here) we can confirm that there are no significant differences between neurotic and schizophrenic parents within the United States sample except on age— the schizophrenics' parents are older. (The other variables considered are social class, occupation, education, and parent's diagnosis.) None of the social variables is significantly associated with D-Score in the United States data.

Thus a detailed examination of the data does not reveal the reason for the discrepancies between the United States and United Kingdom data, but confirms that there are differences between the fathers of schizophrenics in the two samples.

DIAGNOSTIC AND SAMPLING DIFFERENCES BETWEEN CENTRES

If these hypotheses prove insufficient to explain our failure to confirm Singer and Wynne's results, there are two further explanations to consider. It could be that we are not testing comparable groups of patients or of parents, either because of diagnostic differences between our samples or because of selection bias in one of them.

Indeed, TABLES 31–34 confirm that there are significant differences between the parents of patients we diagnose as schizophrenic and the parents of their schizophrenics. Originally we interpreted these differences as being due to differences in method rather than true differences in the populations being sampled. Wynne (personal communication) still holds this point of view in so far as he ascribes our failure to replicate their findings to our method of testing. While our neurotics produce only slightly more deviances than their neurotic controls, their three groups of schizophrenics' parents score considerably higher than ours and have a significantly greater variance in their D-Scores [TABLE 33]. There is no evidence to support Wynne's suggestion that the way we gave the test, however similar or different it was from the N.I.M.H. technique, affected the comparison between our groups of parents.

From a statistical point of view the D-Scores indicate that our schizophrenics do not belong to the same population as theirs.

Is there any other reason to think that we may not be sampling groups of patients comparable with the United States samples?

There have been several careful international diagnostic studies recently which have shown that American-trained psychiatrists diagnose schizophrenia in a much larger proportion of cases than British (twice as much) and most other European-trained psychiatrists (Hordern *et al.*, 1968; Kendell *et al.*, 1971; Cooper *et al.*, 1972). The W.H.O. International Pilot Study of Schizophrenia, in which Wynne and his colleagues participated, also confirms these results (W.H.O., 1973). It follows that Singer and Wynne may have included among their schizophrenics patients we would diagnose as having personality disorders. If we hypothesize that high rates of communication defects and deviances may be related more to personality factors than to schizophrenia, defined in the strict way we use the term, then Singer and Wynne's more impressive results could be due to cases we would diagnose as personality disorder and not as schizophrenia. In this study we confined ourselves to schizophrenics with clearly developed symptoms and signs; 17 out of 20 of our schizophrenics had florid hallucinations and delusions of the type Schnieder (1957) defined as symptoms of the first rank. The recently completed W.H.O. International Pilot Study of Schizophrenia showed that well over 90 per cent of patients with these characteristics would be diagnosed as schizophrenic by psychiatrists from the 9 countries who participated, including the two whose diagnostic practices differed most from the others, namely the Soviet Union and the United States. If the United States study depends on patients who are in many ways different from the United Kingdom sample, then we have chosen the wrong group of patients if we want to replicate their findings.

Alternatively it could be that our control series, which consists of hospitalized patients diagnosed as suffering from neuroses and depression, contains a number of patients that American psychiatrists would call 'Borderline schizophrenia'. In their sample half the parents of borderline patients had scores which overlapped those of schizophrenic parents [see TABLE 27]. Wynne says that patients with the borderline syndrome would be diagnosed as severe personality disorders or as neurosis in Great Britain (personal communication). Although patients with a principal diagnosis of personality disorder were not included in our study the argument would be that we failed to confirm previous findings because our neurotic control group was more deviant than Singer and Wynne's. In fact our control series' mean Deviance scores were scarcely different from those of normal medical students we have tested (Leff and Hirsch, 1972) and are close to the scores of neurotics and normals in Wynne's series, so that, whether true or not, this possibility does little to explain the difference in results, which is mainly due to the comparatively low scores of our parents of schizophrenics.

We have mentioned the possibility of diagnostic differences between our samples, but there is the further possibility of sampling bias which we have not discussed. This could lead to a tendency to select patients or have them referred because of Wynne's unit's known interest in families of schizophrenics and communication disorder. The other possibility is that the sample of schizophrenics is not representative of schizophrenics in general but is biased to include chronic, more severely disturbed patients. Wynne's sample is derived from referrals to his research unit where there is an emphasis on family therapy. Parents of patients must be prepared to co-operate in research and they often participate in psychotherapy when their son or daughter comes to the unit. There is no mention in any of Wynne and Singer's papers of measures taken to avoid the obvious problems of sampling bias which this source of subjects collected over several years must have created. For example, included in Wynne's sample is a special group of patients admitted to another N.I.M.H. unit where they were studied because they were identical twins discordant for schizophrenia; another source of patients was the admission roster of St. Elizabeth's Hospital, the 'state hospital' for Washington, D.C.; and a further sample of patients was derived from referrals from hospitals in the surrounding area. Some of these have a strong psychoanalytic bias (e.g. Chestnut Lodge) and sent patients in response to letters inviting referrals. Others came as referrals from privately practising psychiatrists in the surrounding community, and in other cases the patients were N.I.M.H. admissions who were assigned to various units according to their research interests.

It can be argued that our sample is less open to bias than those of previous studies. The cases were drawn from three psychiatric units which share a local responsibility for a catchment area in London. In addition the international reputation of one of the hospitals (The Maudsley) as a university teaching centre meant that many of the cases which came under consideration in the selection procedure were drawn from other areas as well. However, such cases would be referred because of the hospital's general reputation, and not one in any way pertaining specifically to schizophrenia. Since all eligible cases in the hospitals were systematically included in the series, it is extremely unlikely that any bias towards the inclusion of families with abnormalities of language or communication would be present. This is especially so if one considers the strictness of the selection procedures and the high response rate of 97·5 per cent.

This may not be the case in either the Yale (Wild et al., 1965) or N.I.M.H. sample (Wynne 1971). We are not told of any steps taken to exclude such bias in these investigations. On the other hand it seems possible that centres with an international reputation for their studies of thought and language disorder in families of schizophrenics would be prone to have patients referred to them because such abnormalities had already been noted in the patients elsewhere.

Our patients tended to be acutely ill, 18 of them (45 per cent) experiencing their first admission and none having spent more than a year in hospital during any previous admission. Wynne et al. (to be published) report that 75 per cent of the first degree relatives of their non-remitting schizophrenics and 25 per cent of the relatives of remitting schizophrenics were diagnosed as being schizophrenic themselves. While we did not give a diagnostic interview to any of our parents, the previous history was checked during the selection process. Only one parent of a schizophrenic (and none of the neurotics) had a psychotic illness.

In November and December 1971 we again visited Wynne's unit and carefully examined the case notes of 10 schizophrenic index cases used in their study. At the time the following impressions emerged and were discussed with Dr. Wynne.

1. Their patients were very ill in the sense of psychiatric disability; many of them had spent several years in hospital.
2. It was not their practice to record detailed descriptions of the patient's hallucinations or delusions; in no case was there positive evidence of first rank symptoms in the notes.
3. Many patients were chronic, and had been transferred from other hospitals.
4. Patients were not necessarily evaluated by the research team at a time of florid illness—they may have been chronically ill when they came into the study so the diagnosis was based on past history and symptoms other than delusions and hallucinations.
5. In some cases we would disagree about the diagnosis. For example, the notes of one patient diagnosed as non-relapsing schizophrenia suggested to us that she had been brain damaged at 8 years old and now had an adult autistic syndrome; another patient we thought was a chronic obsessive–compulsive neurotic.

Discussing these impressions with Dr. Wynne, we reached agreement on the conclusion that we were looking at different kinds of patients. In the United Kingdom sample acute psychoses predominated; the patients did not by and large have long-standing illnesses. The United States sample seemed to be more disturbed with chronic conditions, in which florid symptoms were not so prominent. In our study we gave more diagnostic importance to florid symptoms, while in theirs the emphasis was on the 'enduring qualities' of personality abnormality which the United States workers regard as schizophrenic in nature.

These are, of course, little more than our shared impressions and they may not be correct. They are interesting because they fit in with our findings in the review of the literature. The evidence for an association between clinical, personality, or interactional abnormality in the parents and schizophrenia in the offspring was strongest for the group of schizophrenic patients with a poor prognosis, or poor premorbid personality, and for chronically hospitalized schizophrenics. The comparisons we have reported in this chapter between the N.I.M.H. results and our own tend to support this interpretation. Our schizophrenics scored closest to the United States remitting schizophrenics (Dx 5) both in the number of deviances and in the Deviance Rate. Diagnostically Dx 5 is likely to be the group that most closely resembles the

United Kingdom schizophrenics which, as a group, had a low frequency of chronic disability and long-term hospitalization in their previous histories. Therefore, it is important that future studies in this field pay greater attention to the distinction between chronic disabilities and acute manifestations of schizophrenia in their patients.

Wynne places a different emphasis on our findings. He points out that while we discuss our results as a failure to replicate their findings, in fact we did find a significant difference between groups and to that extent *have* replicated their results. He stresses that they too find an overlap between groups in that half the patients they diagnosed as borderline have parents scoring in the schizophrenic range.

As stated above, we do not use the 'Borderline' category. If our neurotics were really borderline, our finding and theirs would be very similar. However, we cannot agree with his formulation for the reasons stated above, namely that it is the low score of our schizophrenics which distinguishes our results from theirs [see TABLE 31]; our parents of neurotics are not significantly more deviant in their communication than theirs.

THE HOUSTON SAMPLE

Our discussion in this chapter has focused on the N.I.M.H. sample, as this represents Singer and Wynne's most recent work. In PART I of this monograph when discussing their work we mentioned their Houston sample. In some way it has advantages over the N.I.M.H. series because there is less likelihood of a bias towards family and communication disorder. The patients were all in a Veterans' Administration Hospital and the Rorschachs were collected as a small part of a much larger study by workers unconnected with Singer and Wynne. The main limitation is that the interviews were taken down by hand rather than tape-recorded and transcribed. Furthermore, there is not sufficient information about the diagnostic criteria for schizophrenia. Our interest in the results for this sample lies in the fact that they are much closer to our own.

For example, Singer and Wynne (1966b) report that the proportion of individual parents in the Houston sample correctly classified using scores from the First Responses was 64 per cent. This compares closely to 61 per cent in our study. They had better success when they considered the parents as pairs, in which case they correctly classified 78 per cent of cases compared to 62·5 per cent in the present series (Singer and Wynne, 1966b). Even more interesting is the fact that when the fathers' scores and mothers' scores were separately compared for differences between groups, there was a significant difference between fathers of schizophrenics and neurotics at the 0·05 level but the scores of mothers did not differ significantly. This is exactly what was found in the present study. Nevertheless, it does seem that their distribution had considerably less overlap than ours in so far as only 42 per cent of their parents of neurotics scored above the lowest scoring schizophrenic (Wynne,

1967). At our request Wynne has re-examined the Houston data to see what relationship there was between words and D-Score in this sample. The analysis confirmed Wynne and Singer's findings in their N.I.M.H. sample that the word count is not a crucial variable; the difference between groups in the D-Score of the Houston sample was unaffected by an analysis which took out the effect of word counts.

The results of this study therefore stand somewhere between Wynne and Singer's N.I.M.H. results and our own findings from the London sample. An attempt to clarify the significance of the Houston sample is confounded by the dearth of detailed information about the range and variation of the D-Scores, and diagnostic details of the sample. We also have reservations about the fact that the subject's responses to Rorschach testing were hand-written rather than tape-recorded and transcribed. The fact that the Houston findings more closely approximate to ours than do the N.I.M.H. results give weight to our view that sampling bias may be an important source of differences between these studies.

CONCLUSION

Turning now to our positive results, we still have to inquire why the fathers of neurotics and schizophrenics in our study used significantly different numbers of words. In a further study (Leff and Hirsch, 1972) of normal subjects we found evidence that the fathers of neurotics were not speaking significantly less than the norm. Hence the difference between them and the schizophrenics' fathers must be due to the excessive verbosity of the latter. It is difficult to ascribe this to a testing artefact as both groups were tested and scored blindly. The place of testing was not the same for all subjects, but again the blind procedures should have eliminated any difference this might have made to the results. If the verbosity of the schizophrenics' fathers is not due to an artefact then it may have an important bearing on aetiology. Pressure of speech in a parent may increase the likelihood of bringing out a schizophrenic abnormality in an otherwise vulnerable offspring. Alternatively it may represent in the father one of numerous genetic factors which contribute additively to a predisposition to schizophrenia in the child. Any explanation which is offered must take account of the fact that about a third of parents of schizophrenics had low Deviance Scores and a similar proportion of neurotics had high Deviance Scores.

Though the findings of this study do not readily suggest an hypothesis about the aetiology of schizophrenia it is important that we do not overlook the fact that under carefully controlled conditions a significant difference did emerge between the groups studied. Further studies are indicated to see if the findings reported here can be repeated in another series, here and elsewhere.

It should be emphasized that our results are incompatible with Wynne and

Singer's 'transactional' hypothesis. [See PART I, CHAPTER V.] They contend that an inability to share a focus of attention, characterized by disruptions, distractions, irrelevance, ambiguities and lack of closure in the speech of parents of schizophrenics, contributes in a crucial way to the experimental factors which predispose to the development of schizophrenia (Singer and Wynne, 1966*a* and *b*; Wynne, 1967, 1968, 1971). They believe that their finding that all parents of schizophrenics have high Deviance Scores supplies the most important evidence to date for their hypothesis that communication disorder in the parents predisposes to schizophrenia in the child. We failed to find the same degree of gross communication disorder in an unbiased sample of parents of schizophrenics. If *our* results are correct then either the theory must be modified to state that communication disorder characterizes the parents of only some schizophrenics, or we must assume that the 41-category Rorschach technique identifies disordered speech in the parents of schizophrenics only on certain occasions, or only in certain parents. Since there is no other adequate evidence for communication deviances in parents, admitting shortcomings in the 41-category Rorschach method is tantamount to accepting that speech abnormalities are only demonstrable in a proportion of parents of schizophrenics. At the same time one must remember that we have shown that a relatively large proportion of parents of neurotics also have high scores. If the present findings are corroborated elsewhere, the conclusion will follow that this technique does not distinguish parents of schizophrenics from other groups to an extent which is likely to be useful for identifying individual subjects for genetic or environmental studies. These issues can now only be resolved by a fresh study designed to answer the questions which our work has raised.

APPENDIX 1

ADDITIONAL CONVENTIONS FOR USE OF THE SINGER AND WYNNE MANUAL

When learning the scoring method outlined in the manual for scoring communication defects and deviances (Singer and Wynne, 1966a), we prepared the following list of modifications to their classification of deviances and the rules for scoring them. The purpose was to clarify areas which we found ambiguous and thereby to reproduce their scoring procedure more reliably. Singer and Wynne agreed to these changes before we began the study proper. They may be of value to workers who wish to use the manual for further studies.

1. Raters will not be told the education or social class of subjects as we are unable to see how this would affect our scoring. Moreover, we are taking it into account in the analysis of our results to see what contribution it makes to the variance.

2. We will not score inaudible material unless the tester indicates in some way that the S. is disrupting the procedure by talking too softly or mumbling, e.g. if tester asks the S. to speak up more than twice in a response. Our reason is that there is considerable background noise and the quality of the tapes is sometimes poor. Wherever possible, abnormalities will be identified by their overt, immediate or surface meaning rather than by what the rater can guess was intended.

3. A given score is only counted once in any single response, that is, it will only contribute to the Deviance Score for that response. When it seems possible to assign either of two closely related or mutually exclusive categories to a single deviance, assign the less pathological, e.g. correcting a simple slip of the tongue (314) may make an abnormally structured sentence (311) normal, so 314 would be assigned. Sometimes, two or more instances of an abnormality appear within a single response which differ in character from each other but are nevertheless varieties of the same category. If it seems possible to assign to each of them one or two different but closely related categories instead of the same one, do so (e.g. 212 and 213, 310 and 312, 181 and 183, 194 and 196). This will weight the scoring more appropriately.

4. Words which seem likely to be typing errors and are not identified by a [sic] will not be scored as 315 or 314, e.g. 'extended' instead of 'extent'.

5. Card rejections. These will only be counted as a response if the subject makes a statement of some sort in the process of rejection. A brief 'Nothing', or 'No', will not count as a response.

6. 110 (a)—Score as a fragment a false start on a sentence which nevertheless has a subject and a verb already given—even if the fragment is immediately corrected. If there are not both a subject and a verb in a false start or possible fragment, we will only score it if there are at least two fully formed incomplete or false starts to the sentence, e.g. 'I just, you see it, it looks like a bat'. 110 (c)—If only a short word such as 'or' or 'to' is left out of a sentence, score 314. If a key word such as a subject or verb or a phrase has clearly been left out of a sentence which would otherwise be complete and normal, score 110, rather than 311 (e.g. Mr. A. I. 1. (p. 2) 3rd sentence):* 'I see where it would (x) with the wing coming out of the tail'. Sentence would be correct if x = 'look like that'.

---

* The reference here is to transcripts of parents which Singer and Wynne sent us for practice scoring.

7. 140—This is given to responses when it is the only possibility or when there is a gross over-all indefiniteness or tentativeness to the passage in addition to more specific deviances within.

8. 160—Certain conditionals or subjunctives are used colloquially as a way of giving an answer and should not be scored 160 unless an 'if' clause is added, e.g. don't score 'I would say that looks like a bat'. But score 'I would say a bat if it was all one colour'. 170 and 212—Are not scored for rhetorical questions on the way to giving a response.

9. 181—Use to score information in the Enquiry which is contradictory to information during the First Viewing, e.g. 1st View: 'He only has two arms and a head'. Enquiry: 'Here is his leg'.

10. 182—If S. refers to 'What I said before' in making a response without specifying what he is referring to, assign 182.

11. 193—This may be used if the subject assigns a label to a blot but then disqualifies the use of the term, e.g. 'That looks like an antennae but I don't know what they are called'. If the S. identifies his uncertainty about the use of a term so the listener is made aware of his possible error, the item may not be scored, e.g. 'I think they look like antlers, or do you call them antennae. I'm not sure of the right terms'.

12. 212 and 213
181 and 183   Scores which have a lot of overlap and will therefore
110 and 311   be regarded as equivalent for reliability ratings.
193, 194 and 196

13. 211—Only to be used when the interruption is obvious from the transcript or is starred by the typist, in which case it will always be scored.

14. 195—In the inquiry we won't score 195 if the subject simply moves on to the next response he remembers that he gave, and the tester does not object or indicate the S. has wrongfully gone ahead. It would seem to us that if a subject is once allowed to go ahead by the tester before the next item is introduced he may then get a set that this is allowed and continue to do it. Since this may largely depend on the tester it seems best not to score such transactions.

15. Do not score a qualification such as: 'Somehow or other, I don't know why, but I thought of a chimney'.

16. 212–0—Certain very common comments like 'So many of these cards look like bats' will not be scored if they are made in connection with a more specific response.

17. 212—S.'s reference to a personal experience. This is scored (+) in the First Viewing, but in the Enquiry it will be allowed (212–0) if the statement is brief and immediately relevant to an explanation of how or why S. saw the blot the way he did.

18. 220—Score if a S. pushes on to another response in the inquiry despite the tester's clear indication not to do so, then or previously, thus taking over the tester's role.

19. (270 v. 320) In addition to its use in manual, we will use category 270 if the S. wrongly assumes that there is something which the blots are or are not meant to look like, e.g. 'There are never any men in these drawings', as if one would expect there to be (Mr. C. X. 5). Also assign 270 if the S. indicates a familiarity with a specific aspect of a blot, e.g. 'Oh, that old boy again' or 'Hello, you again'. However, if the S. is simply indicating recognition of the blots in general, e.g. 'I remember this one too'—don't score the first time but score 320 if it is repeated more than once—as in M.R.'s transcript.

20. 250—Only for references within one response referring to another response.

Simply getting the topics of the First Viewing out of order in the Enquiry will not be scored.

21. Use of 'your'. This is only scored 280 when there is an implied or stated reference to the intent of some party external to the examiner and subject. The colloquial use of 'your' as an impersonal pronoun instead of 'its' or 'the' in describing the blot won't be scored, e.g. 'Here are your eyes, here, here are your arms' (Mr. R.). A change of pronoun would be scored 182—such as 'Here are *your* eyes, here are *its* arms'.

22. 310—If S. uses a wrong term without immediately correcting it, assign 310 unless it is a slip of the tongue (314), e.g. 'It looks like the *pancreas* after the birth of a child' meaning 'placenta'.

23. 311—For small parts of speech which throw listener off—assign 311, e.g. 'That's what it reminded (me?) of it' (Mr. S. V. 2).

24. 320—A stutter or stammer up to 3 times will not be scored, e.g. 'It reminds me of skulls of a, of a, of a cow'. Short phrases of three or more words repeated three or more times consecutively, or repeated three or more times within a response will be scored. Larger phrases and sentences, whether exactly repeated or only approximately repeated, will also be scored. Avoid when there is back and forth exchange with examiner. A rejection may be repeated twice without a penalty.

25. There are several types of somewhat cryptic abnormal remarks which are common and often require multiple scoring:

Examples are: (a) 'looks like grade school'   (317)
                           'reminds me of a state'   (317 and 319)
             (b) 'looks like an abstract'   (317 and 319)
             (c) 'looks like a gink'   (317 and 312)
             (d) 'looks like an ink blot'   (270)
                           'looks like someone has put an ink on paper and blotted it'   (270)

In (d) the S. is reacting to the concrete aspect of the blot rather than what he sees it as.

             (e) 'the flowering business'
                   'the head business'
                   'the skeleton part'
                   'the head part'

These are not scored if part of a larger response in which the meaning is clear. If the meaning is not made more specific score 319. If the phrase stands alone as the complete response, a third score 317 should also be added.

APPENDIX 2

EDUCATION SCALE

The Hollingshead Scale as adapted for subjects educated in Great Britain.

HOLLINGSHEAD DEFINITION	BRITISH DEFINITION	7PT SCALE SCORE
Professional training	Professional training at postgraduate level	1
College graduate	University graduate, Higher National Certificate, diploma in professional training, e.g., teaching or social work	2
Some college	'A' level in 2 or more subjects, attended higher education without getting qualifications, higher matriculation	3
High School graduate	'O' level in 5 or more subjects, matriculation	4
10–11 years of school, some High School	Grammar School, Secondary Modern at least 1 year beyond minimum leaving age. Less than 5 'O' levels, any 'O' levels	5
7–9 years of school, grade school graduate	Did not progress beyond minimum leaving age. No 'O' levels	6
Under 7 years of school, some grade school	Subnormal, special schools	7 (exclude from study)

APPENDIX 3

SOCIAL CLASS OCCUPATION SCALE

REGISTRAR GENERAL	HOLLINGSHEAD–REDLICH	SCALE SCORE
Professional	Higher executive, proprietor of large concern, major professionals	1
Intermediate professional Managers	Business managers, proprietors of medium sized businesses, lesser professionals	2
Manager/Owner small concern	Administrative personnel, small independent businesses, minor professionals	3
Skilled manual	Clerical and sales workers, technicians, owners of little businesses	4
Skilled non-manual	Skilled manual	5
Semi-skilled manual	Machine operator and semi-skilled	6
Unskilled manual and unemployed	Unskilled employees	7

The families' social position is determined from the fathers' 2-factor score:

2-FACTOR SCORE	SOCIAL POSITION
11–17	I
18–31	II
32–47	III
48–63	IV
64–77	V

Calculate the 2-factor score by the formula:

$$\text{2-factor Score} = (\text{Education rating} \times 4) + (\text{Occupation rating} \times 7)$$

APPENDIX 4

CATEGORIES OF COMMUNICATION DEFECTS AND DEVIANCES
(Adapted from Singer, 1967)

I. CLOSURE PROBLEMS

110 Speech fragments
120 Unintelligible remarks
130 Unstable percepts
140 Gross indefiniteness and tentativeness
150 Responses in negative form
160 Subjunctive, 'if', 'might-response'
170 Questions response or tester about response
181 Contradictory information
182 Inconsistent and ambiguous references or shifting points of reference
183 Incompatible alternatives or images

DISQUALIFICATIONS

191 'Derogatory', disparaging, critical remarks, if disqualifying
192 Nihilistic remarks
193 Failures to verify own responses or perception
194 Explicit retractions and denials
195 Forgetting responses or adding additional ones in the Enquiry
196 Implicit partial disqualifications

II. DISRUPTIVE BEHAVIOUR

211 Interruptions of Examiner's speech
212 Extraneous questions and remarks
213 Odd, tangential, inappropriate remarks or answers to questions
220 Non-verbal, disruptive behaviour
230 Humour
240 Swearing
250 Hopping around among responses
260 Negativistic, temporary card rejection followed by a response
270 Concrete-set responses
280 References to 'they' and to the intent of others

III. PECULIAR LANGUAGE AND LOGIC

A. PECULIAR WORD USAGES, CONSTRUCTIONS AND PRONUNCIATION

310 Ordinary words or phrases used oddly or out of context
311 Odd sentence construction
312 Peculiar or quaint, private terms or phrases. Neologisms
313 Euphemisms
314 Slips of tongue
315 Mispronounced words
316 Foreign terms used for no particular reason
317 Cryptic remarks
318 Clang associations, rhymed phrases and word play
319 Abstract or global terms

B. REITERATION

320 Reiteration

C. PECULIAR LOGIC

330 Illogical combinations of percepts and categories. Failure to keep incompatible or alternative percepts, images or concepts distinct
331 *Non sequitur* reasoning
332 Assigning meaning illogically on basis of non-essential attributes of cards
333 Contaminations, condensation

APPENDIX 5

RAW AND TRANSFORMED DATA FOR THE 80 SUBJECTS

Subject No.	Parent	Period	Offspring sex	Offspring diag.	Parent IQ	d	d/r	$\log(1+d/r)$	d/w	$\log(1+d/w)$	d/rA	d/rB	w
9	2	1	1	1	94	5	0·36	0·1335	2·10	1·131400	0·30	0·25	237
10	1	1	1	1	110	14	0·70	0·2304	4·11	1·631200	1·00	6·40	340
11	2	1	1	1	117	25	1·25	0·3522	4·34	1·675220	1·10	1·40	576
12	1	1	1	1	116	31	1·55	0·4065	3·85	1·578970	2·30	0·80	805
13	2	1	1	1	96	51	3·00	0·6021	7·32	2·118660	2·30	4·00	696
14	1	1	1	1	97	67	3·35	0·6385	8·96	2·298570	4·80	1·90	747
15	2	1	1	1	97	7	0·41	0·1492	2·32	1·199960	0·70	0·00	301
16	1	1	1	1	94	14	0·93	0·2856	3·81	1·570690	0·60	1·60	367
19	2	1	1	1	102	18	0·90	0·2788	1·81	1·033180	0·50	1·30	991
20	1	1	1	1	106	6	0·37	0·1367	1·30	0·832909	0·60	0·00	460
21	2	1	2	1	105	6	0·30	0·1139	1·78	1·022450	0·20	0·40	337
22	1	1	2	1	111	44	2·20	0·5051	3·22	1·439830	2·10	2·30	1363
23	2	1	1	1	98	10	0·53	0·1847	1·97	1·088560	0·40	0·67	507
24	1	1	1	1	83	3	0·17	0·0682	0·94	0·662688	0·00	0·38	319
25	2	1	1	1	108	6	0·30	0·1139	1·52	0·924359	0·10	0·50	394
26	1	1	1	1	128	19	0·95	0·2900	2·82	1·340250	0·20	0·85	673
27	2	1	1	1	108	0	0·00	0·0000	0·00	0·000000	0·00	0·00	366
28	1	1	1	1	102	26	1·30	0·3617	7·10	2·091860	1·10	1·50	500
35	2	1	1	1	97	17	0·85	0·2672	3·68	1·543290	0·50	1·20	461
36	1	1	1	1	111	28	1·40	0·3802	1·96	1·085190	1·70	1·10	1423
39	2	1	1	1	121	42	2·10	0·4914	2·90	1·360970	2·60	1·60	1445
40	1	1	1	1	123	30	1·50	0·3979	2·90	1·360970	1·40	1·60	1033
45	2	2	1	1	93	71	3·94	0·6937	6·64	2·033390	3·89	4·00	1069
46	1	2	1	1	118	6	0·32	0·1206	1·54	0·932164	0·10	0·56	388
47	2	2	1	1	93	39	1·95	0·4698	6·13	1·964310	1·20	2·70	636
48	1	2	1	1	88	30	1·50	0·3979	2·42	1·229640	0·40	2·60	1237

Subject No.	Parent	Period	Offspring sex	Offspring diag.	Parent IQ	d	d/r	log (1 + d/r)	d/w	log (1 + d/w)	d/r A	d/r B	w
55	2	2	1	1	88	23	1·21	0·3444	2·74	1·319080	0·80	1·67	838
56	1	2	1	1	116	73	3·65	0·6675	4·73	1·745710	2·60	4·70	1543
63	2	2	2	1	92	7	0·35	0·1303	1·19	0·783901	0·10	0·60	588
64	1	2	2	1	92	35	1·75	0·4393	2·76	1·324410	0·80	2·70	1268
67	2	2	1	1	110	55	2·75	0·5740	8·48	2·249180	2·90	2·60	648
68	1	2	1	1	108	13	0·65	0·2175	2·60	1·280930	0·60	0·70	499
71	2	2	2	1	85	38	1·90	0·4624	3·99	1·607430	1·50	2·30	951
72	1	2	2	1	86	6	0·30	0·1139	0·96	0·672944	0·30	0·30	623
75	2	2	2	1	113	15	0·75	0·2430	2·47	1·244150	0·40	1·10	607
76	1	2	1	1	125	35	1·75	0·4393	3·41	1·483870	1·70	1·80	1024
77	2	2	1	1	135	11	0·55	0·1903	1·02	0·703097	0·30	0·80	1070
78	1	2	1	1	128	36	1·80	0·4472	1·71	0·996949	1·70	1·90	2100
79	2	2	2	1	97	34	1·70	0·4314	3·37	1·474760	1·50	1·90	1008
80	1	2	2	1	115	35	1·75	0·4393	3·07	1·403640	2·00	1·50	1139
1	1	1	1	2	106	18	0·90	0·2788	2·63	1·289230	0·50	1·30	684
2	2	1	1	2	126	15	0·75	0·2430	4·09	1·627270	0·60	0·90	366
3	2	1	1	2	115	16	0·80	0·2553	1·88	1·057790	0·70	0·90	849
4	1	1	1	2	116	8	0·40	0·1461	2·12	1·137830	0·40	0·40	376
5	2	1	2	2	108	6	0·30	0·1139	2·28	1·187840	0·60	0·00	263
6	1	1	2	2	97	5	0·25	0·0969	1·27	0·819779	0·10	0·40	393
7	2	1	2	2	97	39	2·05	0·4843	4·18	1·644800	2·10	2·00	932
8	1	1	2	2	104	37	1·85	0·4548	5·53	1·876400	1·70	2·00	668
17	2	1	2	2	91	1	0·05	0·0212	0·46	0·378436	0·10	0·00	217
18	1	1	2	2	110	4	0·21	0·0828	1·76	1·015230	0·10	0·33	227
29	2	1	2	2	101	3	0·15	0·0607	0·50	0·405465	0·00	0·30	596
30	2	1	2	2	112	11	0·55	0·1903	2·83	1·342860	0·30	0·80	388
31	2	1	1	2	106	4	0·20	0·0792	0·75	0·559616	0·00	0·40	532
32	1	1	1	2	123	4	0·20	0·0792	0·84	0·609765	0·10	0·30	471

Subject No.	Parent	Period	Offspring sex	Offspring diag.	Parent IQ	d	d/r	$\log(1+d/r)$	d/w	$\log(1+d/w)$	$d/r\,A$	d/rB	w
33	2	1	2	2	129	5	0·25	0·0969	1·49	0·912283	0·20	0·30	334
34	1	1	2	2	133	4	0·20	0·0792	0·99	0·688134	0·20	0·20	403
37	2	1	1	2	113	8	0·40	0·1461	1·45	0·896088	0·60	0·20	549
38	1	1	1	2	111	18	0·90	0·2788	3·21	1·437460	0·60	1·20	560
41	2	2	2	2	111	9	0·47	0·1673	2·30	1·193920	0·20	0·78	390
42	1	2	2	2	122	20	1·00	0·3010	2·22	1·169380	0·60	1·40	899
43	2	2	1	2	88	44	2·20	0·5051	3·43	1·488400	2·00	2·40	1280
44	1	2	1	2	101	17	0·85	0·2672	2·46	1·241260	0·60	1·10	690
49	2	2	1	2	88	38	1·90	0·4624	8·11	2·209370	1·50	2·30	468
50	1	2	1	2	100	6	0·30	0·1139	1·29	0·828552	0·10	0·50	464
51	2	2	1	2	105	21	1·10	0·3222	5·25	1·832580	1·00	1·22	400
52	1	2	1	2	117	26	1·30	0·3617	2·29	1·190880	0·70	1·90	1134
53	2	2	2	2	102	11	0·55	0·1903	2·34	1·205970	0·30	0·80	469
54	1	2	2	2	118	35	2·25	0·5119	4·88	1·771550	1·70	2·80	716
57	2	2	2	2	91	71	3·55	0·6580	5·36	1·850020	1·90	5·20	1324
58	1	2	2	2	116	21	1·05	0·3118	2·83	1·342860	0·80	1·30	740
59	2	1	2	2	110	11	0·55	0·1903	5·28	1·837370	0·60	0·50	208
60	1	1	2	2	94	6	0·30	0·1139	2·28	1·187840	0·40	0·20	263
61	2	2	2	2	131	3	0·15	0·0607	0·47	0·385262	0·00	0·30	637
62	1	2	2	2	110	29	1·45	0·3892	3·42	1·486140	0·70	2·20	846
65	2	2	2	2	92	38	2·00	0·4771	2·36	1·211940	1·70	2·34	1606
66	1	2	2	2	98	13	0·65	0·2175	2·07	1·121670	0·40	0·90	628
69	2	2	1	2	104	6	0·30	0·1139	1·01	0·698135	0·20	0·40	594
70	1	2	1	2	119	6	0·30	0·1139	1·18	0·779325	0·20	0·40	505
73	2	2	2	2	100	48	2·40	0·5315	4·42	1·690090	1·40	3·40	1804
74	1	2	2	2	96	0	0·00	0·0000	0·00	0·000000	0·00	0·00	334

Key

Parent	1	... father
	2	... mother
Period	1	... restricted Enquiry
	2	... extended Enquiry
Sex of	1	... male
offspring	2	... female
Diagnosis of	1	... schizophrenia
offspring	2	... neurosis
d		... total number of Deviances
d/r		... number of Deviances per response (Deviance Score)
d/w		... number of Deviances per word × 100 (Deviance Rate)
d/r A		... Deviance Score for First Viewing
d/r B		... Deviance Score for Enquiry
w		... total number of words spoken

REFERENCES

ALANEN, Y. O. (1956) On the personality of the mother and early mother-child relationship of 100 schizophrenic patients, *Acta psychiat. scand.*, **31**, Suppl. 106, 227–34.

ALANEN, Y. O. (1958) The mothers of schizophrenic patients, *Acta. psychiat. scand.*, **33**, Suppl. 124, 1–361.

ALANEN, Y. O. (1966) The family in the pathogenesis of schizophrenic and neurotic disorders, *Acta psychiat. scand.*, **42**, Suppl. 189.

ALANEN, Y. O. (1968) From the mothers of schizophrenic patients to interactional family dynamics, in *The Transmission of Schizophrenia*, ed. Rosenthal, D., and Kety, S., Oxford.

APPERSON, L. B. (1965) Childhood experiences of schizophrenics and alcoholics, *J. genet. Psychol.*, **106**, 301–13.

APPERSON, L. B., and McADOO, W. G. (1965) Paternal reactions in childhood as described by schizophrenics and alcoholics, *J. clin. Psychol.*, **21**, 369–73.

BALES, R. F. (1950*a*) *Interaction Process Analysis*, Cambridge, Mass.

BALES, R. F. (1950*b*) A set of categories for the analysis of small group interaction, *Amer. soc. Rev.*, **15**, 257–63.

BATESON, G., JACKSON, D. D., HALEY, J., and WEAKLAND, J. H. (1956) Toward a theory of schizophrenia, *Behav. Sci.*, **1**, 251–64.

BAXTER, J. C., BECKER, J., and HOOKS, W. (1963) Defensive style in the families of schizophrenics and controls, *J. abnorm. soc. Psychol.*, **66**, 512–18.

BAXTER, J. C., WILLIAMS, J., and ZEROF, S. (1966) Child-rearing attitudes and disciplinary fantasies of parents of schizophrenics and controls, *J. nerv. ment. Dis.*, **141**, 567–79.

BEAVERS, W. R., BLUMBERG, S., TIMKEN, K., and WEINER, M. (1965) Communication patterns of mothers of schizophrenics, *Family Process*, **4**, 95–104.

BECKER, J., and FINKEL, P. (1969) Predictability and anxiety in speech by parents of female schizophrenics, *J. abnorm. Psychol.*, **74**, 517–23.

BECKER, J., and SIEFKES, H. (1969) Parental dominance, conflict and disciplinary coerciveness in families of female schizophrenics, *J. abnorm. Psychol.*, **74**, 193–8.

BEHRENS, M. I., ROSENTHAL, A. J., and CHODOFF, P. (1968) Communication in lower class families of schizophrenics, *Arch. gen. Psychiat.*, **18**, 689–96.

BELL, R. Q. (1968) A re-interpretation of the direction of effects in studies of socialization, *Psychol. Rev.*, **75**, 81–95.

BERGER, A. (1965) A test of the double bind hypothesis of schizophrenia, *Family Process*, **4**, 198–205.

BIRTCHNELL, J. (1970) Early parent death and mental illness, *Brit. J. Psychiat.*, **116**, 281–8.

BORGATTA, E. F. (1964) A note on the consistency of subject behaviour in Interaction Process Analysis, *Sociometry*, **27**, 222–9.

BOWEN, M., DYSINGER, R. H., and BASAMANIA, B. (1959) The role of the father in families with a schizophrenic patient, *Amer. J. Psychiat.*, **115**, 1017–20.

BRODEY, W. (1959) Some family operations and schizophrenia, *Arch. gen. Psychiat.*, **1**, 379–405.

BROWN, G. W., BIRLEY, J. L. T., and WING, J. K. (1972) Influence of family life on the course of schizophrenic disorders: a replication, *Brit. J. Psychiat.*, **121**, 241–58.

BROWN, G. W., MONCK, E. M., CARSTAIRS, G. M., and WING, J. K. (1962) Influence of family life on the course of schizophrenic illness, *Brit. J. prev. soc. Med.*, **16**, 55–68.

BUNCH, J., and BARRACLOUGH, B. (1971) The influence of parental death anniversaries upon suicide dates, *Brit. J. Psychiat.*, **118**, 621–6.

BUSS, A., and LANG, P. (1965) Psychological deficit in schizophrenia. I. Affect, reinforcement, and concept attainment, *J. abnorm. Psychol.*, **70**, 2–24.

CAPUTO, D. V. (1963) The parents of the schizophrenic, *Family Process*, **2**, 339–56.

CHEEK, F. E. (1964a) The 'schizophrenogenic mother' in word and deed, *Family Process*, **3**, 155–77.

CHEEK, F. E. (1964b) A serendipitous finding: sex roles and schizophrenia, *J. abnorm. soc. Psychol.*, **69**, 392–400.

CHEEK, F. E. (1965a) Family interaction patterns and convalescent adjustment of the schizophrenic, *Arch. gen. Psychiat.*, **13**, 138–47.

CHEEK, F. E. (1965b) The father of the schizophrenic, *Arch. gen. Psychiat.*, **13**, 336–45.

CHEEK, F. E. (1966) Parental role distortions in relation to schizophrenic deviancy, *Psychiat. Res. Rep.*, **20**, 54–64.

CIARLO, D., LIDZ, T., and RICCI, J. (1967) Word meaning in parents of schizophrenics, *Arch. gen. Psychiat.*, **17**, 470–7.

CLAUSEN, J. A., and KOHN, M. L. (1960) Social relations and schizophrenia, in *The Etiology of Schizophrenia*, ed. Jackson, D., New York.

COOPER, J. E., KENDELL, R. E., GURLAND, B. J., SHARPE, L., COPELAND, J. R. M., and SIMON, R. (1972) *Psychiatric Diagnosis in New York and London*, London.

COSTELLO, A. J., GUNN, J. C., and DOMINIAN, J. (1968) Aetiological factors in young schizophrenic men, *Brit. J. Psychiat.*, **114**, 433–41.

CREAK, M. (1961) Schizophrenic syndrome in childhood. Progress report of a working party, *Brit. med. J.*, **2**, 889–90.

DELAY, J., DENIKER, P., and GREEN, A. (1957) Essai de description et de définition psycho-pathologique des parents de schizophrènes, *International Congress on Psychiatry, Zurich*, Vol. **4**, pp. 49–56.

DELAY, J., DENIKER, P., and GREEN, A. (1960) Le milieu familial des schizophrènes. II. Methode et approche, *Encéphale*, **49**, 1–21.

DELAY, J., DENIKER, P., and GREEN, A. (1962) Le milieu familial des schizophrènes, III. Resultats et hypothèses, *Encéphale*, **51**, 5–73.

DONNELLY, E. M. (1960) The quantitative analysis of parent behaviour towards psychotic children and their siblings, *Genet. Psychol. Monogr.*, **62**, 331–76.

FARINA, A. (1960) Patterns of role dominance and conflict in parents of schizophrenic patients, *J. abnorm. soc. Psychol.*, **61**, 31–8.

FARINA, A., and DUNHAM, R. (1963) Measurement of family relationships and their effects, *Arch. gen. Psychiat.*, **9**, 64–73.

FARINA, A., and HOLZBERG, J. D. (1967) Attitudes and behaviour of fathers and mothers of male schizophrenic patients, *J. abnorm. Psychol.*, **72**, 381–7.

FARINA, A., and HOLZBERG, J. D. (1968) Interaction patterns of parents and hospitalised sons diagnosed as schizophrenic or nonschizophrenic, *J. abnorm. Psychol.*, **73**, 114–18.

FARINA, A., and HOLZBERG, J. D. (1970) Anxiety level of schizophrenic and control patients and their parents, *J. abnorm. Psychol.*, **75**, 157–63.

FEINSILVER, D. (1970) Communication in families of schizophrenic patients, *Arch. gen. Psychiat.*, **22**, 143–8.

FERREIRA, A. J. (1963) Decision-making in normal and pathologic families, *Arch. gen. Psychiat.*, **8**, 68–73.

FERREIRA, A. J., and WINTER, W. D. (1965) Family interaction and decision making, *Arch. gen. Psychiat.*, **13**, 214–23.

FERREIRA, A. J., WINTER, W. D., and POINDEXTER, E. J. (1966) Some interactional variables in normal and abnormal families, *Family Process*, **5**, 60–75.

FINNEY, D. J., LATSCHA, R., BENNETT, B. M., and HSU, P. (1963) *Tables for Testing Significance in a 2 × 2 Contingency Table*, Cambridge.

FISCHER, M. (1971) Psychoses in the offspring of schizophrenic monozygotic twins and their normal co-twins, *Brit. J. Psychiat.*, **118**, 43–52.

FISHER, S., BOYD, I., WALKER, D., and SHEER, D. (1959) Parents of schizophrenics, neurotics and normals, *Arch. gen. Psychiat.*, **1**, 149–66.

FLECK, S., LIDZ, T., and CORNELISON, A. (1963) Comparison of parent-child relationships of male and female schizophrenic patients, *Arch. gen. Psychiat.*, **8**, 1–7.

FORREST, A. D., HAY, A. J., and KUSHNER, A. W. (1969) Studies in speech disorder in schizophrenia, *Brit. J. Psychiat.*, **115**, 833–41.

FREEMAN, H. E., SIMMONS, O. G., and BERGEN, B. J. (1959) Possessiveness as a characteristic of mothers of schizophrenics, *J. abnorm. soc. Psychol.*, **58**, 271–3.

FREEMAN, R. V., and GRAYSON, H. M. (1955) Maternal attitudes in schizophrenia, *J. abnorm. soc. Psychol.*, **50**, 45–52.

FRITH, C. D., and LILLIE, F. J. (1972) Why does the Repertory Grid Test indicate thought disorder?, *Brit. J. soc. clin. Psychol.*, **11**, 73–78.

FROMM-REICHMANN, F. (1948) Notes on the development of treatment of schizo phrenics by psychoanalytic psychotherapy, *Psychiatry*, **11**, 263–73.

GARDNER, G. G. (1967) The role of maternal psycho-pathology in male and female schizophrenics, *J. cons. Psychol.*, **31**, 411–13.

GARMEZY, N., CLARKE, A. R., and STOCKNER, C. (1961) Child rearing attitudes of mothers and fathers as reported by schizophrenics and normal patients, *J. abnorm. soc. Psychol.*, **63**, 176–82.

GERARD, D. L., and SIEGEL, J. (1950) The family background of schizophrenia, *Psychiat. Quart.*, **24**, 47–73.

GIBSON, R. W. (1958) The family background and early life experience of the manic depressive patient. A comparison with the schizophrenic patient, *Psychiatry*, **21**, 71–90.

GOLDMAN-EISLER, F. (1958) Speech production and the predictability of words in context, *Quart. J. exp. Psychol.* **10**, 96–106.

GUERTIN, W. H. (1961) Are differences in schizophrenic symptoms related to the mother's avowed attitudes toward child rearing?, *J. abnorm. soc. Psychol.*, **63**, 440–2.

HAJDU-GAINES, L. (1940) Contributions to the etiology of schizophrenia, *Psychoanal. Rev.*, **27**, 421–38.

HALEY, J. (1959a) An interactional description of schizophrenia, *Psychiatry*, **22**, 321–32.

HALEY, J. (1959b) The family of the schizophrenic: a model system, *J. nerv. ment. Dis.*, **129**, 357–74.

HALEY, J. (1960) Observation of the family of the schizophrenic, *Amer. J. Ortho-psychiat.*, **30**, 460–7.

HALEY, J. (1968) Testing parental instructions to schizophrenic and normal children; a pilot study, *J. abnorm. Psychol.*, **73**, 559–65.

HEILBRUN, A. B. (1960a) Perception of maternal child rearing attitudes in schizophrenics, *J. cons. Psychol.*, **24**, 169–73.

HEILBRUN, A. B. (1960b) Note on acquiescence set in endorsed attitudes of mothers of schizophrenics and normals, *J. clin. Psychol.*, **16**, 104–5.

HERSOV, L. A. (1960) Persistent non-attendance at school, *J. Child Psychol.*, **1**, 130–6.

HESTON, L. L. (1966) Psychiatric disorders in foster home reared children of schizophrenic mothers, *Brit. J. Psychiat.*, **112**, 819–25.

HESTON, L., and DENNY, D. (1968) Interactions between early life experience and biological factors in schizophrenia, in *Transmission of Schizophrenia*, ed. Rosenthal, D., and Kety, S., Oxford.

HIRSCH, S. R., and LEFF, J. P. (1971) Parental abnormalities of verbal communication in the transmission of schizophrenia, *Psychol. Med.*, **1**, 118–27.

HIRSCH, S. R., GAIND, R., ROHDE, P. D., STEVENS, B. C., and WING, J. K. (1973) Out-patient maintenance of chronic schizophrenic patients with long-acting fluphenazine: double-blind placebo trial, *Brit. med. J.*, **1**, 633–7.

HOLLINGSHEAD, A. B., and REDLICH, F. C. (1958) *Social Class and Mental Illness*, New York.

HORDERN, A., SANDIFER, M. G., GREEN, L. M., and TIMBURY, G. C. (1968) Psychiatric diagnosis: British and American concordance on stereotypes of mental illness, *Brit. J. Psychiat.*, **114**, 935–44.

HORNER, R. F. (1964) Important stimulus variables in the early family relationships of schizophrenic patients, *J. clin. Psychol.*, **20**, 344–6.

HOROWITZ, F. D., and LOVELL, L. L. (1960) Attitudes of mothers of female schizophrenics, *Child Develop.*, **31**, 299–305.

HOTCHKISS, G. D., CARMEN, L., OGILBY, A., and WIESENFELD, S. (1955) The mothers of young male single schizophrenic patients as visitors in a mental hospital, *J. nerv. ment. Dis.*, **121**, 452–62.

KASANIN, J., KNIGHT, E., and SAGE, P. (1934) The parent–child relationship in schizophrenia, *J. nerv. ment. Dis.*, **79**, 249–63.

KAYTON, R., and BILLER, H. B. (1971) Perception of parental sex-role behaviour and psychopathology in adult males, *J. cons. Psychol.*, **36**, 235–7.

KENDELL, R. E., COOPER, J. E., GOURLAY, A. J., COPELAND, M., SHARPE, L., and GURLAND, B. J. (1971) The diagnostic criteria of American and British psychiatrists, *Arch. gen. Psychiat.*, **25**, 123–30.

KETY, S., ROSENTHAL, D., WENDER, P., and SCHULSINGER, F. (1968) The types and prevalence of mental illness in the biological and adoptive families of adopted schizophrenics, in *The Transmission of Schizophrenia*, ed. Rosenthal, D., and Kety, S., Oxford.

KING, A. (1963) Primary and secondary anorexia nervosa syndromes, *Brit. J. Psychiat.*, **109**, 470–9.

KLEBANOFF, L. (1959) Parental attitudes of mothers of schizophrenic, brain-injured and retarded and normal children, *Amer. J. Orthopsychiat.*, **29**, 445–54.

KOHN, M. L. (1968) Social class and schizophrenia: a critical review, in *The Transmission of Schizophrenia*, ed. Rosenthal, D., and Kety, S., Oxford.

KOHN, M., and CLAUSEN, J. A. (1956) Parental authority behaviour and schizophrenia, *Amer. J. Orthopsychiat.*, **26**, 297–313.

KOLVIN, I. (1972a) Infantile autism or infantile psychosis, *Brit. med. J.*, **3**, 753–5.

KOLVIN, I. (1972b) Late onset psychosis, *Brit. med. J.*, **3**, 816–17.

KREITMAN, N., SAINSBURY, P., MORRISSEY, J., TOWERS, J., and SCRIVENER, J. (1961) The reliability of psychiatric assessment: an analysis, *J. ment. Sci.*, **107**, 887–908.

LAING, R. D. (1960) *The Divided Self: a Study of Sanity and Madness*, Chicago.

LAING, R. D. (1961) *The Self and Others: Further Studies in Sanity and Madness*, London.

LAING, R. D. (1967) *The Politics of Experience*, London.

LAING, R. D., and ESTERSON, D. (1964) *Sanity, Madness and the Family*, London.

LANE, R. C., and SINGER, J. L. (1959) Familial attitudes in paranoid schizophrenics and normals from two socioeconomic classes, *J. abnorm. soc. Psychol.*, **59**, 328–39.

LEFF, J. P., and HIRSCH, S. R. (1972) The effects of sensory deprivation on verbal communication, *J. psychiat. Res.*, **9**, 329–36.

LEFF, J. P., and WING, J. K. (1971) Trial of maintenance therapy in schizophrenia, *Brit. med. J.*, **3**, 599–604.

LENNARD, H. L., BEAULIEU, M. R., and EMBREY, N. G. (1965) Interactions in families with a schizophrenic child, *Arch. gen. Psychiat.*, **12**, 166–83.

LERNER, P. M. (1965) Resolution of intrafamilial role conflict in families of schizophrenic patients. I. Thought disturbance, *J. nerv. ment. Dis.*, **141**, 342–51.

LERNER, P. M. (1967) Resolution of intrafamilial role conflict in families of schizophrenic patients. II. Social maturity, *J. nerv. ment. Dis.*, **145**, 336–41.

LEVY, D. M. (1931) Maternal overprotection and rejection, *Arch. Neurol. Psychiat.*, **25**, 886–9.

LIDZ, R. W., and LIDZ, T. (1949) The family environment of schizophrenic patients, *Amer. J. Psychiat.*, **106**, 332–45.

LIDZ, T. (1958) Schizophrenia and the family, *Psychiatry*, **21**, 21–7.

LIDZ, T. (1967) The family, personality development, and schizophrenia, in *The Origins of Schizophrenia*, Excerpta Medica International Congress Series, No. 151.

LIDZ, T. (1968) The family, language, and the transmission of schizophrenia, in *The Transmission of Schizophrenia*, ed. Rosenthal, D., and Kety, S., Oxford.

LIDZ, T., CORNELISON, A. R., FLECK, S., and TERRY, D. (1957a) The intrafamilial environment of the schizophrenic patient. I. The father, *Psychiatry*, **20**, 329–342.

LIDZ, T., CORNELISON, A. R., FLECK, S., and TERRY, D. (1957b) The intrafamilial environment of the schizophrenic patient. II. Marital schism and marital skew, *Amer. J. Psychiat.*, **114**, 241–8.

LIDZ, T., CORNELISON, A. R., TERRY, D., and FLECK, S. (1958) Intrafamilial environment of the schizophrenic patient. VI. The transmission of irrationality, *Arch. Neurol. Psychiat.*, **79**, 305–316.

LIDZ, T., CORNELISON, A. R., SINGER, M. T., SCHAFER, S., and FLECK, S. (1965) The mothers of schizophrenic patients, In *Schizophrenia and the Family*, ed. Lidz, T., Fleck, S., and Cornelison, A. R., New York.

LIDZ, T., FLECK, S., ALANEN, Y. O., and CORNELISON, A. (1963) Schizophrenic patients and their siblings, *Psychiatry*, **26**, 1–18.

LIDZ, T., FLECK, S., and CORNELISON, A. R. (Ed.) (1965) *Schizophrenia and the Family*, New York.

LIDZ, T., WILD, C., SCHAFER, S., ROSMAN, B., and FLECK, S. (1963) Thought disorder in the parents of schizophrenic patients: a study utilizing the Object Sorting Test, in *Schizophrenia and the Family*, ed. Lidz, T., Fleck, S., and Cornelison, A. R., New York.

LINDELIUS, R. (1970) A study of schizophrenia, *Acta psychiat. scand.*, Suppl. 216.

LOEFF, R. G. (1966) Differential discrimination of conflicting emotional messages by normal, delinquent, and schizophrenic adolescents (Doctoral Dissertation, Indiana University), Ann Arbor, University Microfilms, No. 66–1470.

LOVIBOND, S. H. (1954) The Object Sorting Test and conceptual thinking in schizophrenia, *Aust. J. psychol. Res.*, **6**, 52–70.

Lu, Y-C. (1961) Mother–child role relations in schizophrenia, *Psychiatry*, **24**, 133–42.

Lu, Y-C. (1962) Contradictory parental expectations in schizophrenia, *Arch. gen. Psychiat.*, **6**, 219–34.

Lucas, L. (1964) Family influences and schizophrenic reaction, *Amer. J. Orthopsychiat.*, **34**, 527–35.

Lyle, T. K., and Wybar, K. C. (1967) *Practical Orthoptics in the Treatment of Squint*, London.

Mahl, G. F. (1956) Disturbances and silences in the patient's speech in psychotherapy, *J. abnorm. soc. Psychol.*, **53**, 1–15.

Mahl, G. F. (1959) Exploring emotional states by content analysis, in *Trends in Content Analysis*, ed. De Sola Pool, I, Urbana, Illinois.

Magaro, P. A., and Hanson, B. A. (1969) Perceived maternal nurturance and control of process schizophrenics, reactive schizophrenics, and normals, *J. cons. Psychol.*, **33**, 507.

Margolies, J. A., and Wortis, H. Z. (1956) Parents of children with cerebral palsy, *J. Child Psychiat.*, **3**, 105–14.

Mark, J. C. (1953) The attitudes of the mothers of male schizophrenics towards child behaviour, *J. abnorm. soc. Psychol.*, **48**, 185–9.

McConaghy, N. (1959) The use of an Object Sorting Test in elucidating the hereditary factor in schizophrenia, *J. Neurol. Neurosurg. Psychiat.*, **22**, 243–6.

McConaghy, N. (1960) The measurement of an inhibitory process in human higher nervous activity: its relation to allusive thinking and fatigue, *Amer. J. Psychiat.*, **118**, 125–32.

McConaghy, N. (1971) The ocular angle alpha—a genetic marker in the transmission of schizophrenia. Paper to the Fifth World Congress of Psychiatry, Mexico. [In the press.]

McConaghy, N., and Clancy, M. (1968) Familial relationships of allusive thinking in university students and their parents, *Brit. J. Psychiat.*, **114**, 1079–87.

McGhie, A. (1961a) A comparative study of the mother–child relationship in schizophrenia, *Brit. J. med. Psychol.*, **34**, 195–208.

McGhie, A. (1961b) A comparative study of the mother–child relationship in schizophrenia. II. Psychological testing, *Brit. J. med. Psychol.*, **34**, 209–21.

McGhie, A. (1967) Studies of cognitive disorder in schizophrenia, in *Recent Developments in Schizophrenia*. R.M.P.A. Special Publ. 1, ed. Coppen, A., and Walk, A., London.

McKeown, J. E. (1950) The behaviour of parents of schizophrenic, neurotic and normal children, *Amer. J. Sociol.*, **56**, 175–9.

Mednick, S. A. (1966) A longitudinal study of children with a high risk for schizophrenia, *Ment. Hyg. (N.Y.)*, **50**, 522–35.

Mednick, S. A. (1967) The children of schizophrenics: serious difficulties in current research methodologies which suggest the use of the 'High Risk Group' method, in *The Origins of Schizophrenia*, Excerpta Medica International Congress Series, No. 151.

Mednick, S. A., and Schulsinger, F. (1968) Some premorbid characteristics related to breakdown in children with schizophrenic mothers, in *The Transmission of Schizophrenia*, ed. Rosenthal, D., and Kety, S., Oxford.

Mehrabian, A., and Wiener, M. (1967) Decoding of inconsistent communications, *J. pers. soc. Psychol.*, **6**, 109–114.

Mishler, E. G., and Waxler, N. E. (1967) Family interaction patterns and schizophrenia: a multi-level analysis, in *The Origins of Schizophrenia*, Excerpta Medica International Congress Series, No. 151.

MISHLER, E. G., and WAXLER, N. E. (1968a) Family interaction and schizophrenia: alternative frameworks of interpretation, in *The Transmission of Schizophrenia*, ed. Rosenthal, D., and Kety, S., Oxford.

MISHLER, E. G., and WAXLER, N. E. (1968b) *Interaction in Families*, New York.

MISHLER, E. G., and WAXLER, N. E. (1970) Functions of hesitations in the speech of normal families and families of schizophrenic patients, *Language and Speech*, **13**, 102–17.

MORRIS, G. O., and WYNNE, L. C. (1965) Schizophrenic offspring and parental styles of communication, *Psychiatry*, **28**, 19–44.

MOSHER, L. R., POLLIN, W., and STABENAU, J. (1971) Families with identical twins discordant for schizophrenia, *Brit. J. Psychiat.*, **118**, 29–42.

MUNTZ, H. J., and POWER, R. P. (1970) Thought disorder in the parents of thought disordered schizophrenics, *Brit. J. Psychiat.*, **117**, 707–8.

NAMECHE, G., WARING, M., and RICKS, D. (1964) Early indicators of outcome in schizophrenia, *J. nerv. ment. Dis.*, **139**, 232–40.

NATHANSON, I. A. (1967) A semantic differential analysis of parent–son relationships in schizophrenia, *J. abnorm. Psychol.*, **72**, 277–81.

NIELSEN, C. K. (1954) The childhood of schizophrenics, *Acta psychiat. scand.*, **29**, 281–9.

OLSON, D. N. (1972) Empirically unbinding the double bind: review of research and conceptual reformations, *Family Process*, **11**, 69–94.

OLTMAN, J. E., and FRIEDMAN, S. (1965) Report on parental deprivation in psychiatric disorders, *Arch. gen. Psychiat.*, **12**, 46–56.

OLTMAN, J. E., McGARRY, J. J., and FRIEDMAN, S. (1952) Parental deprivation and the 'broken home' in dementia praecox and other mental disorders, *Amer. J. Psychiat.*, **108**, 685–94.

O'NEAL, P., and ROBINS, L. N. (1958) Childhood patterns predictive of adult schizophrenia: a 30-year follow-up study, *Amer. J. Psychiat.*, **115**, 385–91.

OSGOOD, C. E., SUCI, G. J., and TANNENBAUM, P. H. (1957) *The Measurement of Meaning*, Urbana, Illinois.

PALOMBO, S., MERRIFIELD, J., WEIGERT, W., MORRIS, G., and WYNNE, L. (1967) Recognition of parents of schizophrenics from excerpts of family therapy interviews, *Psychiatry*, **30**, 405–12.

PARSONS, A. (1960) Family dynamics in South Italian schizophrenics, *Arch. gen. Psychiat.*, **3**, 507–18.

PAYNE, R. W. (1960) Cognitive abnormalities, in *Handbook of Abnormal Psychology*, ed. Eysenck, H. J., London.

PHILLIPS, J. E., JACOBSON, N., and TURNER, W. J. (1965) Conceptual thinking in schizophrenics and their relatives, *Brit. J. Psychiat.*, **111**, 823–39.

PHILLIPS, L. (1953) Case history data and prognosis in schizophrenia, *J. nerv. ment. Dis.*, **117**, 515–25.

POLLIN, W., and STABENAU, J. (1968) Biological, psychological and historical differences in a series of monozygotic twins discordant for schizophrenia, in *The Transmission of Schizophrenia*, ed. Rosenthal, D., and Kety, S., Oxford.

POLLIN, W., STABENAU, J. R., MOSHER, L., and TUPIN, J. (1966) Life history differences in identical twins discordant for schizophrenia, *Amer. J. Orthopsychiat.*, **36**, 492–509.

POLLOCK, H. M., and MALZBERG, B. (1940) Hereditary and environmental factors in the causation of manic-depressive psychosis and dementia praecox, *Amer. J. Psychiat.*, **96**, 1227–44.

PROUT, C. T., and WHITE, M. A. (1950) A controlled study of personality relationships in mothers of schizophrenic male patients, *Amer. J. Psychiat.*, **107**, 251–6.

RACHMAN, S. (1973) Schizophrenia: a look at Laing's views, *New Society*, **24**, 184–6.

RAPAPORT, D. (1945) *Diagnostic Psychological Testing*, Vol. 1, Chicago.

RAVEN, J. C. (1948) *A Guide to Using the Mill Hill Vocabulary Scale with Progressive Matrices*, London.

REICHARD, S., and TILLMAN, C. (1950) Patterns of parent-child relationships in schizophrenia, *Psychiatry*, **13**, 247–57.

REISS, D. (1967a) Individual thinking and family interaction. I. Introduction to an experimental study of problem solving in families of normals, character disorders and schizophrenics, *Arch. gen. Psychiat.*, **16**, 80–93.

REISS, D. (1967b) Individual thinking and family interaction. II. A study of pattern recognition and hypotheses testing in families of normals, character disorders and schizophrenics, *J. psychiat. Res.*, **5**, 193–211.

REISS, D. (1968) Individual thinking and family interaction. III. An experimental study of categorisation performance in families of normals, those with character disorders, and schizophrenics, *J. nerv. ment. Dis.*, **146**, 384–403.

REISS, D. (1969) Individual thinking and family interaction. IV. A study of information exchange in families of normals, those with character disorders, and schizophrenics, *J. nerv. ment. Dis.*, **149**, 473–90.

REISS, D. (1971) Varieties of consensual experience. III. Contrasts between families of normals, delinquents and schizophrenics, *J. nerv. ment. Dis.*, **152**, 73–95.

REISS, D., and ELSTEIN, A. S. (1971) Perceptual and cognitive resources of family members, *Arch. gen. Psychiat.*, **24**, 121–34.

RICKS, D. F., and NAMECHE, C. (1966) Symbiosis, sacrifice and schizophrenia, *Ment. Hyg. (N.Y.)*, **50**, 541–51.

RINGUETTE, E., and KENNEDY, T. (1966) An experimental study of the double-bind hypothesis, *J. abnorm. Psychol.*, **71**, 136–41.

ROGLER, L. H., and HOLLINGSHEAD, A. B. (1965) *Trapped: Families and Schizophrenia*, New York.

ROMNEY, D. (1969a) Psychometrically assessed thought disorder in schizophrenic and control patients and in their parents and siblings, *Brit. J. Psychiat.*, **115**, 999–1002.

ROMNEY, D. (1969b) The validity of certain tests of overinclusion, *Brit. J. Psychiat.*, **115**, 591–2.

ROSENBERG, S., and KOPLIN, J. (1968) Schizophrenic language—a disattention interpretation, in *Developments in Applied Psycholinguistics Research*, London.

ROSENTHAL, D. (1971) Two adoption studies of heredity in schizophrenic disorders, in *Die Enstehung der Schizophrenie*, ed. Bleuler, M., and Angst, J., Bern.

ROSENTHAL, D., WENDER, P., KETY, S., SCHULSINGER, F., WELNER, J., and OSTER-GAARD, L. (1968) Schizophrenics' offspring reared in adopted homes, in *Transmission of Schizophrenia*, ed. Rosenthal, D., and Kety, S., Oxford.

ROSMAN, B., WILD, C., RICCI, J., FLECK, S., and LIDZ, T. (1964) Thought disorder in the parents of schizophrenic patients: a further study utilising the Object Sorting Test, *J. psychiat. Res.*, **2**, 211–21.

RUTTER, M., and BARTAK, L. (1971) Causes of infantile autism: some considerations from recent research, *J. Aut. child. Schiz.*, **1**, 20–32.

RUTTER, M., and BROWN, G. W. (1966) The reliability and validity of measures of family life and relationships in families containing a psychiatric patient, *Soc. Psychiat.*, **1**, 38–53.

SCHNEIDER, K. (1957) Primäre und sekundäre Symptome bei der Schizophrenie, *Fortschr. Neurol. Psychiat.*, **25**, 487–90.

SCHOPLER, E., and LOFTIN, J. (1969) Thought disorder in parents of psychotic children, a function of test anxiety, *Arch. gen. Psychiat.*, **20**, 174–81.

SHARAN, S. N. (1966) Family interaction with schizophrenics and their siblings, *J. abnorm. Psychol.*, **71**, 345–53.

SHARP, V. H., GLASNER, S., and LEDERMAN, I. (1964) Sociopaths and schizophrenics— a comparison of family interactions, *Psychiatry*, **27**, 127–34.

SHIELDS, J. (1967) The genetics of schizophrenia in historical context, in *Recent Developments in Schizophrenia*, ed. Coppen, A., and Walk, A., London.

SHOBEN, E. J. (1949) The assessment of parental attitudes in relation to child development, *Genet. Psychol. Monogr.*, **39**, 101–48.

SIEGLER, M., OSMOND, H., and MANN, H. (1969) Laing's models of madness, *Brit. J. Psychiat.*, **115**, 947–58.

SINGER, M. T. (1967) Family transactions and schizophrenia. I. Recent research findings, in *The Origins of Schizophrenia*, Excerpta Medica International Congress Series, No. 151.

SINGER, M. T., and WYNNE, L. C. (1963) Differentiating characteristics of parents of childhood schizophrenics, childhood neurotics, and young adult schizophrenics, *Amer. J. Psychiat.*, **120**, 234–43.

SINGER, M. T., and WYNNE, L. C. (1964) Stylistic variables in research on schizophrenics and their families. Unpublished Address presented at Marquette University.

SINGER, M. T., and WYNNE, L. C. (1965) Thought disorder and family relations of schizophrenics, *Arch. gen. Psychiat.*, **12**, 187–212.

SINGER, M. T., and WYNNE, L. C. (1966a) Principles for scoring communication defects and deviances in parents of schizophrenics. Rorschach and T.A.T. Scoring Manuals, *Psychiatry*, **29**, 260–88.

SINGER, M. T., and WYNNE, L. C. (1966b) Communication styles in parents of normals, neurotics and schizophrenics, *Psychiat. Res. Rep.*, **20**, 25–38.

SLUZKI, C. E., BEAVIN, J., TARNOPOLSKY, A., and VERON, E. (1967) Transactional disqualification. Research on the double bind, *Arch. gen. Psychiat.*, **16**, 494–504.

SLUZKI, C. E., and VERON, E. (1971) The double bind as a universal pathogenic situation, *Family Process*, **10**, 397–410.

SOJIT, C. M. (1969) Dyadic interaction in a double bind situation, *Family Process*, **8**, 235–59.

SOJIT, C. M. (1971) The double bind hypothesis and the parents of schizophrenics, *Family Process*, **10**, 53–74.

STABENAU, J. R., TUPIN, J., WERNER, M., and POLLIN, W. (1965) A comparative study of families of schizophrenics, delinquents, and normals, *Psychiatry*, **28**, 45–9.

STRODTBECK, F. L. (1951) Husband–wife interaction over revealed differences, *Amer. sociol. Rev.*, **16**, 468–73.

STRODTBECK, F. L. (1954) The family as a three person group, *Amer. sociol. Rev.*, **19**, 23–29.

THOMAS, A., CHESS, S., and BIRCH, H. C. (1968) *Temperament and Behaviour Disorders in Children*, London.

TIETZE, T. (1949) A study of mothers of schizophrenic patients, *Psychiatry*, **12**, 55–65.

VAZIRI, H. (1961) Fréquence de l'oligophrénie, de la psychopathie et de l'alcoolisme dans 79 familles de schizophrènes, *Schweiz. Arch. Neurol. Psychiat.*, **87**, 160–77.

WAHL, C. W. (1954) Some antecedent factors in the family histories of 392 schizophrenics, *Amer. J. Psychiat.*, **110**, 668–76.

WAHL, C. W. (1956) Some antecedent factors in the family histories of 568 male schizophrenics of the U.S. Navy, *Amer. J. Psychiat.*, **113**, 201–10.

WARING, M., and RICKS, D. (1965) Family patterns of children who became adult schizophrenics, *J. nerv. ment. Dis.*, **140**, 351–64.

WATZLAWICK, P., BEAVIN, J. H., and JACKSON, D. D. (1968) *Pragmatics of Human Communication*, London.

WEAKLAND, J. H. (1960) The 'double-bind' hypothesis of schizophrenia and three party interaction, in *The Etiology of Schizophrenia*, ed. Jackson, D., New York.

WENDER, P., ROSENTHAL, D., and KETY, S. (1968) A psychiatric assessment of the adoptive parents of schizophrenics, in *The Transmission of Schizophrenia*, ed. Rosenthal, D., and Kety, S., Oxford.

WENDER, P., ROSENTHAL, D., ZAHN, T., and KETY, S. (1971) The psychiatric adjustment of the adopting parents of schizophrenics, *Amer. J. Psychiat.*, **127**, 1013–18.

WILD, C., SINGER, M., ROSMAN, B., RICCI, J., and LIDZ, T. (1965) Measuring disordered styles of thinking using the Object Sorting Test on parents of schizophrenic patients, *Arch. gen. Psychiat.*, **13**, 471–6.

WINDER, C. L., and KANTOR, R. E. (1958) Rorschach maturity scores of the mothers of schizophrenics, *J. cons. Psychol.*, **22**, 438–40.

WING, J. K. (1966) *Early Childhood Autism: Clinical Educational and Social Aspects*, Oxford.

WING, J. K., BIRLEY, J. L., COOPER, J. E., GRAHAM, P., and ISAACS, A. (1967) Reliability of a procedure for measuring and classifying 'Present Psychiatric State', *Brit. J. Psychiat.*, **113**, 499–515.

WING, J. K., COOPER, J. E., and SARTORIUS, N. (1974) *The Description and Classification of Psychiatric Symptoms*, London.

WINTER, W., and FERREIRA, A. (1967) Interaction process analysis of family decision-making, *Family Process*, **6**, 155–72.

WITMER, H. (1934) The childhood personality and parent–child relationships of dementia praecox and manic depressive patients, *Smith Coll. Stud. Soc. Wk*, **IV**, 290–377.

WOLMAN, B. B., (1961) The fathers of schizophrenic patients, *Acta psychother.* (Basel), **9**, 193–210.

WORLD HEALTH ORGANIZATION (1973) *The International Pilot Study of Schizophrenia*, Vol. 1, Geneva.

WYNNE, L. C. (1967) Family transactions and schizophrenia. II. Conceptual considerations for a research strategy, in *The Origins of Schizophrenia*, Excerpta Medica International Congress Series, No. 151.

WYNNE, L. C. (1968) Methodologic and conceptual issues in the study of schizophrenics and their families, in *The Transmission of Schizophrenia*, ed. Rosenthal, D., and Kety, S., Oxford.

WYNNE, L. C. (1971) Family research on the pathogenesis of schizophrenia, in *Problems of Psychosis, International Colloquium on Psychosis*, ed. Doucet, P., and Laurin, C., Excerpta Medica International Congress Series, No. 194.

WYNNE, L. C. (to be published). Schizophrenics and their families. I. Research re-directions. (Presented in a condensed version at the Mental Health Research Fund Lecture, London.)

WYNNE, L. C., RYCKOFF, I., DAY, J., and HIRSCH, S. (1958) Pseudo-mutuality in the family relations of schizophrenics, *Psychiatry*, **21**, 205–20.

WYNNE, L. C., and SINGER, M. T. (1963) Thought disorder and family relations of schizophrenics, *Arch. gen. Psychiat.*, **9**, 191–206.

WYNNE, L. C., SINGER, M., BARTKO, J., and TOOHEY, M., Schizophrenics and their families. III. Recent Rorschach communication findings, *Brit. J. Psychiat.* [In the press.]

ZAHN, T. P. (1968) Word association in adoptive and biological parents of schizophrenics, *Arch. gen. Psychiat.*, **19**, 501–3.

ZIGLER, E., and PHILLIPS, L. (1960) Social effectiveness and symptomatic behaviours, *J. abnorm. soc. Psychol.*, **61**, 231–8.

ZUCKERMAN, M., OLTEAN, M., and MONASHKIN, I. (1958) The parental attitudes of mothers of schizophrenics, *J. cons. Psychol.*, **22**, 307–10.

INDEX OF SUBJECTS

Acknowledgement in families of schizophrenics, 57
Acts of speech, implicit and explicit, 86, 102
Adoption studies,
in schizophrenia, 28 *et seq.*, 100
tests of allusive thinking in, 67
Alcoholism, 8, 9, 100
Allusive thinking, 63 *et seq.*, 70
angle alpha related to, 65, 71
Amorphous thinking, 74, 75
definition of, 73
Angle alpha, relation to allusive thinking, 65, 71
Attention, focus of, 72, 73
impairment in families of schizophrenics, 87, 130, 170
relation to verbosity, 87
Attitudes to child-rearing in mothers of schizophrenics, 34
Autism, infantile,
attitudes of mothers, 33
characteristics of parents, 73
distinction from adult schizophrenia, 33

Bannister grid, 67
Body-image boundaries, assessed from Rorschach responses, 70, 78

Chaotic responses,
definition of, 52
in families of schizophrenics, 52
Child Guidance Clinics, records of, 24, 25, 93, 98, 101, 103
Choice fulfilment,
definition of, 52
in families of schizophrenics, 52
Cloze procedure, 84, 85, 102
Communication, 72 *et seq.*
See also Acts of speech, Attention, Chaotic responses, Cloze procedure, Deviance Rate, Deviance Score, Double-bind, Hesitancy of speech, Pseudomutuality, Silences, Speech, Verbosity, Word Count
Control, parental,
in schizophrenia, 36, 37, 50

relation to education, 36, 42
Critical comments by relatives of schizophrenics, 32

Deviance Rate, 147
relation to word count, 148
Deviance Score, 78
calculation of, 125
correlation with age, 77, 82
correlation with education, 77, 82
inter-rater reliability, 134, 158
relation to severity of illness, 79
relation to technique of Rorschach Test, 152
relation to verbal intelligence, 141
relation to word count, 144 *et seq.*
Diagnosis,
American *v.* British, 13, 33, 47, 61, 83, 164
criteria for schizophrenia, 117
Dominance,
definition of, 46
maternal,
in manic-depressive psychosis, 5, 96
in schizophrenia, 5, 8, 11, 13, 18, 23, 35, 38, 40, 47 *et seq.*, 60, 84, 96 *et seq.*
social class and, 9, 10, 96
paternal,
in schizophrenia, 10, 13, 38, 40, 47 *et seq.*, 84, 96 *et seq.*
social class and, 9, 10
Double-bind, 11, 14 *et seq.*, 18, 21, 87 *et seq.*, 109
identification by experts, 89
social background and education and, 88

Emotional divorce, 20, 25, 26, 98
Emotional relationships in families of schizophrenics, 21, 31, 50, 56, 109
Expectations, maternal, in schizophrenia, 11
Expressiveness, definition of, 56

Family therapy interviews, 75

First rank symptoms, 117, 165
Fragmented thinking, 74, 75
definition of, 73

High risk group for schizophrenia, characteristics of, 27
Hypothesis testing by families of schizophrenics, 59

Interaction Process Analysis, 44, 96

Life events, 12

Marital schism, 17 *et seq.*, 24, 25, 26, 96, 98, 109
Marital skew, 18 *et seq.*, 24, 25, 26, 96, 98, 109
Mental retardation,
attitudes of mothers to, 36
incidence in relatives of schizophrenics, 9
Models of schizophrenia,
conspiratorial, 22
psychedelic, 22
psychoanalytic, 22

Neurotic symptoms in schizophrenia, 38

Object Sorting Test, 63 *et seq.*, 70, 74, 77, 83, 141
Over-protection, maternal,
criteria for, 5, 26
in schizophrenia, 5, 8, 11, 23, 26, 35, 38, 41, 50, 93, 94, 104

Parental friction,
definition of, 46
in manic-depressive psychosis, 5
in neurotics, 24
in normals, 7, 8, 9, 10
in presence of schizophrenic offspring and healthy sibling, 55
in schizophrenia, 5, 6, 7, 8, 9, 10, 13, 24, 41, 47, 48, 49, 50, 54, 61, 98, 99
Parental loss,
through bereavement, 6, 9, 11, 12, 100, 118
through separation, 6, 8, 9, 11, 12, 13, 24, 27, 100, 118
Passive father, 6, 10, 18, 48, 50, 51, 95
Physical illness in spouses of schizophrenics, 12

Premorbid personality,
assessment of, 129
attitudes of schizophrenics
with good and poor,
40
importance in interpreta-
tion of research find-
ings, 97 *et seq.*, 167
parents of schizophrenics
with good and poor,
attitudes of, 39 *et seq.*,
47, 49
Rorschach responses of,
69
Pre-schizophrenic children,
characteristics of, 5, 10,
11, 24, 26, 103, 104
influence on parents, 5, 8,
11, 26, 103, 104
Present State Examination,
117
Primary symptoms of
Bleuler, 23
Prognosis of married
schizophrenics, 13
Prospective studies in schizophrenia, 27
Pseudomutuality, 20, 98, 109
Psychiatric disturbance in
parents,
of adopted children, 28, 29
of neurotics, 23
of schizophrenics, 6, 7, 8,
9, 23, 25, 27, 29, 100

Rejection,
by parents of schizo-
phrenics, 9, 37, 41, 95
by parents of sociopaths,
37
Revealed Difference tech-
nique, 44, 94, 99
Risk taking by families of
schizophrenics, 58, 59
Rorschach manual of Singer
and Wynne, 77, 113,
114, 123, 139, 170
use by authors, reliability
of, 134, 158
Rorschach Test, 69, 70, 73,
74, 76, 78, 79, 82
card rejection in, 78, 125

change in technique,
effect on Deviance
Score, 152
effect on word count
153
enquiry, 122
first viewing, 122
procedure, 121

Sample, authors', characteristics of,
age, 126
parents' education, 127
parents' social class, 128
patient's personality, 129
patient's symptoms, 129
et seq.
recent domicile of patients
with parents, 127
sex distribution, 126
Schizoid personality, 20 *et
seq.*, 23, 25
relation to allusive thinking, 63
Schizophrenic spectrum disorder, 29, 30, 100, 105,
107
Schizophreniform psycho-
sis, 23
Schizophrenogenic mother,
6, 23, 25, 26, 95
Severity-of-illness scale, 79
link with Deviance Score,
79
Sex, attitudes of parents of
schizophrenics to, 10, 37
Siblings of schizophrenics,
attitudes of parents to, 10,
46, 55
problem-solving ability
of, 54
psychiatric disturbance in,
23
Silences,
measures of, 83, 102
relation to anxiety, 84
Situational effects in psychological testing, 68
Social class,
effect on attitudes, 41
effect on parental
authority, 9

Social control, lack in
mothers of schizo-
phrenics, 10
Social prestige, desire for,
in parents of manic-
depressives, 10
in parents of schizo-
phrenics, 10
Speech,
disturbance, measures of,
83, 102
relation to anxiety, 84
hesitancy of, 59, 85
Spontaneous agreement,
definition of, 51
in parents of schizo-
phrenics, 50, 51

Thematic Apperception
Test (T.A.T.), 53, 54,
67, 73, 74, 82
Thinking, *see* Allusive thinking, Amorphous think-
ing, Fragmented
thinking, Thought dis-
order
Thought disorder,
Bannister Grid test of, 67
in parents of schizo-
phrenics, 49, 102
Time budget, 31
Twins, monozygotic, dis-
cordant for schizo-
phrenia, 11, 27, 166

Verbosity,
of fathers of schizo-
phrenics, 169
in relation to communica-
tion defects, 84, 147,
154
in relation to impaired
focus of attention, 87
Violence, parental, 12

Withdrawal by mothers of
schizophrenics, 50, 98
Word Association Test, 68,
69
Word Count, relation to
Deviance Score, 144 *et
seq.*

INDEX OF AUTHORS

This index is designed to be used in conjunction with the Reference List and is organized on the basis of particular papers. Where an author's name appears first in the title of a paper, the numbers of the pages on which the paper is referred to are given. Where an author's name appears other than first, the reader is referred to the first-named author of the paper or papers.

Alanen, Y. O. (1956) 50
        (1958) 23, 94, 95, 98, 100
        (1966) 7, 23, 26, 94, 95, 98, 100
        (1968) 23, 94, 95, 98, 100
    See also Lidz, T. *et al.* (1963)
Apperson, L. B. (1965) 41
Apperson, L. B., and McAdoo, W. G. (1965) 41

Bales, R. F. (1950*a*) 43, 96
        (1950*b*) 43, 96
Barraclough, B., *see* Bunch, J. and (1971)
Bartak, L., *see* Rutter, M. and (1971)
Bartko, J., *see* Wynne, L. C. *et al.* (In the press)
Basamania, B., *see* Bowen, M. *et al.* (1959)
Bateson, G., Jackson, D. D., Haley, J., and Weakland, J. H. (1956) 14, 87
Baxter, J. C., Becker, J., and Hooks, W. (1963) 69
Baxter, J. C., Williams, J., and Zerof, S. (1966) 39
Beaulieu, M. R., *see* Lennard, H. L. *et al.* (1965)
Beavers, W. R., Blumberg, S., Timken, K., and Weiner, M. (1965) 76, 87, 91
Beavin, J. H., *see* Sluzki, C. E. *et al.* (1967); Watzlawick, P. *et al.* (1968)
Becker, J., and Finkel, P. (1969) 84, 102
Becker, J., and Siefkes, H. (1969) 41, 47, 60, 61, 97, 99
    See also Baxter, J. C. *et al.* (1963)
Behrens, M. I., Rosenthal, A. J., and Chodoff, P. (1968) 76
Bell, R. Q. (1968) 27, 104
Bennett, B. M., *see* Finney, D. J. *et al.* (1963)
Bergen, B. J., *see* Freeman, H. E. *et al.* (1959)
Berger, A. (1965) 88
Biller, H. B., *see* Kayton, R. and (1971)
Birch, H. C., *see* Thomas, A. *et al.* (1968)
Birley, J. L. T., *see* Brown, G. W. *et al.* (1972); Wing, J. K. *et al.* (1967)
Birtchnell, J. (1970) 101
Blumberg, S., *see* Beavers, W. R. *et al.* (1965)
Borgatta, E. F. (1964) 45
Bowen, M., Dysinger, R. H., and Basamania, B. (1959) 19, 20, 25, 98
Boyd, I., *see* Fisher, S. *et al.* (1959)
Brodey, W. (1959) 19
Brown, G. W., Birley, J. L. T., and Wing, J. K. (1972) 27, 32, 50, 56, 108
Brown, G. W., Monck, E. M., Carstairs, G. M., and Wing, J. K. (1962) 31, 32, 50
    See also Rutter, M. and (1966)
Bunch, J., and Barraclough, B. (1971) 101
Buss, A., and Lang, P. (1965) 63

Caputo, D. V. (1963) 47, 60, 61, 95, 96, 99
Carmen, L., *see* Hotchkiss, G. D. *et al.* (1955)
Carstairs, G. M., *see* Brown, G. W. *et al.* (1962)
Cheek, F. E. (1964*a*) 49, 96
        (1964*b*) 49, 96
        (1965*a*) 49, 50, 60, 96, 99
        (1965*b*) 49, 50, 52, 60, 61, 95, 96, 99
        (1966) 49, 60, 96
Chess, S., *see* Thomas, A. *et al.* (1968)
Chodoff, P., *see* Behrens, M. I. *et al.* (1968)
Ciarlo, D., Lidz, T., and Ricci, J. (1967) 68
Clancy, M., *see* McConaghy, N. and (1968)
Clarke, A. R., *see* Garmezy, N. and (1961)
Clausen, J. A., and Kohn, M. L. (1960) 9
    See also Kohn, M. L. and (1956)

Cooper, J. E., Kendell, R. E., Gurland, B. J., Sharpe, L., Copeland, J. R. M., and Simon, R.
  (1972) 33, 165
    See also Kendell, R. E. *et al.* (1971); Wing, J. K. *et al.* (1974)
Copeland, J. R. M., *see* Cooper, J. E. *et al.* (1972); Kendell, R. E. *et al.* (1971)
Cornelison, A. R., *see* Fleck, S. *et al.* (1963); Lidz, T. *et al.* (1957a and b, 1958, 1963, 1965)
Costello, A. J., Gunn, J. C., and Dominian, J. (1968) 13, 98, 101
Creak, M. (1961) 67

Day, J., *see* Wynne, L. C. *et al.* (1958)
Delay, J., Deniker, P., and Green, A. (1957) 19
                                      (1960) 19
                                      (1962) 19
Deniker, P., *see* Delay, J., *et al.* (1957, 1960, 1962)
Denny, D., *see* Heston, L. and (1968)
Dominian, J., *see* Costello, A. J. *et al.* (1968)
Dunham, R., *see* Farina, A. and (1963)
Dysinger, R. H., *see* Bowen, M. *et al.* (1959)

Elstein, A. S., *see* Reiss, D. and (1971)
Embrey, N. G., *see* Lennard, H. L. *et al.* (1965)
Esterson, D., *see* Laing, R. D. and (1964)

Farina, A. (1960) 47, 49, 60, 61, 97, 98, 99
Farina, A., and Dunham, R. (1963) 47, 61, 97, 98, 99
Farina, A., and Holzberg, J. D. (1967) 38, 47, 61, 97, 98
                                (1968) 47, 61, 97, 98
                                (1970) 84, 85, 102
Feinsilver, D. (1970) 86, 102
Ferreira, A. J. (1963) 51, 60, 61, 96, 99
Ferreira, A. J., and Winter, W. D. (1965) 51, 60, 61, 99
Ferreira, A. J., Winter, W. D., and Poindexter, E. J. (1966) 53, 96
    See also Winter, W. D. and (1967)
Finkel, P., *see* Becker, J. *et al.* (1969)
Finney, D. J., Latscha, R., Bennett, B. M., and Hsu, P. (1963) 127, 128
Fischer, M. (1971) 27
Fisher, S., Boyd, I., Walker, D., and Sheer, D. (1959) 10, 54, 61, 70, 78, 82, 98, 99, 141
Fleck, S., Lidz, T., and Cornelison, A. (1963) 18, 25, 96
    See also Lidz, T. *et al.* (1957a and b, 1958, 1963, 1965); Rosman, B. *et al.* (1964)
Forrest, A. D., Hay, A. J., and Kushner, A. W. (1969) 64
Freeman, H. E., Simmons, O. G., and Bergen, B. J. (1959) 35, 94
Freeman, R. V., and Grayson, H. M. (1955) 35, 94
Friedman, S., *see* Oltman, J. E. and (1965); Oltman, J. E. *et al.* (1952)
Frith, C. D., and Lillie, F. J. (1972) 67
Fromm-Reichmann, F. (1948) 6, 95

Gaind, R., *see* Hirsch, S. R. *et al.* (1973)
Gardner, G. G. (1967) 25, 95, 100
Garmezy, N., Clarke, A. R., and Stockner, C. (1961) 40, 99
Gerard, D. L., and Siegel, J. (1950) 7, 26, 93, 94, 95, 98, 103
Gibson, R. W. (1958) 10
Glasner, S., *see* Sharp, V. H. *et al.* (1964)
Gourlay, A. J., *see* Kendell, R. E. *et al.* (1971)
Graham, P., *see* Wing, J. K. *et al.* (1967)
Grayson, H. M., *see* Freeman, R. V. and (1955)
Green, A., *see* Delay, J. *et al.* (1957, 1960, 1962)
Green, L. M., *see* Hordern, A. *et al.* (1968)
Guertin, W. H. (1961) 38
Gunn, J. C., *see* Costello, A. J. *et al.* (1968)
Gurland, B. J., *see* Cooper, J. E. *et al.* (1972); Kendell, R. E. *et al.* (1971)

Hajdu-Gaines, L. (1940) 6
Haley, J. (1959a) 14, 15, 54
          (1959b) 14, 15, 54
          (1960) 14
          (1968) 89, 92
    See also Bateson, G. *et al.* (1956)
Hanson, B. A., *see* Magaro, P. A. and (1969)
Hay, A. J., *see* Forrest, A. D. *et al.* (1969)
Heilbrun, A. B. (1960a) 38, 40
                (1960b) 38, 40
Hersov, L. A. (1960) 19, 27

Heston, L. L. (1966) 30
Heston, L. L., and Denny, D. (1968) 30
Hirsch, S., *see* Wynne, L. C. *et al.* (1958)
Hirsch, S. R., and Leff, J. P. (1971) 50, 156
Hirsch, S. R., Gaind, R., Rohde, P. D., Stevens, B. C., and Wing, J. K. (1973) 13
    See also Leff, J. P. and (1972)
Hollingshead, A. B., and Redlich, F. C. (1958) 76, 123
    See also Rogler, L. H. and (1965)
Holzberg, J. D., *see* Farina, A. and (1967, 1968, 1970)
Hooks, W., *see* Baxter, J. C. *et al.* (1963)
Hordern, A., Sandifer, M. G., Green, L. M., and Timbury, G. C. (1968) 37, 42
Horner, R. F. (1964) 40
Horowitz, F. D., and Lovell, L. L. (1960) 37, 42
Hotchkiss, G. D., Carmen, L., Ogilby, A., and Wiesenfeld, S. (1955) 22, 93, 94
Hsu, P., *see* Finney, D. J. *et al.* (1963)

Isaacs, A., *see* Wing, J. K. *et al.* (1967)

Jackson, D. D., *see* Bateson, G. *et al.* (1956); Watzlawick, P. *et al.* (1968)
Jacobson, N., *see* Phillips, J. E. *et al.* (1965)

Kantor, R. E., *see* Winder, C. L. and (1958)
Kasanin, J., Knight, E., and Sage, P. (1934) 5, 8, 11, 26, 93, 94, 103
Kayton, R., and Biller, H. B. (1971), 41
Kendell, R. E., Cooper, J. E., Gourlay, A. J., Copeland, M., Sharpe, L., and Gurland, B. J.
    (1971) 13, 33, 61, 83, 165
    See also Cooper, J. E. *et al.* (1972)
Kennedy, T., *see* Ringuette, E. and (1966)
Kety, S., Rosenthal, D., Wender, P., and Schulsinger, F. (1968) 29, 100
    See also Rosenthal, D. *et al.* (1968); Wender, P. *et al.* (1968, 1971)
King, A. (1963) 27
Klebanoff, L. (1959) 36, 104
Knight, E., *see* Kasanin, L. *et al.* (1934)
Kohn, M. L. (1968) 62, 106
    See also Clausen, J. A. and (1960)
Kohn, M. L., and Clausen, J. A. (1956) 9, 41, 70, 96, 97, 101
Kolvin, I. (1972a) 33
        (1972b) 33
Koplin, J., *see* Rosenberg, S. and (1968)
Kreitman, N., Sainsbury, P., Morrissey, J., Towers, J., and Scrivener, J. (1961) 81
Kushner, A. W., *see* Forrest, A. D. *et al.* (1969)

Laing, R. D. (1960) 20
        (1967) 21
Laing, R. D., and Esterson, D. (1964) 21, 22
Lane, R. C., and Singer, J. L. (1959) 40
Lang, P., *see* Buss, A. and (1965)
Latscha, R., *see* Finney, D. J. *et al.* (1963)
Lederman, I., *see* Sharp, V. H. *et al.* (1964)
Leff, J. P., and Hirsch, S. R. (1972) 165, 169
Leff, J. P., and Wing, J. K. (1971) 129
    See also Hirsch, S. R. and (1971)
Lennard, H. L., Beaulieu, M. R., and Embrey, N. G. (1965) 51. 53, 61, 96
Lerner, P. M. (1965) 48, 97, 99
        (1967) 48, 60, 97, 99
Levy, D. M. (1931) 5
Lidz, R. W., and Lidz, T. (1949) 6, 101
Lidz, T. (1967) 16, 26, 43
        (1968) 16, 18
Lidz, T., Cornelison, A. R., Fleck, S., and Terry, D. (1957a) 17, 43, 55, 95, 96
                                                    (1957b) 17, 24, 25, 43, 54, 55, 96, 98
Lidz, T., Cornelison, A. R. Singer, A. T. Schafer, S., and Fleck, S. (1965) 7, 55
Lidz, T., Cornelison, A. R., Terry, D., and Fleck, S. (1958) 18, 54, 55
Lidz, T., Fleck, S., Alanen, Y. O., and Cornelison, A. (1963) 18
Lidz, T., Fleck, S., and Cornelison, A. R. (1965) 60
Lidz, T., Wild, C., Schafer, S., Rosman, B., and Fleck, S. (1963) 64, 68
    See also Ciarlo, D. *et al.* (1967); Fleck, S. *et al.* (1963); Lidz, R. W. and (1949);
    Rosman, B. *et al.* (1964); Wild, C. *et al.* (1965)
Lillie, F. J., *see* Frith, C. D. and (1972)
Lindelius, R. (1970) 27, 101
Loeff, R. G. (1966) 91
Loftin, J., *see* Schopler, E. and (1969)

Lovell, L. L., *see* Horowitz, F. D. and (1960)
Lovibond, S. H. (1954) 63
Lu, Y-C. (1961) 10, 93
          (1962) 10, 93, 103
Lucas, L. (1964) 12, 101
Lyle, T. K., and Wybar, K. C. (1967) 65

Magaro, P. A., and Hanson, B. A. (1969) 41
Mahl, G. F. (1956) 83, 102
Malzberg, B., *see* Pollock, H. M. and (1940)
Mann, M., *see* Siegler, M. *et al.* (1969)
Margolies, J. A., and Wortis, H. Z. (1956) 27
Mark, J. C. (1953) 34, 37, 93, 94, 95
McAdoo, W. G., *see* Apperson, L. B. and (1965)
McConaghy, N. (1959) 63, 64, 68, 70
              (1960) 65
              (1971) 65
McConaghy, N., and Clancy, M. (1968) 65, 70
McGarry, J. J., *see* Oltman, J. E. *et al.* (1952)
McGhie, A. (1961a) 10, 37, 41, 95, 98
            (1961b) 37, 41
            (1967) 63
McKeown, J. E. (1950) 8, 98
Mednick, S. A. (1966) 27
               (1967) 104
Mednick, S. A., and Schulsinger, F. (1968) 27, 104
Mehrabian, A., and Wiener, M. (1967) 91
Merrifield, J., *see* Palombo, S. *et al.* (1967)
Mishler, E. G., and Waxler, N. E. (1967) 91
                  (1968a) 7, 35, 46, 60, 61, 68, 82, 85, 94, 97, 102, 114
                  (1968b) 46, 55, 60, 61, 68, 82, 85, 94, 97, 102, 114
                  (1970) 55, 85
Monashkin, I., *see* Zuckerman, M. *et al.* (1958)
Monck, E. M., *see* Brown, G. W. *et al.* (1962)
Morris, G. O., and Wynne, L. C. (1965) 72, 75
     See also Palombo, S. *et al.* (1967)
Morrissey, J., *see* Kreitman, N. *et al.* (1961)
Mosher, L. R., Pollin, W., and Stabenau, J. (1971) 11
     See also Pollin, W. *et al.* (1966)
Muntz, H. J., and Power, R. P. (1970) 66

Nameche, G., Waring, M., and Ricks, D. (1964) 26, 94
     See also Ricks, D. F. and (1966)
Nathanson, I. A. (1967) 41
Nielsen, C. K. (1954) 8, 96, 100

Ogilby, A., *see* Hotchkiss, G. D. *et al.* (1955)
Olson, D. N. (1972) 91
Oltean, M., *see* Zuckerman, M. *et al.* (1958)
Oltman, J. E., and Friedman, S. (1965) 11, 101
Oltman, J. E., McGarry, J. J., and Friedman, S. (1952) 12
O'Neal, P., and Robins, L. N. (1958) 24, 101, 103
Osgood, C. E., Suci, G. J., and Tannenbaum, P. H. (1957) 47
Osmond, H., *see* Siegler, M. *et al.* (1969)
Ostergaard, L., *see* Rosenthal, D. *et al.* (1968)

Palombo, S., Merrifield, J., Weigert, W., Morris, G., and Wynne, L. (1967) 75, 81, 82
Parsons, A. (1960) 19
Payne, R. W. (1960) 63, 64
Phillips, J. E., Jacobson, N., and Turner, W. J. (1965) 66
Phillips, L. (1953) 38, 46, 129
     See also Zigler, E. and (1960)
Poindexter, E. J., *see* Ferreira, A. J. *et al.* (1966)
Pollin, W., and Stabenau, J. (1968) 11, 26, 93, 104
Pollin, W., Stabenau, J. R., Mosher, L., and Tupin, J. (1966) 11, 93, 104
     See also Mosher, L. R. *et al.* (1971); Stabenau, J. R. *et al.* (1965)
Pollock, H. M., and Malzberg, B. (1940) 101
Power, R. P., *see* Muntz, H. J. and (1970)
Prout, C. T., and White, M. A. (1950) 8, 98

Rachman, S. (1973) 21, 22
Rapaport, D. (1946) 63

Raven, J. C. (1948) 120
Redlich, F. C., *see* Hollingshead, A. B. and (1958)
Reichard, S., and Tillman, C. (1950) 7
Reiss, D. (1967*a*) 57
  (1967*b*) 59
  (1968) 59, 61, 86, 97, 102
  (1969) 59, 60
  (1971) 60
Reiss, D., and Elstein, A. S. (1971) 68
Ricci, J., *see* Ciarlo, D. *et al.* (1967); Rosman, B. *et al.* (1964); Wild, C. *et al.* (1965)
Ricks, D. F., and Nameche, G. (1966) 26, 94, 103
  See also Nameche, G. *et al.* (1964); Waring, M. and (1965)
Ringuette, E., and Kennedy, T. (1966) 88, 92
Robins L. N., *see* O'Neal, P. and (1958)
Rogler, L. H., and Hollingshead, A. B. (1965) 12, 101
Rohde, P. D., *see* Hirsch, S. R. *et al.* (1973)
Romney, D. (1969*a*) 66, 70
  (1969*b*) 66, 70
Rosenberg, S., and Koplin, J. (1968) 63
Rosenthal, A. J., *see* Behrens, M. I. *et al.* (1968)
Rosenthal, D. (1971) 29
Rosenthal, D. Wender, P., Kety, S., Schulsinger, F., Welner, J., and Ostergaard, L. (1968) 29, 31
  See also Kety, S, *et al.*, (1968); Wender, P. *et al.*, (1968, 1971)
Rosman, B., Wild, C., Ricci, J., Fleck, S., and Lidz, T. (1964) 64, 65, 68, 70, 82, 141
  See also Lidz, T. *et al.* (1963); Wild, C. *et al.* (1965)
Rutter, M., and Bartak, L. (1971) 33
Rutter, M., and Brown, G. W. (1966) 32
Ryckoff, I., *see* Wynne, L. C. *et al.* (1958)

Sage, P., *see* Kasanin, J. *et al.* (1934)
Sainsbury, P., *see* Kreitman, N. *et al.* (1961)
Sandifer, M. G., *see* Hordern, A. *et al.* (1968)
Sartorius, N., *see* Wing, J. K. *et al.* (1974)
Schafer, S., *see* Lidz, T. *et al.* (1963, 1965)
Schneider, K. (1957) 117, 165
Schopler, E., and Loftin, J. (1969) 7, 35, 64, 67, 70, 82, 114, 159
Schulsinger, F., *see* Kety, S. *et al.* (1968); Mednick, S.A. *et al.* (1968); Rosenthal, D. *et al.* (1968)
Scrivener, J., *see* Kreitman, N. *et al.* (1961)
Sharan, S. N. (1966) 54, 61, 97, 99
Sharp, V. H., Glasner, S., and Lederman, I. (1964) 37
Sharpe, L., *see* Cooper, J. E. *et al.* (1972); Kendell, R. E. *et al.* (1971)
Sheer, D., *see* Fisher, S. *et al.* (1959)
Shields, J. (1967) 100, 113
Shoben, E. J. (1949) 35
Siefkes, H., *see* Becker, J. and (1969)
Siegel, J., *see* Gerard, D. L. and (1950)
Siegler, M., Osmond, H., and Mann, H. (1969) 21
Simmons, O. G., *see* Freeman, H. E. *et al.* (1959)
Simon, R., *see* Cooper, J. E. *et al.* (1972)
Singer, J. L., *see* Lane, R. C. and (1959)
Singer, M. T. (1967) 70, 78
Singer, M. T., and Wynne, L. C. (1963) 73, 77, 81
  (1964) 72, 73, 102
  (1965) 74, 81, 129
  (1966*a*) 72, 77, 82, 102, 114, 122, 123, 125, 138, 170
  (1966*b*) 77, 78, 82, 102, 114, 134, 136, 168, 170
  See also Lidz, T. *et al.* (1965); Wild, C. *et al.* (1965); Wynne, L. C. and (1963); Wynne, L. C. *et al.* (In the press)
Sluzki, C. E., Beavin, J., Tarnopolsky, A., and Veron, E. (1967) 92
Sluzki, C. E., and Veron, E. (1971) 92
Sojit, C. M. (1969) 90, 91
  (1971) 90
Stabenau, J. R., Tupin, J., Werner, M., and Pollin, W. (1965) 48, 61, 65, 70
  See also Mosher, L. R. *et al.* (1971); Pollin, W. *et al.* (1966); Pollin, W. and (1968)
Stevens, B. C., *see* Hirsch, S. R. *et al.* (1973)
Stockner, C., *see* Garmezy, N. *et al.* (1961)
Strodtbeck, F. L. (1951) 43, 44, 99
  (1954) 43, 44, 99
Suci, G. J., *see* Osgood, C. E. *et al.* (1957)

Tannenbaum, P. H., *see* Osgood, C. E. *et al.* (1957)
Tarnopolsky, A., *see* Sluzki, C. E. *et al.* (1967)
Terry, D., *see* Lidz, T. *et al.* (1957*a* and *b*, 1958)
Thomas, A., Chess, S., and Birch, H. C. (1968) 104
Tietze, T. (1949) 7
Tillman, C., *see* Reichard, S. and (1950)
Timbury, G. C., *see* Hordern, A. *et al.* (1968)
Timken, K., *see* Beavers, W. R. *et al.* (1965)
Toohey, M., *see* Wynne, L. C. *et al.* (In the press)
Towers, J., *see* Kreitman, N. *et al.* (1961)
Tupin, J., *see* Pollin, W. *et al.* (1966); Stabenau, J. R. *et al.* (1965)
Turner, W. J., *see* Phillips, J. E. *et al.* (1965)

Vaziri, H. (1961) 9, 100
Veron, E., *see* Sluzki, C. E. *et al.* (1967); Sluzki, C. E. and (1971)

Wahl, C. W. (1954) 9
        (1956) 9
Walker, D., *see* Fisher, S. *et al.* (1959)
Waring, M., and Ricks, D. (1965) 25, 29, 94, 98, 99, 100
   See also Nameche, G. *et al.* (1964)
Watzlawick, P., Beavin, J. H., and Jackson, D. D. (1968) 14, 15
Waxler, N. E., *see* Mischler, E. G. and (1967, 1968*a* and *b*, 1970)
Weakland, J. H. (1960) 14
   See also Bateson, G. *et al.* (1956)
Weigert, W., *see* Palombo, S. *et al.* (1967)
Weiner, M., *see* Beavers, W. R. *et al.* (1965)
Welner, J., *see* Rosenthal, D. *et al.* (1968)
Wender, P., Rosenthal, D., and Kety, S. (1968) 28, 100
Wender, P., Rosenthal, D., Zahn, T., and Kety, S. (1971) 31, 67, 69, 70
   See also Kety, S. *et al.* (1968); Rosenthal, D. *et al.* (1968)
Werner, M., *see* Stabenau, J. R. *et al.* (1965)
White, M. A., *see* Prout, C. T. and (1950)
Wiener, M., *see* Mehrabian, A. and (1967)
Wiesenfeld, S., *see* Hotchkiss, G. D. *et al.* (1955)
Wild, C., Singer, M., Rosman, B., Ricci, J., and Lidz, T. (1965) 77, 81, 159, 166
   See also Lidz, T. *et al.* (1963); Rosman, B. *et al.* (1964)
Winder, C. L., and Kantor, R. E. (1958) 69
Williams, J., *see* Baxter, J. C. *et al.* (1966)
Wing, J. K. (1966) 33
Wing, J. K., Birley, J. L. T., Cooper, J. E., Graham, P., and Isaacs, A. (1967) 117
Wing, J. K., Cooper, J. E., and Sartorius, N. (1974) 117
   See also Brown, G. W. *et al.* (1962, 1972); Hirsch, S. R. *et al.* (1973); Leff, J. P. and (1971)
Winter, W., and Ferreira, A. (1967) 45, 50, 53
   See also Ferreira, A. J. and (1966)
Witmer, H. (1934) 5, 93, 96, 98
Wolman, B. B. (1961) 19
World Health Organization (1973) 33, 165
Wortis, H. J., *see* Margolies, J. A. and (1956)
Wybar, K. C., *see* Lyle, T. K. and (1967)
Wynne, L. C. (1967) 72, 78, 114, 135, 168, 170
       (1968) 72, 73, 77, 114, 135, 156, 170
       (1971) 72, 77, 78, 113, 114, 135, 166, 170
Wynne, L. C., Ryckoff, I., Day, J., and Hirsch, S. (1958) 20, 98
Wynne, L. C., and Singer, M. T. (1963) 73
Wynne, L. C., Singer, M., Bartko, J., and Toohey, M. (In the press) 166
   See also Morris, G. O. and (1965); Palombo, S. *et al.* (1967); Singer, M. T. and (1963, 1964, 1965, 1966*a* and *b*)

Zahn, T. P. (1968) 69
   See also Wender, P. *et al.* (1971)
Zeroff, S., *see* Baxter, J. C. *et al.* (1966)
Zigler, E., and Phillips, L. (1960) 49
Zuckerman, M., Oltean, M., and Monashkin, I. (1958) 35, 36, 41, 42, 95